Income Redistribution and Social Security

INTERNATIONAL STUDIES IN ECONOMIC MODELLING

Series Editor
Homa Scobie

Executive Director
European Economics and Financial Centre
P. O. Box 2498
London W2 4LE
Tel (071) 229-0402
Fax (071) 221-5118

---

1 **Economic Modelling in the OECD Countries**
H. Motamen-Scobie
2 **Modelling the Labour Market**
Edited by M. Beenstock
3 **Input–Output Analysis**
Current developments
Edited by M. Ciaschini
4 **Models of Disequilibrium and Shortage in Centrally Planned Economies**
C. Davis and W. Charemza
5 **Economic Modelling at the Bank of England**
Edited by S. G. B. Henry and K. D. Patterson
6 **Recent Modelling Approaches in Applied Energy Economics**
Edited by O. Bjerkholt, O. Ølsen and J. Vislie
7 **International Commodity Market Models**
Advances in methodology and applications
Edited by O. Güvenen, W. C. Labys and J.-B. Lesourd
8 **Dynamic Models for the Inter-relations of Real and Financial Growth**
H. Ekstedt and L. Westberg
9 **Economic Models of Trade Unions**
Edited by P. Garonna, P. Mori and P. Tedeschi
10 **International Energy Economics**
Edited by Thomas Sterner
11 **International Trade Modelling**
Edited by M. G. Dagenais and P.-A. Muet
12 **Continuous Time Econometrics Theory and applications**
Edited by Giancarlo Gandolfo
13 **Empirical Approaches to Fiscal Policy Modelling**
Edited by Alberto Heimler and Daniele Meulders
14 **Inflation**
Penelope A. Rowlatt
15 **Modelling the Structure of the Economy**
Maurizio Ciaschini
16 **Econometric Modelling of World Shipping**
Michael Beenstock and Andreas Vergottis
17 **Income Redistribution and Social Security**
An application of microsimulation
J. H. M. Nelissen
18 **Economic Progress and Growth**
Edited by Homa Motamen-Scobie

Income Redistribution and Social Security

J. H. M. Nelissen

Department of Social Security Economics and
Department of Demography
Tilburg University, The Netherlands

CHAPMAN & HALL

London · Glasgow · Weinheim · New York · Tokyo · Melbourne · Madras

Published by Chapman & Hall, 2–6 Boundary Row, London SE1 8HN, UK

Chapman & Hall, 2–6 Boundary Row, London SE1 8HN, UK

Blackie Academic & Professional, Wester Cleddens Road, Bishopbriggs, Glasgow G64 2NZ, UK

Chapman & Hall GmbH, Pappelallee 3, 69469 Weinheim, Germany

Chapman & Hall Inc., One Penn Plaza, 41st Floor, New York NY10119, USA

Chapman & Hall Japan, Thomson Publishing Japan, Hirakawacho Nemoto Building, 6F, 1-7-11 Hirakawa-cho, Chiyoda-ku, Tokyo 102, Japan

Chapman & Hall Australia, Thomas Nelson Australia, 102 Dodds Street, South Melbourne, Victoria 3205, Australia

Chapman & Hall India, R. Seshadri, 32 Second Main Road, CIT East, Madras 600 035, India

First edition 1994

Typeset in 10/12 pt Sabon by Pure Tech Corporation, Pondicherry, India
Printed in Great Britain by T. J. Press, Padstow, Cornwall

ISBN 0 412 57090 4

A catalogue record for this book is available from the British Library

Library of Congress Catalog Card Number: 93–74441

Printed on permanent acid-free text paper, manufactured in accordance with the proposed ANSI/NISO Z39.48-1992 and ANSI/NISO Z39.48-1984 (Permanence of paper)

Contents

Introduction to the Series

There has been a growing dependence in the past two decades on modelling as a tool for better understanding of the behaviour of economic systems, and as an aid in policy and decision making. Given the current state of the art globally, the introduction of a series such as this can be seen as a timely development. This series will provide a forum for volumes on both the theoretical and applied aspects of the subject.

International Studies in Economic Modelling is designed to present comprehensive volumes on modelling work in various areas of the economic discipline. In this respect one of the fundamental objectives is to provide a medium for ongoing review of the progression of the field.

There is no doubt that economic modelling will figure prominently in the affairs of government and in the running of the private sector, in efforts to achieve a more rational and efficient handling of economic affairs. By formally structuring an economic system, it is possible to simulate and investigate the effect of changes on the system. This in turn leads to a growing appreciation of the relevance of modelling techniques. Our aim is to provide sufficient space for authors to write authoritative handbooks, giving basic facts with an overview of the current economic models in specific areas and publish a useful series which will be consulted and used as an accessible source of reference.

The question may arise in some reader's minds as to the role of this series *vis-à-vis* other existing publications. At present, no other book series possesses the characteristics of International Studies in Economic Modelling and as such cannot fill the gap that will be bridged by it. Those journals which focus in this area do not present an exhaustive and comprehensive overview of a particular subject and all the developments in the field. Other journals which may contain economic modelling papers are not sufficiently broad to publish volumes on all aspects of modelling in a specific area which this series is designed to cover.

A variety of topics will be included encompassing areas of both micro and macroeconomics, as well as the methodological aspects of model construction. Naturally, we are open to suggestions from all readers of, and contributors to, the series regarding its approach and content.

Finally, I would like to thank all those who have helped the launch of this series. The encouraging response received from authors who have contributed the forthcoming volumes and from the subscribers to the series has indicated the need for such a publication.

Homa Scobie
European Economics and Financial Centre
London, 1992

Preface

This study has its origin in 1984, when I prepared a paper for the 1985 Conference of the International Union for the Scientific Study of Population (IUSSP). I had just finished a report on the effect of demographic changes on the demand for social security benefits [Nelissen and Vossen (1985)]. From this study it appeared that the demographic structure would affect, in particular, the expenditures for old age pensions and I wondered how income distribution would be changed by the increasing contribution rate. A simple simulation model showed that the lifetime redistributive impact of the Dutch state pension is considerably smaller than a period analysis suggests [Nelissen (1987b)]. This conclusion puzzled me more and more and I began asking how one could reach a realistic simulation of the lifetime income redistribution and how one would implement the other social security schemes in the Netherlands. I soon discovered that lifetime income redistribution by the social security system is an unexploited field of research. The reason also soon became clear. Data is not available and analytical models are intractable. Therefore, I decided to 'construct' my own database, to simulate a long-term socio-economic panel, which resulted in the microsimulation model NEDYMAS.

In constructing that database I have been helped by the developments in computer hardware that took place in the second half of the 1980s. Without the decentralization of computer facilities it would probably have been impossible to develop and test such an extended model within a rather limited period. The latter would also have not been possible without the aid of Paul Vermaseren, who takes pleasure in tackling problems that seem unsolvable at first glance and for whom it is a challenge to make computer programmes run as quickly as possible. Through his good offices, the project got a strong impulse at the right time.

I am also grateful to Toon van den Aker (who died much too early, in 1992) for his advice with respect to the plan of the microsimulation model and for his help in programming the ALGOL68 version of the model. The size of the computer programme in combination with a cramping compiler made it necessary to translate the programme into another language. A choice was made for FORTRAN. The translation into FORTRAN was realized for the greater part by Willem Spoeltman, who did the job with great accuracy. Other help has been provided by Rob Vossen, who created the figures in chapter 6, by John Schell, who verified chapter 5 and by Frans van Poppel, who helped me with my search for demographic data covering the 1940s and 1950s.

At various points I have benefited greatly from discussions with colleagues and friends. Ad Vossen, Jan Bartlema, Frank van Tongeren and Otto Hellwig provided me with constructive comments and suggestions.

Another form of support has been provided by Gerard Frinking. He has always allowed me freedom in my way of working. He was also always present if facilities had to be created or the financing of the project incurred risks. Thanks are especially due for his dedication in finding financial support for the project within the research programmes *The Redistributional Effects of Social Security*, financed by the Department of Education (during the period 1985–1990) and the *Research Program for Population Studies*, financed from 1991 by the Dutch Scientific Organization NWO (grant no. 18.051).

I am also grateful to Arie Kapteyn and Jos Berghman, who supervised this study. Their efficient way of working has always impressed me, as has their stimulating support throughout the execution of the project.

Last, but not least, I would like to say a special thank you to Anne McDonald for her invaluable help in correcting my English. Although it must have been a laborious – and probably often dull – job, she has done it in a most pleasant manner.

Jan Nelissen
Tilburg
April 1993

Dutch terminology and abbreviations

(Dutch abbreviations are used throughout the book.)

AAW	Algemene Arbeidsongeschiktheidswet / General Disablement Benefits Act
ABP	Algemeen Burgerlijk Pensioenfonds / Civil Servants Pensions Fund
ABP–IP	Invaliditeitspensioen ingevolge het ABP / Disability Pension under the ABP
ABP–OP	Ouderdomspensioen ingevolge het ABP / Old Age Pension under the ABP
ABP–WP	Weduwen-, weduwnaars- en wezenpensioen ingevolge het ABP / Widows, Widowers and Orphans Pension under the ABP
ABW	Algemene Bijstandswet / General Social Assistance Act
AKW	Algemene Kinderbijslagwet / General Family Allowances Act
AOW	Algemene Ouderdomswet / General Old Age Pensions Act
AWBZ	Algemene Wet Bijzondere Ziektekosten / General Exceptional Medical Expenses Act
AWW	Algemene Weduwen- en Wezenwet / General Widows and Orphans Pensions Act
DSO	Doorbetaling Overheidspersoneel ingeval van ziekte / Sickness Payments for Civil Servants
IOAW	Inkomensvoorziening voor Oudere en Gedeeltelijk Arbeidsongeschikte Werkloze Werknemers / Provision for Older and Partly Disabled Unemployed Employees
IW	Inhoudingswet Ambtenaren / Civil Servants Deduction Act
IZA	Instituut Ziektekostenvoorziening Ambtenaren / Health Costs Provision for Civil Servants
KKZ	Kinderbijslagwet Kleine Zelfstandigen / Self-Employed Persons Family Allowances Act
KTO	Kindertoelage Overheidspersoneel / Civil Servants Family Allowances Provision
KW	Kinderbijslagwet / Family Allowances Act
KWL	Kinderbijslagwet voor Loontrekkenden / Wage-Earners Family Allowances Act
KWR	Kinderbijslagwet voor Rentetrekkers / Benefit Receiving Persons Family Allowances Act
NWW	Nieuwe Werkloosheidswet / New Unemployment Insurance Act
TW	Toeslagenwet / Supplementary Benefits Act
WAO	Wet Arbeidsongeschiktheidsverzekering / Disablement Insurance Act

WP–PS	Werknemerspensioenen in private sector / Private Pensions for Employees
WRO	Wachtgeldregeling Overheidspersoneel / Civil Servants Unemployment Benefit
WW	Werkloosheidswet / Unemployment Insurance Act
WWV	Wet Werkloosheidsvoorziening / Unemployment Provisions Act
ZFB	Ziekenfondsbesluit / Decree Health Insurance Fund
ZFW	Ziekenfondswet / Health Insurance Fund Act
ZW	Ziektewet / Sickness Benefit Act

PART ONE

Introduction

1 Introduction

1.1 PURPOSE AND STRUCTURE

The purpose of this book is to study the redistributive impact of social security schemes on income distribution for different birth generations in the Netherlands. In view of the role that income plays in the socio-economic behaviour of individuals and households, concern with income distribution has always been an important element in public discussion. In the Netherlands, for example, wage policy and wage negotiations in the 1970s were dominated by the demand for income equalization by the trade unions [Windmuller, De Galan and Van Zweeden (1983: ch. 7)]. At the end of the 1970s, the debate shifted to cuts in expenditures. But continuing retrenchments over the past decade have led to a renewed interest in (re)distributive issues. From 1983, the government paid special attention to income policy, income developments and income distribution through a yearly publication.[1] An overview of the development and results of the income distribution policy in the Netherlands can be found in Van Wijngaarden (1986).

Treating income and income distribution in terms of income in a particular year, however, is too simplistic a view [Pestieau (1989) and Atkinson (1983)]. In this way, changes in, for example, the population structure or changes in educational attainment, are not taken into consideration. This does not matter if we only want to compare changes in two or three successive years. However, it can result in serious deviations if we are looking for developments over a period of, say, five years [*e.g.* Mookherjee and Shorrocks (1982)]. At the individual level, demographic changes (*e.g.* marriage, childbirth or divorce), are of greater importance to individual income development than socio-economic changes (such as becoming unemployed), Klevmarken (1983). This implies that one cannot limit oneself

[1] The series started with Ministerie van Sociale Zaken en Werkgelegenheid (1983) following critical remarks made in Parliament. Discussion led to the annual publication of a report on income policy, see Ministerie van Sociale Zaken en Werkgelegenheid (several years).

to the situation in a particular year but also has to take account of system dynamics.[2] In section 1.3, we will deal in more detail with the arguments for opting for a lifetime approach.

When speaking of income and its distribution, social security benefits and social security payments cannot be ignored. This is also one of the roles of the state in the income formation process. In Western society, the social security system has a large impact on the distribution of disposable income. Until World War II, the social security system provided an answer to the socio-economic insecurity of industrialization, which started with the Industrial Revolution. Since then, social security systems have become a structural stabilizer in the Western economic system. It is generally accepted that it is the task of the state to provide all its citizens with a minimum income under all circumstances. This involves protecting individuals against the financial consequences of sickness, accident, disability, old age, unemployment or death, and providing them with compensation for the costs of health, children and physical or mental handicaps. This concept has become an integral part of the economic process and is indissolubly linked to the process of income formation and income redistribution [Van Zweeden (1983: 21)]. As a result, we do not only want to know the allocative consequences of government policy [Wolfson (1979b: 30–31)].

The choice of a lifetime approach when speaking of income distribution and the meaning of social security schemes in this respect, results in the aforementioned goal: **to analyse the redistributive impact of social security schemes**. Our analysis refers to the Netherlands and is limited to the **birth cohorts 1930–1960**.

The book is divided into nine chapters. Chapter 1 introduces the subject. Chapter 2 gives an overview of related studies. Chapter 3 describes the technique of microsimulation, its advantages and disadvantages. That chapter also describes the structure of our microsimulation model, called **NEDYMAS** (**NE**therlands **DY**namic **M**icro-**A**nalytic **S**imulation model). Chapter 4 describes the field of application, the Netherlands. The model contains three main modules: the demographic module, the labour force participation and income formation module and the social security module. These main modules are described in chapters 5, 6 and 7, respectively. Chapter 8 analyses the results. The last chapter, chapter 9, draws together some conclusions.

The present chapter deals with the following subjects: the definition of social security (section 1.2); annual versus lifetime income (section 1.3); the notion of (re)distributive effects (section 1.4); how to measure lifetime

[2] For this reason, the Netherlands Central Bureau of Statistics started a pilot study on the construction of statistics on income changes in September 1983. As a consequence, it now supplies us not only with the traditional purchasing power figures, but also with dynamic ones. Van de Stadt (1988).

income and its inequality (section 1.5), and the way in which we tackle the problem, namely, through microsimulation (section 1.6). We consider each in turn.

1.2 SOCIAL SECURITY

The concept of social security can be defined in various ways. The definitions vary from a very limited scope to a very broad one. Here, we confine ourselves to the definitions currently in use in the Netherlands.

Broadly defined, social security has been considered as an element of the integral socio-economic policy. Veldkamp (1978: 4) defines social security as the totality of institutions and provisions which aim to guarantee a certain level of subsistence. It does this by among others, substituting the income as much as possible in the case of a loss of income source; by compensating – directly or indirectly – the costs which can barely be met; and by taking away the causes of the insufficient income or its disappearance. In this definition all measures which guarantee, substitute or are complementary to income, are considered as social security arrangements. This means that, in addition to the traditional social insurances and other social provisions (discussed below), provisions such as housing grants, scholarships, full employment policy, and so on, are also considered as social security elements. The main point of departure in this definition is the focus on the guarantee for a certain level of existence. This also holds for other broad definitions of social security. For example, Halberstadt (1978: 74) defines social security as the entirety of individual claims, which – automatically or otherwise – can be expressed in money. Another important characteristic element is that no reference is made to the corporate nature of the schemes, so that, as a consequence, all pension provisions, irrespective of the level of regulation, form part of it. Also, so-called tertiary income (section 4.2) is included under this definition.

The current definition of social security in its broad sense in the Netherlands [Ministerie van Sociale Zaken en Werkgelegenheid (1982)], considers social security as the totality of legal measures which are aimed at guaranteeing continuity in individuals' spending opportunities. On the basis of this definition, social security may be divided into four components:

(a) Social insurances;
(b) Pension insurances;
(c) Other social provisions;
(d) Social benefits, directly paid by the employer.

Social insurances comprise all legal arrangements which are primarily aimed at **income redistribution** between persons or social groups whereby the right to a benefit is based on the insurance concept. Voluntary insurances, for which participation depends on legalized entry requirements, are also considered as social insurances.

Pension insurances include all arrangements, which are primarily aimed at the **redistribution of the income of persons over time**. They are based on a labour relation. Pension insurances are financed by a capital reserve system. This implies that a relationship is created between the insured person and the pension fund. In other words, the insured person has a personal claim to the pension fund.

Other social provisions include all arrangements in the field of social security, where the benefits are **financed directly by the state**. No specific premiums are levied: these provisions are financed from public funds.

Social benefits paid directly by the employer, refer to payments to (former) employees on the basis of a **labour relation**.

We will limit ourselves to the above definition of social security, because it is also used by the Dutch government. Another important reason for this limitation is that to use a broader definition would require a substantial extension of the model (*e.g.* housing grants) or would cover a field on which too little information is available (*e.g.* the impact of full employment policy).

In addition to the broad definition, the limited definition is also used very often. In the limited definition, social insurances and the corresponding complementary provisions are included under social security. In some cases, primary social provisions – such as the minimum wage and the legal holiday allowances – are also treated as being part of social security (in both the broad and the limited definition).

1.3 ANNUAL OR LIFETIME INCOME

To gain insight into the relative positions of persons or groups of persons, it is not sufficient to look at the order in any one year. Income level and its composition in any one year depend too much on chance. Transitory income has a large impact on income over a limited period. According to Friedman (1957), 15 to 30% of the variance in household incomes in urban areas can be explained by transitory income elements. Since the 1950s, this percentage has probably grown. Income flow over a longer period is subject to this to a lesser extent.

In addition to past experiences, future expectations are also important. This is particularly true if one analyses social security schemes, because '. . . the social services typically involve payments by workers to support non-workers such as children, pensioners, the sick or the unemployed. Since individuals do not remain in these dependent categories throughout their lives, current beneficiaries will, at other times, be supporting people who are similar to themselves but at a different stage of their life-cycle or of their fortunes . . .' [Layard (1977: 46)].

This is another argument against the use of a limited period in our analysis: the impact of the social security system on the income distribution of each individual also depends on the stage of the life cycle the individual is in at that particular moment. Income differences between persons at one moment can be compensated for in another period. Both Deleeck (1974) and Pestieau (1990) give examples of a society in which each income increases with age by the same proportion. If we suppose that the initial income, the age at which the initial income is earned and the age of dying do not differ, all young people in this society would be relatively poor, and all old people relatively rich. Income distribution, as measured at any time, would be unequal. However, the income distribution on a lifetime basis would be completely equal. Everyone receives the same income during his or her life.

Lillard (1977: 42) gives analogous reasons: '. . . among recent entrants into the labour force low earnings may reflect high levels of investment in training which will be compensated by high earnings at later stages of the life cycle . . .'. The reverse holds for those who can invest less in this area. Income differences can also be caused by differences in earning capacity, which continue to exist during an individual's entire life. A cross-section analysis does not allow us to distinguish these two sources of income differences.

Another point is that some forms of public expenditure – for example, education and employment programmes – bear the character of an investment, through which the complete gain is only partly measured. Generally, one can say that income differences on an annual basis are partly the consequence of differences in human capital investments (Mincer, 1974). A further objection against the use of annual incomes is that the integral public income policy is not exclusively focused on annual incomes.[3] A practical rather than a methodological objection is that non-positive incomes are not considered.

Another important argument for considering the redistributive impact of social security schemes is that a '. . . pure social insurance system will significantly affect the pattern in which income is received over an individual's lifetime, but will have no impact on income distribution across individuals . . . it does not represent an increase in the well-being of some individuals at the expense of others but merely a change in the timing of income receipt across individual lifetimes . . .' [Burkhauser and Warlick (1981: 403)]. Of course, the social security system does not merely consist of pure social insurances, but insurance elements are present in at least a part of almost all schemes (not including the pure welfare programmes, such as some social assistance schemes).

[3] *E.g.* Ministerie van Sociale Zaken en Werkgelegenheid (1983: especially 12–13) and the discussion on the so-called '*meerjarige minima*' during the 1980s. The introduction of the AOW can also be considered as a policy directed to long-term income policy: a redistribution of income during a person's life.

There are other reasons for concentrating on the lifetime redistributive impact of the social security system. According to [Aaron (1977) and Cohen and Friedman (1972)] individuals from high-income backgrounds generally start working at a later age and have a higher life expectancy than those in low-income groups. Consequently, the former pay contributions during a shorter period, but receive certain types of benefits (*e.g.* old age pensions) over a longer period. Furthermore, certain contributions are tax deductible, which favours those who earn high incomes. This is strengthened by the progressive nature of the tax system.

Although the aforementioned arguments favour the use of the lifetime approach, its application is limited. This is the result of both practical and methodological problems. The most important practical difficulty is the lack of sufficient data. Only for the US is longitudinal income data available, covering a sufficiently large sample over a long period.[4] Usually, a cross-section approach is used to solve this problem. However, this approach gives a distorted picture of lifetime income [*e.g.* Nelissen (1987a: 60 and 63) for the Netherlands]. It does not take into account the career effect, technological developments, changes in the demand–supply proportions of types of labour, and so on.

It is also often argued that it would not be feasible to take account of the changes in household size and composition during a person's lifetime. Nowadays, standardization methods are available to solve this problem. As to the absence of income data during a sufficiently long period, the reader is referred to section 4.4.

The two main methodological objections against the use of the lifetime income concept are the uncertainty with respect to future income flows and the valuation of the elements of the income flow in the course of time [Ritzen (1979: 94–98)]. The first problem cannot be avoided if we want to use the lifetime income approach for those who are still alive. Uncertainty about their future incomes will continue to exist, irrespective of the methods and models used. Factors which cannot be predicted will always be at work.

The other problem, the valuation of the income flows – ideally measured by the consumption streams – with respect to each other over time, is that individuals do not have the same risk aversion. In practice, we cannot use different utility functions for the different people. This is all the more serious since we cannot speak of a perfect capital market. This would imply that persons with consumption streams having the same present value at some discount rate can have different utility and different present value for their discounted incomes. Layard (1977) shows that a low discount rate

[4] The Longitudinal Employer–Employee Data, which covers one per cent of all wage earners since 1957 and the Michigan Panel Study of Income Dynamics which is held from 1968 on [see Atkinson, *et al.* (1988: 622–623)].

justifies the resulting issue best. Another possibility is to get an idea of the problem by using a range of alternative discount rates.

Other objections against the use of lifetime income [Von Weiszäcker (1978), especially the discussion of the paper] are:

- Transfers between different times in the life cycle are not without costs, both in a material and an immaterial sense;
- People are generally unable to value events up to the end of their lives, which argues for a high discount rate;
- The expectation of a high income in the future does not remove current poverty.

In spite of these objections, we have opted for the concept of lifetime income in this study. One reason is, as Pestieau (1989: 4) notes, the fact that '... it makes more sense than that of yearly income as it takes into account the possibility of averaging consumption expenses from an income stream fluctuating over years ...'. In other words, the transitory elements have to be filtered out as much as possible. A second reason is a more pragmatic one. Knowledge of the income redistribution by social security is available for annual income. By comparison, knowledge of the lifetime impact is very scarce and is almost always limited to old age pensions. Studies on the impact of all or almost all social security schemes do not exist. In view of the discussion on the redistributive effects of social security, one cannot limit oneself to an annual approach. Knowledge of long-term effects are necessary.

1.4 THE NOTION OF (RE)DISTRIBUTIVE EFFECTS

The redistributive impact of social security, or – more generally – state interventions, depends on the moment at which it is investigated [Wolfson (1979a) and De Wulf (1979)]. If one opts for administrative entrance, one opts for the effect at the moment of intervention on the person who has to pay *e.g.* taxes or premiums, or who receives benefits. This effect is called the impact incidence or the statutory incidence. If we look at the purpose, we get the legislative incidence, and if we look at the result, we are dealing with the effective incidence or economic incidence.

The statutory incidence can be compared with a cross-section approach, which is beyond our scope. While we are interested in the result in the first instance, and less so in the purpose of the system (which is mostly not very clear), we prefer economic incidence. We would also prefer to involve the external effects of the social security system in the determination of its impact. It is generally accepted that external effects are at work, but almost no information is available on its total size. In this study, we will not go into this matter.

Another question which is raised is how income transfers from and to the state are valued by both receivers and payers. Purely collective goods will not be valued against production costs by users [Wilms (1984)]. However, this study only looks at unbound transfers – lack of data means we were unable to investigate the beneficial aspects of the AWBZ and the ZFW.

The way in which the incidence is analysed depends, in turn, on the purpose of the research. Several types can be distinguished.[5] The only suitable one for our purpose is the net incidence. This is the only one which takes into account payments and benefits. It would be ideal to make an integral comparison between the current system and a hypothetical state of nature without a social security system, which serves as a benchmark. In other words, one has to find an appropriate counterfactual, which gives a '. . . full set of general equilibrium changes in relative prices and incomes that would occur if transfer programs were removed . . .' [Danziger, Haveman and Plotnick (1981: 1006)]. The largest changes are expected to take place in savings and labour supply, and so, primary income formation is influenced. However, there are no available studies implementing these ideas. Behrens and Smolensky (1973), Meerman (1978), and Reynolds and Smolensky (1977) reach the conclusion that the true pre-transfer income cannot be measured.

Söderström (1984) tries '. . . to gain some idea of the form and content of social policy when it does not benefit certain individuals at the expenses of others . . .' (p. 21), which he calls the Stoic ideal. However, such an approach requires several assumptions, all of which can be debated at least to the same extent as a comparison with the current system [*e.g.* Van Mierlo (1978)].

Besides, the effect of the existence of a social security system on savings and labour supply is not clear from empirical studies. Danziger, *et al.*'s conclusion with regard to the savings impact (in the US) is that these are '. . . depressed (. . .) by 0–20% relative to their value without these programs, with the most likely estimate lying near the lower end of this range . . .' [Danziger, *et al.* (1981: 1006)]. Their guesstimate for the labour supply in the US is a decrease by about 4.5%. In comparing the effect of the growth of the social security system in the Netherlands and the US between 1974 and 1980, Haveman (1985) concludes that 'transfer generosity' implied a reduction in labour supply by about 2.7 percentage points in the Netherlands and 0.7 points in the US. His conclusions, however, have been criticized by, among others, Pen (1985). Furthermore, research on search behaviour among the unemployed does not support the hypothesis. Van den Berg (1988), and Ten Have and Jehoel (1985) discuss this hypothesis in relation to the Netherlands.

So, we opt for a marginal net incidence approach. In this, the redistribution is measured as the difference between post-transfer income and pre-

[5] Wolfson (1979b: 156–157), which is derived from Musgrave and Musgrave (1976: 379–380).

transfer income, in which the latter is obtained from the former by reducing this by the benefits and increasing it by the premium payments. This means that we look at the primary response to or incidence of the social security system (in terms of its redistributive effect). This means that the emphasis is on 'target efficiency' [Golladay and Haveman (1977: 2)]. The indirect effects – via changes in labour supply, consumption patterns, and, as a consequence, changes in production structure and, therefore, labour demand – are not implied. If we also want to cover these indirect effects, we would need a disaggregated general disequilibrium model. Such a model is not available at present and it will take many years to develop one. The current version of NEDYMAS is a first step to its construction.

The foregoing implies that – disregarding those income elements that we cannot model – we compare secondary lifetime income and primary lifetime income. Danziger, *et al.* (1981: 1007) make the point that true pre-transfer income is probably more equally distributed than pre-transfer income measured in this way. Therefore, the net result has to be considered to be an upper limit of the redistributive effects.

In this way, we only look at who pays for, and who benefits from, the social security system and what each net gain or loss amounts to. We have to realize that our benchmark is an arbitrary one. However, if we assume that social security is '. . . randomly put into place, that its net redistribution would never have otherwise occurred, and that the private sector took no steps to self-insure against the redistribution . . .' [Kotlikoff (1985: 492)], which is plausible for particular redistributive elements of the system, this approach seems to be the most reasonable.

1.5 MEASURING LIFETIME INCOME AND ITS INEQUALITY

The level of inequality in lifetime income also depends on the way income is measured, that is to say, how income flows in the past and the future are determined and how they are discounted.

In determining income we can start from two approaches, the historical method and the hypothetical method; Blomquist (1976). The first method uses observed sequences of annual incomes of different individuals. The advantage is that real existing income histories are being compared. However, there are also a number of disadvantages: much data over a very long time are needed. And we can only work with the distribution for deceased persons, or with truncated lifetime incomes.

The hypothetical method states an income generating function for the individuals distinguished in the database and, so, simulates lifetime income histories. With this method there are no difficulties with truncated distributions and less data is needed. We have opted for the second method (section 6.4).

The reasons for discounting are that the income development differs across occupations and different types of education, it is affected by periods of unemployment, and so on. Individuals are assumed to distribute earnings over time in such a way that they maximize their lifetime utility. At first glance, we would be inclined to choose the market interest rate as the optimal discount rate. People have to borrow or lend money against this market rate. However there is no single market rate. Other objections can also be raised [Hancock and Richardson (1985)]. So, the rate is not applicable to those who have no opportunity to borrow or to lend. People can have problems determining the real interest rate from the nominal one, which implies behaviour other than when the real rate is known. Also, individuals are not always inclined to borrow and lend continuously, even if this would be an optimal strategy. Because human capital is rather illiquid, it is reasonable to assume that the required rate of return on investments in human capital has to exceed the market interest rate. Besides, time preferences will differ between individuals.

For these reasons, several authors have examined subjective discount rates. The estimates vary from about 6 [male graduate teachers in Zabalza (1979)[6]] to more than 35% [see Holbrook (1967), involving individuals with a very short time horizon].

In spite of the objections raised against the use of one 'objective' discount rate, which is the same for every individual, we will not use the subjective approach. We do not have data on time preferences for the Netherlands at our disposal. As a compromise, we will compare the results for different discount rates (section 8.4), a method which is fairly common [*e.g.* Blomquist (1976), Göbel (1983) and Davies, *et al.* (1984)].

The next question to be answered is: do we consider the redistributive impact of the social security system for the population as a whole? Treating income distribution for the total population at a certain moment, *e.g.* the population of the Netherlands on 1 January 1980, implies that we compare people belonging to different birth cohorts, who have experienced different economic opportunities and, therefore, different economic growth opportunities during different phases in their lives. Besides, the income distribution depends on the population structure at the time of investigation. For this reason we have decided to evaluate lifetime income of different birth generations separately.

A further question concerns the measures to be used in determining the redistributive impact of the social security system. There is no measure which can be applied generally. All measures concentrate on specific aspects of the distribution or cover mainly a limited segment of the distribution. We prefer to use the Theil coefficient, which has the advantage of being easy to break down. Besides, information will be given by means of the

[6] For female teachers, Zabalza finds a subjective discount rate of 31%.

contribution of the various social security benefits and contributions per decile and by means of the benefit–tax ratio per decile.

1.6 HOW THE PROBLEM IS TACKLED

The most important problem in analysing the impact of social security on lifetime income is the almost complete absence of data that could permit a longitudinal approach. That is why we opted for the hypothetical method in section 1.5. This implies that we have to construct our own database. Looking at the conditions for receiving a social security benefit (chapter 7), many of the characteristics at the micro level have to be known, *e.g.* age, marital status, sex, household size and composition, income, (former) economic activity, labour supply, income of other household members, and so on. In constructing our database, we, therefore, have to obtain a picture of the demographic and economic structure of the population. A suitable method for this purpose – and probably the only one – is microsimulation.[7] With the aid of microsimulation complex systems with mutual dependencies can be described. We need to operate at the micro level, because most of the processes we need to study – for example, claims for a private pension, family allowances, a benefit from the General Assistance Act – are at work at that level, and the process context cannot be formulated adequately at the macro level. This is especially true for redistributive aspects. Classical methods are inappropriate for that purpose. In theory, a microsimulation model can be formulated as a Markov process. In practice, however, the size of '. . . such a process for even a simple model overwhelms all existing resources for its solution . . .' [Sadowsky (1977: 3)].

The method has been intensively applied in research into the distributional effects of changes in the social security system. An overview of its use in the US is provided by Haveman (1987). The notion of microsimulation is simple. Starting from a representative sample, the characteristics of the sample population are adjusted for each period. In this way, a fictional panel is created. As a consequence, individual socio-economic life histories can also be simulated and the method provides us with the '. . . capability of examining the entire distribution of effects, not just an aggregate or a mean . . .' [Haveman and Hollenbeck (1980: xxii)]. The simulated individual impacts can be aggregated, the total costs of schemes can be derived, the number of households that are affected by an arrangement, the impact

7 Other ways used to simulate features of the life cycle are (1) the utilization of cross-section data for one year and thus creating synthetic cohorts [*e.g.* Ghez and Becker (1975)]; (2) the construction of pseudo-cohorts based on cross-section surveys in different years, in which the same people are not surveyed [*e.g.* Browning, Deaton and Irish (1985)]. However, both methods '. . . fail, to a greater or lesser extent, to capture the enormous degree of change in people's circumstances over time . . .' [Harding (1990: 6)].

on the income distribution and – in the case of the presence of sufficient behavioural responses in the model – the effects of policy (changes) on labour supply, employment, savings and so on can be evaluated [Haveman (1987: 216)]. Chapter 3 which follows deals with the method in more detail.

2

Overview of related studies

There has been little research into the field of the lifetime redistributive impact of social security schemes. In their article on the effect of income transfer programmes on – among other factors – income distribution, Danziger, *et al.* (1981: 1014) state '. . . no studies measure the redistributive effect of all transfers using a lifetime or even a multiyear accounting period . . .'. This is still the case. This does not mean, however, that there are no studies on the lifetime redistributive impact of social security schemes. However, all the available studies are limited to only one aspect of social security, *viz.* pensions provisions. In particular, the redistributive impact of the Old Age Insurance (OAI) in the US has been the subject of discussion. This discussion has been conducted in view of the reform proposals to solve the financing problems of the OAI in the long run. The redistributive aspects of these studies will be discussed below.

Old age pension schemes have also been the subject of discussion in other countries, including the former West Germany and Canada. The most important aspect from the point of view of this book is the way in which the problem was tackled in these countries, *viz.* extended microsimulation models, whereas the studies in the US are heavily restricted by the assumptions made. For example, the latter studies generally do not have a longitudinal character. By contrast, the microsimulation approach opens the possibility for longitudinal studies.

Most of the US studies use the so-called insurance model [see Thompson (1983) and Meyer and Wolff (1987b)], which considers the pooling among persons of the risk of income losses as the essential element of social security, to analyse the redistribution. In this model the expected value of insurance protection is compared with its tax price, measured in terms of benefit-contribution ratios, net present values or internal rates of return. The other approach to analysing lifetime redistribution is the so-called annuity-welfare model, which decomposes benefits into an annuity component (the insurance part) and a transfer or adequacy component.

First, we look at studies that concentrate on a specific cohort without distinguishing different income levels within that cohort. A number of examples of this approach applied to the Old Age Survivor's Insurance (OASI), can be found in Aaron (1982: ch. 6). One example is Moffit (1982) from which it is clear that all US cohorts who had already retired have received benefits worth more than the contributions they have paid. Aaron claims that the net benefit even rises the later the cohort is born. This is caused by the extension of the social security system in the 1960s and 1970s. These generations only paid social security contributions during a part of their working lives or not at all, whereas they generally can claim a benefit without limitations. Similar studies forecast a net future benefit from social security (in terms of a positive rate of return) in the US [*e.g.* Russell (1982) and Leimer and Petri (1981)]. However, it is not reasonable to think that the increase in the net benefit will also hold for all future generations and everywhere; *e.g.* Nelissen (1987b) for the lifetime incidence of Dutch state pensions. For the US there are also results which contradict the above findings. Boskin, Avrin and Cone (1983) and Feldstein and Pellechio (1978) find that future retirees will have smaller net benefits than the current retirees and that young workers will receive a negative net benefit. Explanations for this contradiction are the differences in the considered period and the use of different discount rates.

Aaron (1977) studies the redistributive impact of OASI for 14 year olds in 1966, using the 1967 Survey of Economic Opportunity (SEO), adjusting for assumed growth rates in earnings. He distinguishes between factors such as sex, race, level of education and married versus unmarried persons. His most striking result is the negative correlation between level of education and the benefit-cost ratio for white households. This is caused by longevity and a later year of entrance in the labour market. These factors more than offset the progressivity in the contributions. For nonwhites the relation between level of education and the benefit-cost ratio is somewhat irregular. His other findings are consistent with expectations. One-earner couples have a higher benefit-cost ratio than two-earner couples, who in turn have a higher ratio than single females and single males. Because Aaron normalizes his results, we are not able to compare the (absolute) results with other studies.

Okonkwo (1976) used longitudinal age-earnings profiles from four US censuses and life expectancies by sex, race and education to estimate internal rates of return. His results are analogous to those of Aaron (1977).

Next, there are studies that also look at different income groups within a cohort. Chen and Chu (1974) calculated tax-benefit ratios and rates of return for representative workers who retired in 1974 and for workers entering the labour force at 18 and 22 in 1974, assuming that these entrants retire at 65. They show lower tax-benefit ratios and higher rates of return for workers with average earnings than for those with maximum taxable earnings. The same holds for 1974 retirees in comparison with 1974 entrants. Chen and Chu made their calculations for various hypothetical groups. Their results show that the tax-benefit ratio for the 1974 retirees (using constant 1973 prices) is between 0.09 and 0.46, whereas the rate of return varies between 6.1 and 13.1%. For 1974 entrants aged 22 the tax-benefit ratio is between 0.53 and 1.57 and the rate of return between 1.4 and 5.1%. For the 18-year-old entrants these figures are 0.65–1.86 and 1.1–4.3% respectively.

Freiden, Leimer and Hoffman (1976) analysed a sample of case histories of US workers who retired between 1967 and 1970. The rate of return of benefits over taxes paid '. . . was very much higher for the low-income retirees than for the high. On a lifetime basis the sharply regressive feature of the payroll tax was more than overcome by the highly progressive feature of the benefit structure . . . However, at this stage of the art of lifetime income analysis, it is probably fair to say that the issue of long-run equity of the Social Security system is still open to question . . .' (Moss, 1978: 136). Aaron (1977), for example, found the reverse for future retirees.

More extended are the Pellechio and Goodfellow (1983) results. They estimate the present value in 1983 (including the 1983 amendments) of future benefits and past and future contributions for a set of representative workers aged 25, 40 and 55 in 1983. They consider the complete OASDI programme (thus including survival and disability benefits) for six earnings levels. Net present value increases by age under *ceteris paribus* conditions. The highest values are reached for one-earner married couples (and within this group the net present value is highest for middle-income) and lowest for single males. With the exception of one-earner couples, the net present value is highest for the low earners.

The OASDI has also been investigated by Ferrara and Lott Jr. (1985), who calculate rates of return for 12 hypothetical family types, entering the labour force in 1983. Higher income earners have been assumed to enter the labour force at older ages than low-income earners. The resulting rates of return are given in table 2.1 (Ferrara and Lott Jr., 1985: 22).

Table 2.1 *Rates of return for 12 family types by Ferrara and Lott Jr. (1985)*

Single maximum-income earner	– 1.5
Two maximum-income spouses	– 1.0
Maximum-income spouse, average-income spouse	– 0.5
Maximum-income spouse, low-income spouse	– 0.5
Maximum-income spouse, nonworking spouse	0.0
Single average-income worker	0.0
Two average-income spouses	0.5
Average-income spouse, low-income spouse	1.0
Average-income spouse, nonworking spouse	1.5
Two low-income spouses	1.5
Single low-income worker	1.5
Low-income spouse, nonworking spouse	2.75

So, low-income, one-earner families receive the highest real internal rate of return. Families with maximum earnings receive a zero or a negative rate of return.

Leimer and Petri (1981) use a long-run macrosimulation model of the US economy to analyse the intergenerational welfare consequences of the OASI system. This tracks a series of cohorts through time and contains long-term demographic and economic changes, a detailed modelling of social security and important linkages between social security and the economy. In this way, the authors are able to compare the welfare consequences of the current pay-as-you-go system with a hypothetical system, based on funding. From this comparison it appears that cohorts born between 1953 and 1984 will prefer the funding system, whereas for the other birth cohorts the pay-as-you-go system has to be preferred.

A study comparable to Ferrara and Lott Jr. (1985) is that of Hurd and Shoven (1985). Their study does not include the 1983 amendments (the increased age of eligibility for future retirees and the partial taxation of benefits). The most important point of the latter study is that it takes account of previous contributions by persons who were already dead in the year that serves as the starting point. All the above studies neglect this issue. This affects the results to a large degree for widows and widowers at all ages and the effect is larger as the cohort is older. At the age of about 70, all categories are influenced strongly by this aspect. At this age, only half of the paid taxes of nonwhites are considered, when the taxes of the dead are not taken into account. For whites the proportion amounts to about two-thirds.

Hurd and Shoven use the Social Security Administration's Retirement History Survey, referring to 11 000 households in 1969, whose head was aged between 58 and 64. These households were reinterviewed every two years until 1979. They found that the median rate of return of couples in 1969 was 8.39, which is much greater than what is generally assumed to be offered by other investments. In 1979 the rate of return is generally somewhat lower as a consequence of changes in the system (*e.g.* double indexing). Looking at the rates of return by wealth quartile, what is most striking is that these hardly differ in spite of the considerable progressivity of the social security benefit schedule. This means that this is apparently neutralized by the taxes paid by the deceased. Simulations for future generations show that the real rate of return declines monotonically and substantially with cohort age. For example, the median-income single female retiring in 1970 has an expected real rate of return of 9.1%, for those retiring in 2000 the rate amounts to 3.8% and in 2020 3.3%. It appears that '... the intergenerational transfers are extremely large and the intragenerational distribution of transfers is quite different (more progressive) for the currently young than it is for the presently elderly ...' [Hurd and Shoven (1985: 213)].

Boskin, Kotlikoff, Puffert and Shoven (1987) compute the expected present value of Social Security retirement (OAI) benefits and taxes for households of different marital circumstances, incomes and age cohorts using the 1985 social security and income tax laws. Looking at the intergenerational transfers, they find that the internal rate of return declines rapidly for the cohorts born between 1915 and 1960. Thereafter, the internal rate of return is more or less constant. For the younger cohorts it holds that the increased life expectancy offsets the increased taxation of benefits. Using a real discount rate of 3%, the present value of transfers for single-earner couples is negative as early as the 1945 cohort for earnings levels above $10 000 (at the 1985 wage index). Intragenerational analysis also shows that one-earner couples have a higher rate of return than singles with the same earnings history, whereas single females benefit more than single males from the system. These differences are due to the receipt by couples of an inflation-indexed joint survivor annuity, with the initial benefit level set at 150% of the single person's benefit, and to differences in life expectancy between males and females. A last important result is their finding that higher income households receive a lower real rate of return than lower income households.

We mentioned Moffit (1982) earlier. He estimates net benefits at time of entry into labour force – covering the period 1942–77 – for eight cohorts. In this way he also takes account of contributions and survivor's benefits of persons dying before reaching retirement age. He finds that net benefits increase for successive cohorts, but that the rate of growth declines.

Burkhauser and Warlick (1981) analyse the old age survivor's insurance in the United States, using the annuity-welfare model. Various authors looked at the redistributive impact of the OASI, using only annual data [*e.g.* Bridges (1974), Danziger (1977) and Ozawa 1976)]. These all conclude that OASI redistributes income to a large extent. However, Burkhauser and Warlick show that this does not hold if one uses a life cycle framework. They consider various income brackets – within cohorts – to determine the value of lifetime wealth increment in 1972. All income categories show positive redistributive benefits. In terms of absolute dollars, high-income groups receive at least as much as low-income groups. The middle-income groups profit most from the system. In percentages of the OASI benefit the upper 70% of the income distribution receives about the same percentage (64–77%). It appears that the net gain from OASI was larger for older than for younger retirees, and that it was roughly proportional across earnings classes. The system favours very low income recipients and those who are only part of their life insured under the OASI (such as some groups of government employees, so-called double-dippers) by the existence of minimum provisions. It also favours older cohorts, because the older the cohort the fewer the years of OASI payments.

Meyer and Wolff (1987b) use the same data and – with some minor adjustments – the same method to isolate the effect of household characteristics and programme parameters on the redistributive impact of old age insurance (by contrast with Burkhauser and Warlick, they do not include survivors' benefits). They find that earlier retirement cohorts receive a larger net benefit from OASI than later retirement cohorts, that the system benefits women relative to men due to differences in longevity, but that married women with significant earnings have hardly any positive net benefits. This is due to the existence of dependent's benefits, with the result that married women barely gain an increase in benefits from labour force participation.

Boskin, Avrin and Cone (1983) also use the annuity-welfare model to analyse the pre-1983 amendment situation. They use social security longitudinal earnings tapes, including covered earnings from 1937 to 1975. For those who had not reached the age of 65, earnings were predicted separately for males and females using an estimating equation based on positive 1972 earnings. These predicted earnings were indexed over time using 7% for inflationary earnings and the assumption of a 1.5% per year earnings increase due to productivity. The discount rate amounts to 3% net of inflation. Their results show that families contribute more over time. Families of those who were already retired in 1977 pay less than 10% of those who were between 25 and 34 years old in 1977. For the latter group the net result is a negative one: they pay more than they will receive. The former group receives about six times their contribution. For younger cohorts up to and including the cohort aged 35 to 44 in 1977, the net result in terms of their contribution is positive, but is getting smaller. They also give information for four income brackets. From this it is clear that redistribution between income classes is fairly limited. The net benefits, in 1977 dollars, discounted to year of retirement vary between $36 587 and $42 476 for the oldest cohort and between $5972 and – $1923 for the youngest cohort. The average lifetime benefit for these two cohorts amounts to $49 400 and $73 577, respectively.

In the early 1970s some studies in the UK were also published. These concern the impact of the proposed National Superannuation, an old age benefit in which both the benefits and contributions are earnings-related. Prest (1970) gives results for persons retiring in 1969 under the assumption that the proposed system would have been in operation in the past. He finds that single men have a lower benefit contribution ratio than married couples and that redistribution from richer to poorer is substantial. Atkinson (1970) shows results for various birth generations. His findings are in line with Prest's. Atkinson also shows that the redistributive effect under the current system – in which benefits are earnings-related – is more limited than under a system in which benefits are flat-rated. Atkinson concludes that younger generations are worse off than older generations.

Shimono and Tachibanaki (1985) compare the redistributive effect of the Japanese and British pension systems in the framework of a two-period analysis. In both systems contributions are a percentage of income up to a contribution limit. In the Japanese system, benefits are a fixed amount plus a percentage of the income, again up to a certain income limit. The English system also has a fixed amount, but if earnings were above this amount, the benefit is increased by a percentage of the difference between earnings and the fixed amount. Their findings are not surprising: the flat element in the level of benefit has a positive effect on redistribution; an increase of the proportional rate of contribution reduces lifetime income inequality and the existence of a maximum limit of income for the determination of contribution and benefit weakens the redistributive impact. However, the assumptions in the two-period model are restrictive and the results cannot, therefore, be compared with those of the other studies reviewed here.

The results of Nelissen (1987b) for the Netherlands are analogous to the conclusions for the US. This is striking, because the Dutch pension system consists of flat-rate benefits, whereas benefits are proportional to income (up to the so-called maximum premium income). It appears that redistribution between income groups is limited. The larger part of redistribution takes place from unmarried men and women to married couples.

The disadvantage of all the studies above is that life cycle income has been based on a relatively short period. It would therefore be preferable to include longitudinal pre-retirement economic status and earnings. This course has been adopted by Wolfson (1988 and 1989). He looks at, among other things, the redistributional impact of a homemaker pensions proposal under the public earnings-related Canada and Quebec Pensions Plans (C/QPP). In his view, the analysis only makes sense in a life cycle context, since the proposal is related to both labour market and demographic behaviour in the past. Therefore, a suitable analysis requires longitudinal microdata on the dynamics of marriage, fertility, divorce, labour force participation and earnings. In the absence of such data, the life cycle analysis is only possible using synthetic or simulated data. These data have been produced using a Monte Carlo life cycle microsimulation model. The homemaker pension proposal treats homemakers with actual earnings below half the average wage as if they had earnings equal to half this average wage. Homemakers are defined as any adults caring for a child under age 18, for a spouse, or for a dependent and infirm relative living in the same house. In this way the proposal ensures a minimum flat-rated pension for homemakers. Wolfson concludes that the proposal tends to be mildly redistributive from higher to lower lifetime income groups, whereas it does not benefit women as much as might be expected (but almost equal in value to men and women).

These results are criticized by Kennedy (1990), who uses the same microsimulation model, but adds financial consistency at the macro level. Under his assumptions, the highest income groups benefit from the proposal and females do have profits from the homemaker pension proposal at the cost of men.

Another application of microsimulation in the field of old age pensions has been carried out by Wagner (1984) to derive the intergenerational distributional aspects of the German *gesetzlichen Rentenversicherung*. His conclusions do not differ substantially from the ones mentioned above. He also finds that redistribution from the higher to the lower incomes is limited. In spite of some rules that benefit non-employed persons, the system benefits those with smooth career patterns.

Microsimulation models have been used previously to study pensions, see *e.g.* Schulz (1982), but lifetime redistribution was not one of the areas covered. Research into the redistributional aspects of the complete social security system are not available. The only approximation of a lifetime social security incidence known to the author comes from Davies, St. Hilaire and Whalley (1984), Harding (1992) and Falkingham, Hills and Lessof (1993). Davies, *et al.* use a limited and restrictive microsimulation model of life cycle saving and bequest behaviour of Canadian households [Davies (1982)]. They do not distinguish between various social security schemes (such as old age pensions, unemployment schemes, disability schemes) but use an average net benefit. It is not known to what extent different schemes contribute to the lifetime incidence. The lifetime paths of the income and tax streams are based on the 1971 Statistics Canadian Survey of Consumer Finances (SCF). Their conclusion is that lifetime redistribution of social security is less than the annual one, '. . . since transfers are less concentrated in the lower deciles in the lifetime data . . .' [Davies, *et al.* (1984: 644)]. Harding uses a pseudo-cohort of 2000 males and 2000 females 'born' in 1986 in Australia, who live for up to 95 years in a world which does not change; a steady-state world has been assumed. She distinguishes between several types of social security income. Harding's (1992) conclusion is in agreement with that of Davies, *et al.* (1984). Falkingham *et al.* (1993) is analogous to Harding (1992), but refers to a steady-state approach based on the British situation in 1985.

An important element in determining the redistributive impact of social security schemes is the lifetime distribution of earnings. Research has been carried out on this related subject several times. Fase (1969) examined the lifetime income for a number of professions in the Netherlands. However, the method is only applicable to homogeneous groups. Cohort studies covering about 15 years are available – Creedy, *et al.* (1980) – and for an overview Göbel (1983: 12–13). Neither method, however, is able to determine the development in individual incomes.

Göbel (1983), on the other hand, treats some cohorts who were born around 1910, based on data from the German Pensions Insurance. He uses the historical method, so that no lifetime incomes for persons still in their active period can be determined. Soltow (1965) also uses this method. The hypothetical method has been applied by Summers (1956), Blinder (1974) and Blomquist (1976). The earnings functions as derived by Klevmarken and Quigley (1976), Weiss and Lillard (1978) and Abowd and Killingsworth (1983) belong to the same category, although they do not focus on lifetime income. Hain and Helberger (1986) use the microsimulation approach to derive lifetime income. A version of this income function [see Wagner (1983)] was also used by Wagner (1984) in his analysis of the *gesetzliche Rentenversicherung* in the former West Germany.

Also related to the above is the research into the demand for social security benefits, which has been intensively analysed in the 1970s, especially in the US. The analyses were by means of microsimulation models. Its main purpose, however, was not primarily the analysis of distributional effects, but of the extent to which the social welfare programmes met their goals, how efficient they were, which side effects the programmes had, and so on. Haveman (1987) provides an overview.

To recapitulate: most studies concentrate on old age pensions. First, we discussed studies that compare complete cohorts, without looking at the income distribution within cohorts. We then considered a number of studies on the redistributive impact for different income groups within a specific cohort. From the survey it is clear that workers '. . . with low covered earnings receive more in benefits per dollar of earnings and taxes paid than do workers with high earnings . . .' [Aaron (1982: 78)]. Couples receive more than singles with the same earnings. Low-income, one-earner families receive the highest real internal rate of return. Those who start working relatively late in life generally receive a higher net benefit than those who enter working life relatively early. The older the generation, the larger the net benefit. A higher life expectancy (which is positively correlated with income) also leads to relatively higher net benefits; Okonkwo (1973), Freiden, Leimer and Hoffman (1976), Aaron (1977), Leimer (1978) and Nelissen (1987b). Most studies do not use a life cycle framework, because they only consider the programme as existing at the moment the research was carried out and, consequently, do not consider changes in the programme. This can have important impacts. Moreover, life cycle income has been based on a relatively short period. The latter problem has been solved by the use of microanalytic simulation models.

In conclusion, research into the redistributive impact of social security schemes on lifetime income has been limited to old age public pensions and the significance of the greater part of these studies is limited by the treatment of life cycle income and changes in the programme under consideration. The latter does not hold for the studies in which an extended microsimulation model has been used (Canada and the former West Germany).

3

Microsimulation

3.1 INTRODUCTION

The microsimulation approach was proposed by Orcutt (1957 and 1960), as was the first – limited – application [Orcutt, *et al.* (1961)]. Microsimulation is a '. . . technique of computerised modelling within which the decision making process is replicated for individual decision makers within the system . . .' [Bonsall (1979: 82)]. Microsimulation analyses the behaviour of a system using characteristics of the micro-units distinguished in the system, whereby, with the aid of a model that reproduces the functioning of the system under study, individuals' characteristics are adjusted for each period. A microsimulation system acts on a microdata base, generally containing thousands of actors (*e.g.* individuals, firms) and this microdata base is adapted – or aged – from period to period. The process is shown in figure 3.1.

In our application, the system under study is the social security system in the Netherlands. The micro-units in the microdata base are individuals, living in the Netherlands, and emigrants. These individuals are related to other members in his or her household, if present. The microdata base contains the characteristics of all these micro-units. Those characteristics which are recorded include age, marital status, level of education, number of children, economic activity, labour supply, wage income, various social security benefits and payments, year of immigration and year of emigration. A complete list can be found in section 3.3. The model is implemented in a computer programme, containing a set of relationships that describe (part

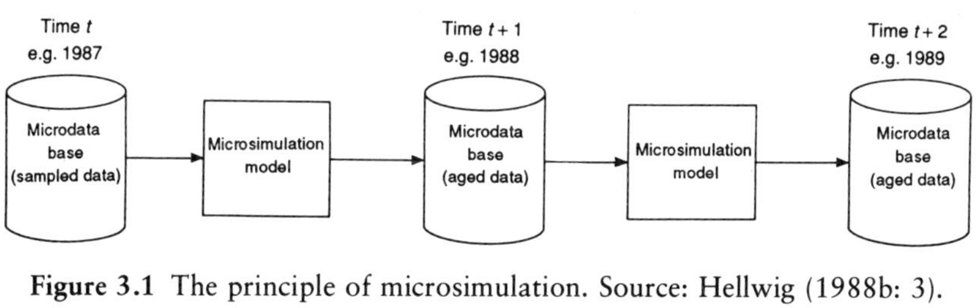

Figure 3.1 The principle of microsimulation. Source: Hellwig (1988b: 3).

of) the economy. The programme describes (preferably by applying behavioural assumptions) the changes in the individuals' characteristics and describes the conditions which, for example, determine whether an individual has to pay social security premiums or receives social security benefits; in both cases equations determine how much has to be paid or received.

Each characteristic of the individuals – such as sex, year of birth – has to have the possibility of being fixed or changed over time by means of a behavioural model which ages it. The behavioural hypotheses can be formulated in various ways: tables, regression equations, probability distributions, decision trees, transition probabilities, institutional rules, and so on. The required parameters generally have to be estimated from data. These data are often derived from the microdata base or are obtained externally. By applying the behavioural assumptions we can determine how the situation of each of the micro-units changes as a consequence of internal and external factors which influence the system in question. The model is 'solved' by simulation. No analytical solution is obtained. So, the result is not unique. Other initial values for the random generator (see the next section) will give other solutions. The reliability of the results, therefore, depends on the number of micro-units distinguished in the microsimulation system and the number of (repeated) runs.

In the next section we will deal with the method and its advantages and drawbacks in more detail. Section 3.3 describes the general structure of the NEDYMAS model.

3.2 MICROSIMULATION: PROS AND CONS

Figure 3.2 A list of individuals and some of their attributes.

Label	Age	Sex	Marital Status	Education	Occupation
01.1	30	Male	Divorced	3	11
02.1	21	Male	Single	2	19
03.1	25	Male	Married	4	16
03.2	23	Female	Married	4	3
04.1	54	Male	Married	4	3
04.2	55	Female	Married	2	3
04.3	28	Female	Single	2	21
04.4	33	Male	Single	2	16
04.5	20	Male	Single	2	21
05.1	46	Male	Married	4	11
05.2	41	Female	Married	2	18
05.3	21	Female	Single	2	6
06.1	69	Male	Married	4	20
06.2	60	Female	Married	4	21
07.1	44	Male	Divorced	3	9

Source: Clarke (1986: 249).

The essence of microsimulation lies in the programme which focuses on multi-actor, multi-level and multi-process synthesis [Caldwell (1987)]. For this, a bottom-up strategy is applied. The state representation of the components of the system of interest forms the basis of each modelling strategy. As the name suggests, the micro-level representation of individuals in terms of social, economic and demographic characteristics, together with other possible relevant spatial and activity attributes, forms the basis of microsimulation [Clarke (1986)]. The information with respect to individuals, for example, is stored in the form of lists which are updated (list processing). An example of such a list is given in figure 3.2.

This storage method forms the key to the application of microsimulation. The advantage of list processing as compared with storage via an occupancy matrix, for example – the method which is used for macrosimulation, among other applications – is that the storage space needed is relatively small, even if only a limited number of characteristics are used. The number of records to be stored via list processing in microsimulation – which uses a discrete **event** model – increases linearly with the number of micro-units, whereas storage via an occupancy matrix in macrosimulation – which uses a discrete **time** model – is multiplicatively related to the number of states. This is the consequence of working with decision unit probabilities instead of with transition probabilities [Hayes (1989)]. For example, if a population is broken down by sex (male and female), age (20 five-years groups) and, say, five household types, we have $2 * 20 * 5 = 200$ states, which implies that we have to store $200 * 200$ groups. In the case of microsimulation we only need 3^*n elements, n being the number of simulated persons. In both cases we must also store the transition probabilities. Considering only the demographic part, and using 100 000 individuals, NEDYMAS requires 9 900 000 bytes or about 10 megabytes. To get the same information by macrosimulation would need about 1.6×10^{24} states, and consequently a matrix of about 2.5×10^{48} cells [Nelissen (1989)]. The macrosimulation approach also has the disadvantage that it cannot tell us who is whose partner or child, or deal with continuous variables. This is not a problem with the microsimulation approach. When using more than a very limited number of variables – and certainly in the case of continuous variables such as income – the micro/macro storage ratio will be close to zero [*e.g.* Keilman (1987)]. This means that microsimulation is able to provide information which cannot be obtained from such a macro approach.

How is microsimulation applied in practice? As we discussed above, a microsimulation model comprises a microdata base of micro-units and a micromodel. With the aid of the micromodel a representative continuation of the sample is obtained at the end of each period. This process is called ageing of the population, as given schematically in figure 3.3.

To illustrate this, we will take the modelling of mortality. The decision whether an individual will or will not undergo a potential transition is simulated with the aid of the Monte Carlo method. This means that the conditional probability of an individual undergoing that event has to be given.

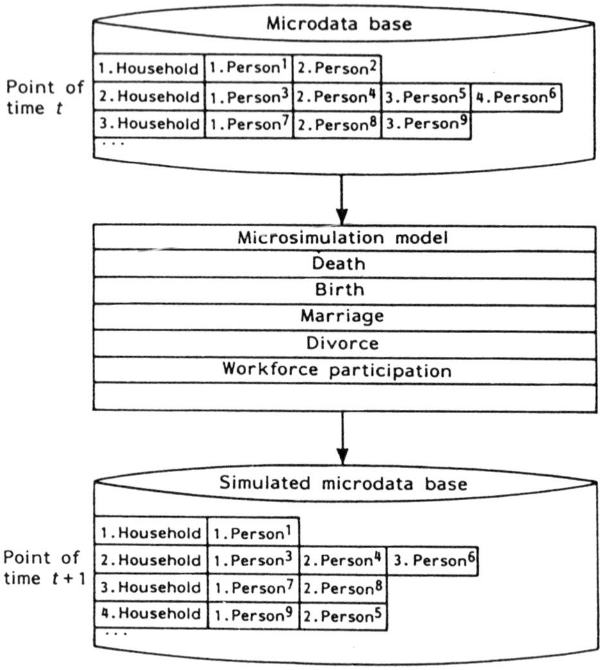

Figure 3.3 The principle of microsimulation.

For example, for a 77-year-old divorced woman the probability of dying was 6.75% in 1968. We then randomly draw a number from the uniform [0, 1] distribution. If this number is smaller than or equal to the probability of dying of 0.0675, the woman is expected to die. If the number is larger than 0.0675, the woman will remain alive. If she dies, we investigate whether she had children (who have become orphans). So, decisions (or events) at the level of an individual can have implications for other individuals. Microsimulation creates a synthetic database which reflects the (developments in the) demographic and economic structure of the population. A stylized example is given in figure 3.4. Hendricks, Holden and Johnson (1977) used microsimulation to produce a simulated set of family and earning histories from 1960 to 2000, using the DYNASIM model, for the Office of the Secretary of Health, Education and Welfare.

Figure 3.4 An example of microsimulation.

1986 (sample data)						1987 (aged data)					
	ID	Age	Sex	Job	Income		ID	Aged	Sex	Job	Income
Household 1						Household 1					
P1	1	47	M	Yes	38 000	P1	1	48	M	Yes	38 000
P2	2	44	F	No	0	P2	2	45	F	No	0
P3	3	20	M	Yes	23 000	P3	4	16	M	No	0
P4	4	15	M	No	0						
Household 2						Household 2					
P1	5	79	F	No	14 000	P1	3	21	M	Yes	25 000
						P2	8	19	F	No	0
Household 3						Household 3					
P1	6	37	M	Yes	32 000	P1	6	38	M	Yes	35 200
P2	7	38	F	No	0	P2	7	39	F	Yes	14 175
P3	8	18	F	No	0						
Household 4						Household 4					

Source: Hellwig (1988b).

The simulated population can be considered as the realization of a stochastic process, as a random sample from the real population. The simulated and observed population will differ randomly for two reasons. First there is the variance related to the specification of the initial sample population. The second reason is the variance associated with the sampling approach for selecting the particular members of the population whose characteristics have changed for each year of the simulation; this is called Monte Carlo variability [Orcutt, *et al.* (1976: ch. 11)].

We can identify a number of types of microsimulation models [Social and Cultural Planning Agency (1985: 46–47) and Merz (1988: 4–9)]. First, we can distinguish between standard and empirical simulation models. Standard simulations refer to stylized calculations (*e.g.* for specific types of households or persons). Empirical simulations use empirical data. This enables us to determine more accurately the number of persons to which some calculations refer and the relevance of any changes. In the following, we limit ourselves to empirical models. A first differentiation is based on the question of whether the time aspect in the population is ignored or not. This results in static and dynamic microsimulation models, respectively. The static models measure only first-order effects: it is assumed that the sample structure of the micro-units does not change. Weighing factors adjust the microdata base to the population in the future. These models are only suitable for short- and medium-term simulations. In dynamic models, the sample characteristics are aged each period and micro-units are allowed to change their behaviour as a consequence of changes in the system. Children and immigrants can be added to the sample and household situations are allowed to change by *e.g.* marriage or divorce. So, the number of micro-units in dynamic models generally changes in time, whereas the number remains constant in the static models. Dynamic models are as originally proposed by Orcutt and they explicitly model the demographic processes. This does not imply that static models do not contain behavioural relationships; only the transition probabilities are assumed not to change.

Within the dynamic type, two subtypes can be distinguished: longitudinal models and cross-sectional models, respectively. In the longitudinal approach the complete life history of each separate micro-unit is simulated in one run, without interaction with other micro-units. In the cross-sectional approach all micro-units are aged for the first year, and then all these micro-units pass through the second year of the simulation, and so on. In this way interaction between micro-units is continuously possible. The life history of one individual is only known if all micro-units have passed through the whole simulation period. The absence of interaction in the longitudinal approach is a very great drawback. The disadvantage of the cross-sectional models is that they require more information, and using this information, are also more expensive in terms of computer programme development, computer time, and so on. But, its advantage is clear: we get a more realistic approximation of reality. A discussion can also be found in Hayes (1989). Because of their costs, the number of applications of dynamic cross-sectional models is rather limited. Extensive models – covering not only household dynamics, but also socio-economic characteristics – are only available in the US, the former West Germany, and now also in the Netherlands (also considered the next section). An overview of these three types of microsimulation is given in figure 3.5.

The most important advantages of microsimulation are as follows [Social and Cultural Planning Agency (1985: 48–49); Orcutt, Glazer, Harris and Wertheimer (1980: 86); Arrow (1980: 258–260); Orcutt and Glazer (1980: 124–125) and Hellwig (1988a: 30–32):

(a) Microsimulation takes place at the level at which most decisions are made, namely that of micro-units. The micro-unit is the natural starting point for analysis. Aggregation is, therefore, unnecessary and connected problems can be avoided. So, there is no need to translate behavioural relations at the micro level to the macro level. This is especially important in the field of social sciences because aggregation of theories to the macro level has not been carried out except under very restrictive assumptions [for example, Kirman (1989)]. This also implies that no information is ever lost through aggregation. Different types of institutional rules – *e.g.* in the field of taxes and social security – can also be modelled.
(b) Modern social scientists break problems down into manageable parts. This leads to problems when trying to put the parts together again. In many cases, the quantitative revolution in social sciences has resulted in a strengthening of the imbalance of analysis over synthesis. Microsimulation can contribute to the reverse [Caldwell (1987)].

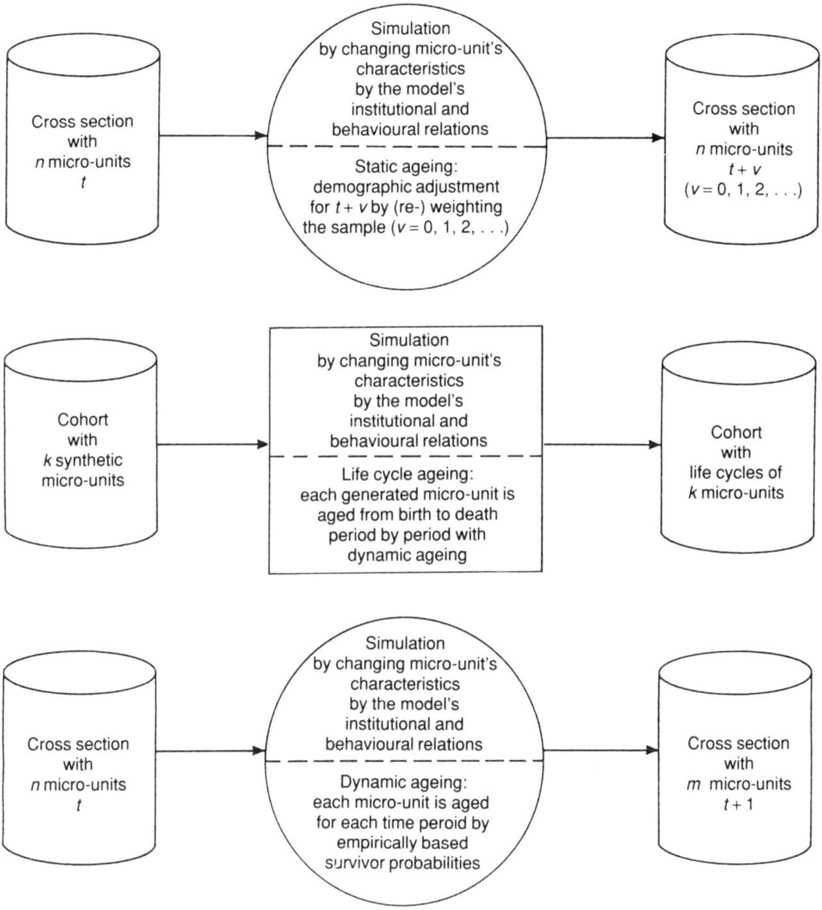

Figure 3.5 Static, dynamic and longitudinal microsimulation.
Source: Merz (1988: 6).

(c) There is hardly any loss of data. In principle, all micro-data can be used. As a result, there is a great deal of available information, and there is full representation and treatment of the heterogeneity in household and individual characteristics. It is possible, for example, to generate the income distribution in a particular year; this is virtually impossible with macro-models. In this manner we can also gain insight into the question of how many and which households are affected by specific measures of, for example, the social security system, and how this influences further behaviour [Bekkering, *et al.* (1989), for example, discuss such processes in the field of tax legislation].

(d) The most complicated interrelationships can be described; in such cases paramount importance is attached to the explicit treatment of dynamics in simulating the system. For example, the determination of eligibility for a social welfare benefit or for a rent rebate is relatively easy with the aid of the microsimulation model, which can also determine its effect on, for example, the labour supply of various household members.
(e) It is relatively easy to maintain consistency, which is a general methodological problem in, for example, modelling household and family dynamics [Galler (1988)].
(f) Assumptions and hypotheses with respect to the micro-units can be introduced or changed at any time. The model is very flexible in view of its use of modules: each process is generally implemented in a separate module. These modules can be developed independently of other modules. In a microsimulation model alternative policies can be modelled and calculated very quickly.
(g) The method is intuitively appealing because it uses existing units (*e.g.* individuals).

It goes without saying that microsimulation also has a number of drawbacks [Social and Cultural Planning Agency (1985: 49–51); Klevmarken (1980); Hoschka (1986) and Hellwig (1988a: 32–34)]. However, it is preferable to speak of (practical) problems rather than disadvantages, as follows:

(a) The behavioural hypotheses are often based on insufficient knowledge (such as the behavioural hypotheses which form the basis of demographic decisions). As a consequence all microsimulation models have only a limited number of behavioural responses, particularly in the field of household formation.
(b) Large databases are needed, or have to be simulated. In the Netherlands, such databases are limited. One of the available databases is the Socio-Economic Panel, but in view of the costs involved, it could not be used for our purpose.
(c) The construction and maintenance of microsimulation models requires large-scale investments in manpower, computer capacity and computer time. In view of the high costs of microsimulation in comparison with other methods (case studies, mental models, regression models, demographic and social accounts) it is surprising that the method has been applied at all. It is estimated that the development of the German SPES/Sfb3 models required 100 to 150 man years, DYNASIM about 55 man years and the Darmstad model about 15 man years [Hellwig (1988c: 6) and Social and Cultural Planning Agency (1990: 16)].
(d) In addition to variance related to the specification of the initial sample population, Monte Carlo variability results from the sampling approach to selecting the members of the model population whose characteristics change. By repeating the runs, we can gain deeper insight into the magni-

tude of this phenomenon [Orcutt, *et al.* (1976) and Nelissen (1989)]. Microsimulation does not give a unique solution.

The drawbacks associated with microsimulation also apply to other methods which try to give the same type of output. Microsimulation is certainly expensive in terms of computer capacity, manpower, and so on. This is, however, inherent to its nature: using large input to give very detailed results. The Monte Carlo variability problem can be reduced by using larger microdata bases or by repeating the runs, so that a distribution for the desired result can be derived. However, to a certain extent this is a relative problem: the solution to the problems treated with microsimulation models cannot be solved analytically. Essentially, the choice is between having no solution or a solution subjected to Monte Carlo variability. Moreover, '... models that don't have to be solved can be changed or added to freely and easily ...' [Bergmann (1990: 101)].

Micro models are the most appropriate instruments for an analysis of the problem under investigation. With the aid of micromodels, we can incorporate first-order effects (direct effects as a consequence of changes in *e.g.* institutional relations) and second-order effects (behavioural effects as a consequence of the reallocation of activities by the micro-units). This method also yields ideal information on the distribution of the effects. However, this type of model cannot be used directly to process so-called third-order effects (as a consequence of the spillover to other markets and the cyclical consequences). This can be solved, in practice, by constructing a (limited) meso- or macromodel around the micromodel [for example, Golladay and Haveman (1977); Orcutt, *et al.* (1976) and Hansen, *et al.* (1987)], although problems with regard to the simultaneity and consistency of the model remain. The model dynamics are also often limited because the structure is recursive. This can be alleviated by restricting the period of analysis to a week or a month instead of a year [for example, Bennett and Bergmann (1986)].

Common meso- and macromodels cannot be disaggregated to provide the information needed, in particular the distribution of the effects, especially if knowledge of the other household members is needed. A comparison between the microsimulation approach and other models used for policy analyses can be found in Greenberger, Crenson and Crissey (1976: ch. 4).

All in all, we can conclude that a micro approach has to be preferred for our purpose and, given the requirements to solve the problem, microsimulation is the appropriate method.

3.3 THE GENERAL STRUCTURE OF NEDYMAS

Our model NEDYMAS is a dynamic cross-sectional model. Demographic processes are explicitly simulated, which implies that the size of the microdata base changes during the simulation period. The sample passes through time year by year. For each person in the micro database we investigated which personal characteristics changed, and to what extent, each year. In section 3.1 we stated that the heart of microsimulation modelling is formed by its state representation of the components of the system of interest. This is executed by drawing up a list of attributes for each individual in the sample. The attributes for each individual, used by NEDYMAS, are given in table 3.1.

Table 3.1 *Attributes used in NEDYMAS*

001	identification no.	sequence number of individual generated
002	sex	male, female
003	marital status	0 = unmarried and non-cohabiting, 1 = married, 2 = divorced and non-cohabiting, 3 = widowed and non-cohabiting, 4 = unmarried and cohabiting, 5 = divorced and cohabiting, 6 = widowed and cohabiting
004	year of birth	year of birth of the individual
005	year of death	year in which the individual died
006	id. no. mother	pointer to the mother
007	id. no. father	pointer to the father
008	year of leaving his parental home	year in which the individual left parental home or both parents have died
009	degree of urbanization	0 = unknown, 1 = place of residence has less than 50 000 inhabitants (in 1982), 2 = 50 000 up to 400 000 inhabitants, 3 = 400 000 inhabitants or more
010	level of education	see chapter 6, table 6.1.
011	level of partner's education	see chapter 6, table 6.1.
012	end of education	year in which the education process is left
013	part-time education	Boolean for being in part-time (true) or full-time (false) education
014	year of emigration	year in which the individual emigrates
015	year of immigration	year in which the individual immigrates
016	empartner	Boolean indicating whether a married or cohabiting man emigrates with (false) or without (true) his partner
017	siblings	number of siblings
018	no. of children	number of children, including partner's children born before the current marriage or cohabitation and excluding children of whom a former partner has been granted custody
019	no. of children at former partner	number of children of whom a former partner has been granted custody
020	year of cohabitation	year in which the cohabitation started
021	year of marriage	year in which the marriage was contracted
022	year of divorce	year in which both partners divorced or dehabitated
023	year of widowhood	year in which the partner died
025	id. no. partner	pointer for the partner
026	id. no. former partner	pointer for the former partner

Table 3.1 (*Contd.*)

027	old people's home	Boolean that is true if one lives in an old people's home, otherwise false
028–047	id. nos. children	pointers to the children, with the exclusion of children of whom a former partner has been granted custody
048–067	id. nos. children at former partner(s)	pointers to the children of whom a former partner has been granted custody (up to the age of 22); the last two pointers are used as pointers to the mother and father, respectively, if the mother or father has died and could claim benefits from the Civil Servants Pension Fund (ABP)
068	economic activity	1 = employee, 2 = self-employed, 3 = retired, 4 = unemployed, but before not an employee or civil servant, 5 = civil servant, 6 = unemployed employee, 7 = unemployed civil servant, 8 = conscript, 9 = disabled employee, 10 = disabled civil servant, 11 = disabled, not being 9 or 10, 12 = student, 13 = housewife or houseman, 14 = unemployed, before disabled employee, 15 = unemployed, before disabled civil servant, 16 = unemployed, before disabled, not being 14 or 15
069	percentile	the percentile of the income distribution to which the individual belongs
070	labour force participation	the proportion of the current labour time; 0 = unemployed or not available for the labour market; 1 = full-time; between 0 and 1 part-time
071	year of unemployment	last year in which one became unemployed
072	month of unemployment	month in which one became unemployed
073	year of employment	year in which one entered economic activity working for the last time
074	month of employment	month in which one entered economic activity working for the last time
075	no. of count children	number of children counting for the child allowance acts
076	aow years	number of years one is insured for the AOW
077	aow voluntary	Boolean, which is true if one is insured voluntarily for the AOW (emigrants only)
078	abw	Boolean, true if one receives an ABW benefit in the current year
079	rww	Boolean, true if one can claim an RWW benefit
080	ioaw	Boolean, true if one can claim an IOAW benefit
081	aaw	1 = high basis, 2 = low basis (see section 7.5.)
082	prinkvv	income concept, on the basis of which the premiums for the AOW, AWW, AKW, AWBZ and AAW are determined
083	prinkwv	income concept, on the basis of which the premiums for ZFW, ZW, WAO, WW and NWW are calculated
084	prinkwv 1	income concept, on the basis of which the premiums for ZFW are calculated, when one is retired
085	benefit basis	the salary on the basis of which the WW, WWV, NWW and WAO benefits are determined

Table 3.1 (*Contd.*)

086	taxable income	taxable income
087	wealth	personal wealth
088	wealth abw	household wealth in accordance with ABW definition
089	child allowance	the amount of child allowances one receives
090	benefit abw	the amount of ABW benefits one receives
091	labour[6]	the number of months one was employed this year
092	labour[5]	the number of months one was employed last year
093	labour[4]	the number of months one was employed two years ago
094	labour[3]	the number of months one was employed three years ago
095	labour[2]	the number of months one was employed four years ago
096	labour[1]	the number of months one was employed five years ago
097	upcs	unemployment pay for civil servants; 0 = no rights, −1 = claim for a short benefit, + 1 = claim for other type
098	upcs1	Boolean, which is true if one can claim a upcs in the current year
099	duration upcs	number of months one can claim unemployment pay for civil servants
100	type upcs	type of upcs one can claim; 1 = *Rijkswachtgeldbesluit 1959*, 2 = *Uitkeringsregeling 1966*, 3 = other
101	upcs amount	amount received from unemployment pay for civil servants
102	midsum[2]	income in the last but one year as civil servant, relevant to ABP benefits
103	midsum[1]	income in the last year as civil servant, relevant to ABP benefits
104	term of office abp	the term of office built up for the ABP pensions
105	term of office abp1	the term of office built up for the ABP pensions, relating to the change on October 1st, 1986
106	old age abp	amount received from ABP old age pension
107	disability abp	amount received from ABP disablement benefit
108	widowhood abp	amount received from ABP widowhood and orphan benefit
109	wage	the before tax labour income
110	net wage rate	the after tax labour income per hour
111	gross income	wage plus benefits
112	net income	the after tax income in the current year
113	scholarship	Boolean, which is true if one receives a scholarship
114	non-wage income	the amount of non-wage income one receives
115	payment aow	the amount one pays for the AOW
116	benefit aow	the amount one receives from the AOW
117	extra allowance aow	the amount one receives from the AOW as an extra allowance, if one's partner is younger than 65 years and has a limited income
118	payment aww	the amount one pays for the AWW
119	benefit aww	the amount one receives from the AWW

Table 3.1 (*Contd.*)

120	payment akw1	the amount one pays for child allowances (self-employed only)
121	payment akw2	the amount one's employer pays for child allowances (employees only)
122	payment akw3	the amount the state, as employer, implicitly pays for child allowances (civil servants only)
123	benefit akw	the amount one receives from child allowances
124	year of disablement	year in which one became disabled
125	percentage disabled	the percentage of being disabled
126	disabled	Boolean, which is true if one is disabled
127	benefit aaw	the amount one receives from the AAW (lifetime)
128	benefit aaw1	the amount one receives from the AAW in the current year
129	payment aaw1	the amount one pays for the AAW (self-employed only)
130	payment aaw2	the amount one's employer pays for the AAW (employees only)
131	benefit wao	the amount one receives from the WAO
132	payment wao1	the amount one pays for the WAO
133	payment wao2	the amount one's employer pays for the WAO (employees only)
134	basis wao	the amount on which the WAO benefit is based
135	benefit dso	the amount one receives as sickness benefits from the state (civil servants only)
136	payment dso	the amount the state, as employer, pays for sickness insurance (civil servants only)
137	benefit zw	the amount one receives from the ZW
138	payment zw1	the amount one pays for the ZW
139	payment zw2	the amount one's employer pays for the ZW (employees only)
140	months ww	number of months one received a WW benefit
141	ww	Boolean, which is true if one can claim a (N)WW benefit
142	benefit ww	the amount one receives from the (N)WW
143	payment ww1	the amount one pays for the (N)WW
144	payment ww2	the amount one's employer pays for the (N)WW (employees only)
145	wwv	the number of months one receives a WWV benefit
146	benefit wwv	the amount one receives from the WWV
147	year rww	year in which one starts receiving a new RWW benefit
148	month rww	month in which one starts receiving a new RWW benefit
149	year ioaw	year in which one starts receiving a new IOAW benefit
150	month ioaw	month in which one starts receiving a new IOAW benefit
151	benefit ioaw	the amount one receives from the IOAW
152	tw	Boolean, which is true if one can claim a TW benefit
153	duration tw	the number of months in the current year, for which one can claim a TW benefit

Table 3.1 (*Contd.*)

154	basis tw	the income which serves as a starting-point for the TW claim
155	benefit tw	the amount one receives from the TW
156	nww high	Boolean, which is true for individuals that can claim a benefit, that exceeds 70% of the last salary, as a consequence of the temporary provisions at the time of introduction of the NWW
157	nww	the number of months one can claim an NWW benefit
158	nww continued	the number of months one can claim an NWW *Vervolguitkering* benefit
159	zfw	Boolean, which is true if one is compulsorily insured for the ZFW
160	payment zfw1	the amount one pays for the ZFW
161	payment zfw2	the amount one's employer pays for the ZFW (employees only)
162	payment awbz1	the amount one pays for the ABWZ (self-employed only)
163	payment awbz2	the amount one's employer pays for the AWBZ (employees only)
164	tax	the tax amount paid in the current year
165	tax group	the tax group one belongs to (see section 6.5)
166	tax transfer	the income free of tax, which is not earned by the individual in question and which is added to the partner's income free of tax
167	epsilon	the draw out of the normal distribution to generate income mobility (see section 6.4.4)
168	aowt	the aow amount received in the current year
169	lifetime wages	the sum of wages, received during life
170	lifetime taxes	the sum of taxes, paid during life

The storage of this list of attributes requires 512 bytes per individual. Each time one of the attributes is changed, the attribute in question is overwritten. If one wants to keep some data for further analysis, they have to be transferred to tape. The next step, after the adaptation of a micro-representation, is the specification of an initial population. We prefer to use a real sample of individuals and households along with their attributes. However, such a sample is not available. A first useable sample can be derived from the 1947 Census data, *e.g.* NCBS (1951b, 1951c, 1952 and 1954). The construction of this initial population is described in sections 5.12, 6.2 and 6.3.7. As a consequence, the first generation which can be followed over time is the generation born in 1930.

Once the initial population has been determined, our analysis can be carried out by updating the characteristics of the individuals (and thus the households) during the period under investigation. Here, the Monte Carlo sampling procedure is applied. NEDYMAS has been organized modularly. This means that we do not have a massive programme, but rather a set of subprogrammes, which can be used – partly or completely – at will. For example, the demographic modules can be used to generate the household structure.

The modules which are used in the current version of NEDYMAS and the sequence of treatment are given in table 3.2.

Table 3.2 *Programme module sequencing for each individual in NEDYMAS*

Order	Programme module	Eligibility
	A. Demographic module	
1.	Incrementation	Each person
2.	Immigration	Adding persons who have not lived before in the Netherlands to the datafile
3.	Family reunification	Adding persons whose partner or parents immigrated earlier to the datafile
4.	Emigration	Each family and each person over 16
5.	Return immigration	Each family and each person over 16 who had emigrated before
6.	Old people's home	Each couple and each person over 60
7.	Death	Each person
8.	First marriage selection	Each unmarried person over 14
9.	Remarriage selection	Each previously married person
10.	Divorce	Each married couple
11.	Dehabitation[1]	Each couple living together without being married
12.	Cohabitation selection	Each person over 14 who is not living with someone, married or unmarried
13.	Fertility	Women aged 15–49 years old
14.	Splitting off of children	Persons younger than 40 years of age
	B. Labour and income module (first part)	
15.	Education	Each person over 5
16.	Scholarship	Each person in vocational colleges or at university
17.	Income percentile	Each employed person
18.	Transitions from school	Each person who leaves school
19.	Transitions from disablement	Each disabled person
20.	Transitions from military service	Each conscript
21.	Transitions from being employed	Each employed person
22.	Transitions from being unemployed	Each unemployed person
23.	Transitions from the state houseman/housewife	Each houseman/housewife
24.	Retirement	Each person aged 65
25.	Labour income	Each person employed for part of the year
	C. Social security module	
26.	Private pension premiums	Each employee
27.	Pension premiums for civil servants	Each civil servant
28.	Deduction civil servants	Each civil servant
29.	AOW benefits	Each person over 64, with the exception of most married women up to 1987 (see section 7.2)
30.	AWW benefits	Widows and widowers and their children a)
31.	Widow, widower and orphan pensions under the ABP	Each person, whose partner or father or mother has been insured under the ABP a)

Table 3.2 (*Contd.*)

Order	Programme module	Eligibility
32.	Family allowances	Each family with children a)
33.	AAW benefits	Each disabled person a)
34.	ZW/DSO benefits	Each employee and civil servant
35.	WAO benefits	Each disabled former employee
36.	Disablement pensions under the ABP	Each disabled former civil servant
37.	Old age pensions under the ABP	Each person who has ever been insured under the ABP
38.	Unemployment benefits for civil servants	Each person who was a civil servant before becoming unemployed a)
39.	WW/NWW benefits	Each person who was an employee before becoming unemployed a)
40.	WWV benefits	Each person who was an employee before becoming unemployed and who can not (no longer) claim a WW benefit a)
41.	TW benefits	Each person who receives an NWW, a WAO, an AAW or a ZW benefit a)
42.	IOAW benefits	Older and partly disabled unemployed employees a)
43.	ABW benefits	Each family a)
44.	ZFW premiums	Each employee and some groups of benefit receivers
45.	ZW premiums	Each employee
46.	WAO premiums	Each employee
47.	WW/NWW premiums	Each employee
48.	AOW premiums	Each person aged 15 to 65
49.	AWW premiums	Each person aged 15 to 65
50.	Family allowances premiums	Each person aged 15 to 65 (up to 1 July 1988)
51.	AAW premiums	Each person aged 15 to 65
52.	AWBZ premiums	Each person aged 15 to 65
	B. Labour and income module (second part)	
53.	Taxes	Each person

a) under certain conditions

This means that – like all microsimulation models – NEDYMAS is a recursive model. First, all demographic transitions are made in the model. Next, education is considered, and thereafter changes in economic activity, with the resulting labour income. Lastly, the income transfers and taxes are modelled. As a consequence, changes in, for example, current year labour income do not affect the education process or the demographic block. There is one (partial) exception: labour income in the current year partly affects the possible change in economic activity.[2] This is graphically shown in figure 3.6.

[1] The term 'cohabitation' is used only for people living together without being married. If such individuals decide to dissolve their consensual union, we speak of 'dehabitation'.

[2] The decision which refers to labour supply uses the expected labour income for the current year. The changes in economic growth (section 6.4.3) are taken into account in this exception.

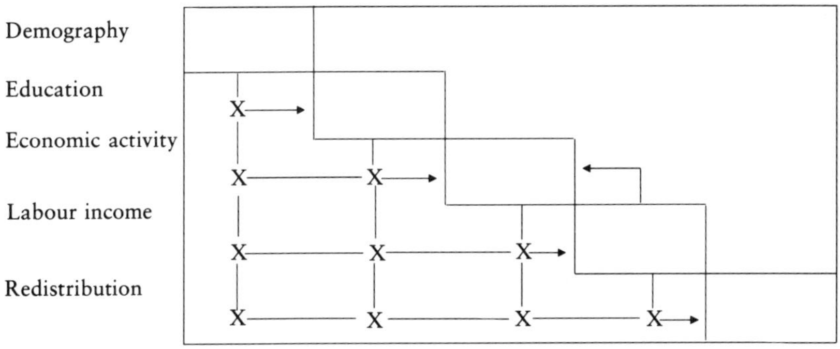

Figure 3.6 The recursive structure of NEDYMAS.

Another problem in programming the model is the simultaneity of the processes. Generally, the periodicity of the data is one year, whereas the periodicity of the processes in the real world is much less. The processes can take place at any time within the year, also within one block, *e.g.* the demographic module. Therefore, more processes can take place simultaneously within one year. This simultaneity influences the calculation of the transition probabilities, when opting for a sequential ordering of events. In NEDYMAS the problem is solved by using the appropriate occurrence-exposure rates, so that the sequence in which the processes are simulated has been taken into account. In this way, a random determination of the sequence in which the processes and the individuals to be simulated are executed – as proposed by Hellwig (1988c: 11–12) – is not necessary.

Carrying out an analysis with the aid of NEDYMAS requires a few simple control modules. The specification of a simulation requires the writing of a number of these control modules (to determine the simulation process and the desired output), compiling them (translation of the programme into machine code) and linking them with the other modules needed. Unlike macroeconomic models, there is no comfortable computer software for microsimulation. The existing models are implemented in an *ad hoc* manner. This is understandable, since microsimulation programming requires more efforts than the management of the structure of time series data. We also opted for an *ad hoc* approach. The computer programme has been written in FORTRAN and its source code amounts to about 40 000 lines.

Analyses with NEDYMAS can only be run under batch, not interactively. However, testing and debugging the programme can be executed in an interactive way. The disadvantage of this method of organization is that the programme is not user-friendly. An experienced programmer, who is

However, the changes in the working population in proportion to the total population are not considered.

familiar with the programme, is needed to carry out modifications. The advantage, on the other hand, is that programme development is fairly simple. Moreover, there is greater flexibility, with the user able to write his or her own routines.

NEDYMAS needs a six pass[3] per year system until 1990, a seven pass per year system in 1990 and a nine pass per year system from 1991. This large number of passes is needed because various probabilities can only be computed after the execution of certain modules (this holds, for example, for leaving the parental home), or because some checks and – if required – some corrections have been made (for example, the number of immigrants) and so on. The way in which the model runs through the various modules is shown in table 3.3.

Table 3.3 *The six/nine pass system of NEDYMAS*

	Start	Initializations – new immigrants – calculating various demographic transition rates
PASS 1		Family reunification new immigrants – new emigration – return emigration – return immigration
	Break	Adding any remaining immigrants (married women and children)
PASS 2		Old people's home – mortality – marriage – divorce – dehabitation – cohabitation
	Break	Matching persons for marriage and cohabitation – calculating birth rates and leaving parental home rates – calculating inflow, outflow and throughflow probabilities for the education submodule
PASS 3		Fertility – splitting off of children – entering school – repeating, removing and outflow from school
	Break	Initializations for the labour market and income formation module
PASS 4		Income percentile – scholarship – transitions between the various socio-economic positions – determination term of office
	Break	Comparison between numbers of simulated employed and unemployed persons and the observed (or forecasted) numbers, respectively and possible adaptations
PASS 5		Labour income – private pension premiums – pension premiums for civil servants – deduction civil servants – determination of labour [1] up to and including labour [6] (see table 3.2)
	Break	Determination of level of benefits (only from 1991 on) and the new division in percentiles
PASS 6/5		Benefits AOW, AWW, ABP pensions, child allowances, AAW, ZW, WAO, WW, WWV and NWW
	Break	(necessary because the following benefits can only be calculated if all household members have gone through pass 6/5)
PASS 7/6		Benefits TW, IOAW and ABW
	Break	Determination of premium percentages of the employee insurances (from 1991 on)
PASS 8/6		Premiums for the employee insurances (from 1991 on) and determination of the transfer of tax allowances between partners (from 1990 on)
	Break	Determination of premium percentages of the general insurances
PASS 9/6		Premiums for the general insurances and determination of taxes

[3] A pass is defined as a sequence of (sub)modules through which each individuals goes, before the next individual is treated.

The external data required – *e.g.* for the calculation of transition probabilities – are stored sequentially, whereas the list of attributes of the sample population members is stored using random access capability. This random access capability makes it very easy to execute interactions. If the receipt of a benefit depends on the characteristics of other household members, it is almost impossible to determine the eligibility for a benefit when applying sequential storage.[4] The disadvantage, however, is that the process is relatively expensive in input–output operation in comparison with sequential storage, and that more expensive disks have to be used instead of tapes. To save computer time, the input–output operations for the list of attributes is written in machine code.

[4] For that reason benefit eligibility can only be treated in the first operating version of DYNASIM – DYNASIM/MASH – which uses a random–access method in the right way and is less sophisticated in the second version – DYNASIM/MASS – which uses a sequential method [Devine and Wertheimer (1981: 55)].

4

Field of application: the Netherlands

This chapter contains information on the Netherlands, the country that serves as our field of application. First, we briefly describe the Dutch social security system and indicate which schemes have been implemented in the NEDYMAS model (section 4.1). We then go on to define the income concept (4.2), the income unit (4.3) and income standardization (4.4).

4.1 A BIRD'S-EYE VIEW OF THE DUTCH SOCIAL SECURITY SYSTEM

The social security system in the Netherlands contains two important subsystems: a need-based minimum system and a wage-related system. In most other countries emphasis, in general, is placed on one of these systems. This means that we are in a position to compare how both systems work.

The Dutch social security system was primarily built up in the years after the Second World War. Its development can be called ambiguous. No choice has been made between the two types of social security systems, the Atlantic need-based minimum approach and the Continental wage-related approach [Veldkamp (1984) and Muffels, Nelissen and Nuyens (1988: 2–3)]. Thereby, one can distinguish two types of social insurance in the Netherlands, general insurances and employee insurances, respectively. Both are based on the pay-as-you-go system.

The general insurances are Atlantic oriented: flat-rate benefits, covering all residents. Premiums, which are proportional to income, have to be paid by all residents up to a fixed maximum income. The solidarity principle is the starting point, not the insurance principle. At present, the following schemes are general insurances: AOW, AWW, AKW, AWBZ and AAW.[1]

Employee insurances only apply to employees in the private sector. The insurance or equivalence principle is the point of departure. These insurances

[1] A description of these schemes (and the schemes mentioned hereafter) can be found in chapter 7.

are compulsory insurances for these employees. The employee insurances are genuine insurances: on the one hand, premiums are a fixed proportion of income (which can be seen as the insured risk[2]), whereas on the other hand, benefits are related to the (former) income.[3] Both are limited by a fixed maximum income. At present, the following employee insurances are in operation: ZW, WAO, NWW and ZFW.

Social provisions in the Netherlands are mainly intended to support those who cannot provide for themselves. The following schemes can be considered as social provisions: IOAW, TW, ABW and KKZ.

There are a number of state arrangements for civil servants and employees in public firms. They are comparable to the employee insurances. Besides their duration, these arrangements differ, in particular, in the way the premiums are paid: they are paid by the state in its capacity as employer and employees are exempt from payment. The most important schemes are: WRO, DSO, IZA, KTO. In addition a large number of pension provisions exist for both civil servants and private employees. The largest pension fund is the ABP.

Table 4.1 gives information on the size distribution of the Dutch social security system. This table is based on the broad definition of the Department of Social Affairs. From this table, the important role of the social security system in the income redistribution process is immediately clear. At present about one-third of the Dutch net national income is redistributed in the form of social security benefits. If we also take account of fund raising by pension funds, the percentage exceeds 40% of the national income. The main element is social insurances. These constitute about two-thirds of total benefits. Both social provisions and supplementary pensions account for about 15%, whereas direct payments by the employer constitute no more than a few per cent of the total social security benefits.

Table 4.1 *The size distribution of the Dutch social security system (total benefits in 10^9 Dutch guilders)*

Type	1950	1960	1970	1980	1988
– social insurances	53	63	72	72	68
*general insurances	(11)	(23)	(34)	(42)	(40)
*employee insurances	(42)	(39)	(38)	(30)	(28)
– supplementary pensions	26	20	14	12	16
– social provisions	11	9	8	12	13
– direct payments	11	9	7	5	4
– total as a % of NI	11	14	21	32	34
– total benefits	2	6	24	102	136

Sources: Ministerie van Sociale Zaken en Werkgelegenheid (1984: 95–101 and 1989: 152–155) and NCBS (30)

[2] However, these insurances cannot be seen as actuarial insurances, because premiums are not differentiated by the real risk of becoming unemployed or the real risk of becoming disabled.
[3] This does not hold for the ZFW. This act regulates the provision of medical and surgical treatment or its compensation (see section 7.14).

The starting point for our analysis is the current definition of social security in its broad sense. However, information on some schemes is lacking. We deal with the following social security arrangements[4] in our analysis[5]:

(a) in the field of unemployment provisions:
WW (1952–1986) 7.8 / NWW (1987–) 7.10 / WWV (1965–1986) 7.9 / WRO (1947–) 7.17
(b) in the field of longlasting disability:
AAW (1976–) 7.5 / WAO (1967–) 7.6 / ABP–IP (1947–) 7.18
(c) in the field of sickness and shortlasting disability:
ZW (1947–) 7.7 / DSO (1947–) 7.7
(d) in the field of old age, widowhood and orphanhood:
AOW (1957–) 7.2 / AWW (1959–) 7.3 / ABP–OP (1947–) 7.18 / ABP–WP (1947–) 7.18 WP–PS (1947–)[6] 7.16
(e) in the field of family allowances:
KW (1947–1962) 7.4 / KWR (1947–1962) 7.4 / KWL (1963–1979) 7.4 / KKZ (1963–1979) 7.4 / AKW (1963–) 7.4 / KTO (1947–1979) 7.4
(f) in the field of health costs[6]:
ZFB (1947–1966) 7.14 / ZFW (1967–) 7.14 / AWBZ (1968–) 7.15
(g) other social provisions:
ABW (1965–)[7] 7.13 / IOAW (1987–) 7.11 / TW (1987–) 7.12
(h) other social security premiums:
IW (1981–) 7.19

The extent to which the various social security schemes are treated can be derived from table 4.2.

Table 4.2 *Coverage of the various social security schemes in this book*

Type	1950	1960	1970	1980	1988
Benefit side					
– social insurances	40	69	72	72	70
– supplementary pensions	34	33	39	40	42
– social provisions	83	71	67	69	74
– direct payments	75	94	98	96	97
– total	47	64	69	69	67
Financing side					
– social insurances	56	82	91	92	99
– supplementary pensions	100	100	100	100	100
– total	72	87	92	93	99

Sources: Ministerie van Sociale Zaken en Werkgelegenheid (1984: 95–101 and 1989: 152–155) and own calculations

[4] An extended description will be given in chapter 7.
[5] The period considered is given in parentheses. The section in which the arrangement is described is given next.
[6] Only premium payments.
[7] For the greater part, see the description in chapter 7.

In terms of total benefits, we cover 47% in 1950 and about 70% from 1970 onwards. The benefit side has not been covered for 100% because of the lack of data in the field of supplementary pensions and the compensation for medical expenses. Less than half the supplementary pensions are treated, while we are not able to simulate the private pension benefits. The multiplicity of kinds of private pensions and the absence of a module for intra-job mobility in our microsimulation model makes it impossible to simulate these pensions in a realistic way at the moment. So, only pensions under the ABP are included. A future version of NEDYMAS [Nelissen (1992)], will attempt to investigate the effect of omitting private pensions.

With the exception of the 1940s and 1950s, 70% of social insurance benefits have been included in NEDYMAS. The benefits under the ZFW, the AWBZ and some health insurances – such as for some groups of civil servants – are not taken into consideration in the model. Here, data do not enable us to study the income distribution. These health cost insurances accounted for 28% of social insurances in 1950, 21% in 1960 and 29% in 1988. This means that apart from these health cost insurances, almost all social insurances have been included in the model from about 1957. Up to 1967, the former Accident Insurance Act and the Disablement Act (in combination with the Temporary Act for Disabled Pension Receivers) also account for a substantial proportion of the social insurances benefits, *e.g.* 16% in 1950 and 9% in 1960. However, the Temporary Act for Old Age Pensions, which operated until the introduction of the AOW in 1957, has not been included. This law accounted for 16% of the social insurances benefits in 1950. The remaining deviation between total benefits and benefits included in the model may be attributed to the Voluntary Advanced Retirement scheme and the insurance against the risk of unemployment due to weather conditions. Both comprise only a few per cent. A future version of NEDYMAS [see Nelissen (1991a and b)], will also be able to give an indication of the effect of the ZFW and AWBZ benefits.

Between 70–80% of other social provisions are covered. Not included are arrangements for social work provision (WSW), arrangements for artists (BKR), special pensions for groups of war victims and home care. The WSW formed 11% of the other social provisions in 1987 (the minimum), and 23% in 1970 (the maximum). Home care ranged between 2–9%, special pensions between 4–9% and the BKR about 1%.

Social benefits directly paid by the employer are almost completely covered. The only elements which are not included are the Voluntary Advanced Retirement for Civil Servants (about 2% in 1987) and the Breadwinner and Income Compensation for Soldiers (25% in 1950 to less than 1% in 1987).

On the financing side, we limit ourselves to social insurances and supplementary pensions. The other social provisions and benefits paid directly by the employer – i.e. the state – are both financed by public funds. The percentages equal the percentages for these schemes at the benefits side, augmented by the premiums for the compulsory ZFW, the AWBZ and private pensions. The Accident Insurance Act and the Disablement Act (in combination with the Temporary Act for Disabled Pension Receivers) are not included. This explains the lower percentages in 1950 and 1960. From about 1965 onwards, more than 90% of the financing side is covered, and up to 99% in 1987.

The remainder of this section contains data on the contribution level and the benefit levels of the social insurances. An extended description of the various schemes can be found in chapter 7. Here, emphasis is on the amounts and premium percentages. These figures are important in interpreting the redistributional impact of the social security schemes as described in chapter 8.

The contribution rates (in per cent) for the general insurances and the maximum income to which these premiums have to be paid (the annual ceiling) are shown for a number of years in table 4.3. The premium percentages are the sum of both employers' and employees' premium percentages.

Table 4.3 *Premium percentages and annual ceiling for the general insurances*

	AOW	AWW	AKW	AAW	AWBZ	Ceiling (Dfl.)
1960	5.5	1.25	–	–	–	7 450
1965	8.7	1.5	1.8	–	–	12 000
1970	9.5	1.5	2.075	–	1.245	17 450
1975	10.4	1.5	1.2	–	2.7	31 750
1980	10.25	1.35	2.0	4.2	3.2	46 400
1985	11.7	1.4	3.95	6.05	4.25	63 200
1990	14.3	1.25	0	1.15	5.4	42 123

We see that the AOW percentage more than doubles between 1960 and 1985, which is mainly due to structural increases of the benefit in the 1970s and to the change in the age composition of the Dutch population. The further rise between 1985 and 1990 is caused by the change in the annual ceiling following the Oort tax reform (chapter 6). The AWW percentage remains constant. By comparison, the AKW percentage strongly varies, for several reasons: the abolition of the specific family allowances schemes for employees, civil servants and self-employed persons and the implementation of these schemes into the AKW, and the changes in the extent to which the contributions are financed by public funds (see also table 4.5). The AWBZ percentage continuously grows due to its extended coverage of medical and surgical treatments and increasing health care costs.

Table 4.4 *Premium percentages and ceilings for the employee insurances*

	KB	ZW	WW	WAO	ZFW	Ceiling ZFW	Ceiling others	Franchise WAO
1950	5.0	4.0	–	–	3.6	3 750	3 432	–
1955	5.0	4.0	1.4	–	4.0	6 000	4 992	–
1960	5.3	4.2	1.44	–	4.8	7 450	6 240	–
1965	3.0	5.1	1.16	–	5.4	10 000	8 424	–
1970	3.3	6.3	1.0	5.3	7.5	12 480	23 140	–
1975	3.5	7.85	1.16	9.2	9.2	23 400	42 640	–
1980	–	8.05	1.27	14.1	8.1	34 320	61 100	14 560
1985	–	6.57	3.55	16.15	9.2	40 820	68 120	23 660
1990	–	6.35	3.18	12.15	7.9	43 500	68 900	23 920

The premium percentages for the employee insurances (table 4.4) reflect the changes in the risk and the changes in the contributions from public funds. These contributions vary considerably over time and are shown in table 4.5. The KB percentage in 1965 is remarkably lower than before. This is a consequence of the introduction of the AKW in 1963, which partly took over the obligations of the KB. In the ZW it is assumed that employees pay 1%. This percentage has grown over time due to changes in sick leave. The large increase in the WW percentage in the 1980s is caused by the withdrawal of contributions from public funds in combination with an increase in unemployment. The rise in the number of disabled persons increased the WAO percentage. In the second half of the 1980s the increase in the percentage stopped. This was due to the reform in 1987 (which diminished the benefit level from 80% to 70% of the former wage) and the fact that the franchise has not always been adjusted for inflation.

Table 4.5 *Percentual contribution from public funds*

	Total	AOW	AWW	AKW	AAW	AWBZ	KB	ZW	WW	WAO	ZFW
1955	3.4	–	–	–	–	–	4.6	2.9	31.9	–	4.5
1960	3.6	1.7	1.4	–	–	–	2.5	0	24.2	–	0
1965	5.7	6.2	1.1	1.1	–	–	0.3	0	23.9	–	0
1970	5.6	3.7	0.4	0.5	–	40.9	5.1	0	19.5	0	0
1975	8.5	6.7	0.4	27.7	–	24.9	1.4	0	43.7	0	0
1980	15.5	10.4	7.1	52.4	7.7	24.4	–	0	23.8	8.7	5.4
1985	3.0	0.5	0.5	0.3	2.9	3.3	–	0	0.1	0	0
1989	9.2	0.3	0	100	0.3	12.1	–	0	0	0	13.0

The level of the benefits under the AOW, AAW and AWW has been linked to the net minimum wage since the early 1970s. For example, the net AOW benefit for a married couple equals the net minimum wage, whereas for a single person the AOW benefit amounts to 70% of the net minimum wage. The benefit rate, defined by the gross pension benefit of a married couple divided by gross average income, amounted to 0.30 in 1957, 0.32 in 1961,

0.46 in 1966, 0.51 in 1971 and about 0.60 from 1976 [Verbon (1988: 24)]. The AKW benefit for a child increases as the number of children rises. The level of the benefit is not only determined by income developments but also by other – political – reasons. The benefit rate for the AKW for the first child amounts almost continually to just over 3%. For subsequent children, the benefit rate varies. For example, the benefit rate for the second child amounted to almost 0.05 in 1963, 0.05 in 1975 and about 0.04 in 1990. For the sixth child the benefit rate was 0.05, 0.08 and, again, 0.05, respectively.

The wage-related benefits under the ZW, WW and WAO amounted to 80% of the (former) wage up to 1987, and 70% afterwards. But in 1969 a minimum level was introduced (the net minimum wage). Also a maximum benefit holds, which equals the premium ceiling. For further details, see chapter 7.

4.2 THE INCOME CONCEPT

The income concepts available differ in three respects:

(a) the period to which the income refers;
(b) the definition of the imputed unit; and
(c) the elements which form part of the income.

It is also possible to distinguish between the way in which the income is standardized. In this section emphasis is on point c). The other points are considered in the following sections.

A general definition of income in a fixed period – the Haig-Simons definition [Hofstra (1980)] – is the amount which equals the consumption in that period, plus the change in wealth during that period. In this definition income is consumed or saved. If it is saved, this results in an increase in wealth. However, this definition is not unequivocal in all respects, *e.g.* the housing services of an owner-occupied home. We must also bear in mind our goal, being the analysis of the income redistributive effect of social security schemes. Therefore, we opt for another point of departure.

Almost all income elements can be classed under three main components: rewards from production factors, unbound income transfers and bound income transfers. These three income components correspond to three types of income sources: primary, secondary and tertiary sources. Primary income is created in the production process and contains the entirety of wages, profits and other income from wealth (such as rent and interest). Secondary income is derived from primary income after deduction of contributions for social security (both employees' and employers' premiums) and income taxes and augmented with unbound income transfers. Tertiary income equals secondary income plus the received transfers from state, bound to goods and services, minus the paid transfers to state, bound to goods and services. A schematic overview referring to the Netherlands is given in table 4.6.

Table 4.6 *Primary, secondary and tertiary income*

+ 1	profits from entrepreneurship or free profession, with the exclusion of acquisition costs and depreciation
+ 2	wages, salaries, bonuses, commissions, royalties, and so on (gross)
+ 3	employers' premium payments for social security and pensions
+ 4	other income (dividend, interest, rent, and so on), with the exclusion of acquisition costs
=	**Primary income**
+ 5	received pension transfers
− 6	paid pension premiums
+ 7	unbound income supplements from social provisions (primary provisions under the ABW)
+ 8	income transfers from social insurances and social provisions
+ 9	family allowances for children up to the age of 16 years old
− 10	premiums social insurances, with the exclusion of the ZFW premium
− 11	direct taxes, in which the absence of tax expenditures – with the exclusion of acquisition costs – is assumed
+ 12	received alimony
− 13	paid alimony
=	**Secondary income**
+ 14	money value of the advantage bound to the use of endowed or freely provided goods and services, for which exclusion of use is possible and which are financed by material state expenditures
+ 15	money value of the 'use' of pure public goods
+ 16	tax advantages of the use of goods and services
+ 17	money value bound to provisions as under 14, but financed by social insurances
− 18	indirect taxes
− 19	money value of payments in kind
− 20	other payments to state, bound to goods and services (school fees, premiums ZFW, charges ZFW and AWBZ, and so on)
=	**Tertiary income**

Source: Social and Cultural Planning Agency (1981: 45).

The main part of the redistribution process by social security takes place in the transition from primary to secondary income, whereas tertiary income also contains some social security components (the ZFW in particular and some provisions in the field of the AAW and AWBZ). However, the available data do not provide us with sufficient information to analyse the distribution of deliveries by the ZFW, the AWBZ and provisions in kind by the AAW, by *e.g.* income. This also holds for the charges included in the AWBZ and ZFW. As a consequence, we are not able to determine the redistributive impact of the items, which specifically belong to the tertiary income component, with the exclusion of the ZFW contributions for the compulsorily insured. Therefore, we take the secondary income as a starting point for our analysis.[8] [9]

[8] An advantage of this choice is that the problems involved in the treatment of so-called tax expenditures can be avoided. For a discussion, see Van de Stadt (1988: ch. 3).

[9] In the Netherlands, some other income concepts are also frequently used. The Netherlands Central Bureau of Statistics uses original income ('*gevormd inkomen*'), total income ('*totaalin-*

Using the secondary income as the income unit creates some problems. Our model is not able to simulate nonlabour income, because it contains no module for private consumption. So, savings cannot be determined and, as a consequence, neither can wealth or income from wealth. This means that our model does not generate income components which belong to item 4 in table 4.6. With respect to the acquisition costs, we only take account of the so-called 4% rule (see section 6.5).

Item 5, the received pension transfers can only be inserted for civil servants. As we discussed, private pension benefits cannot be treated in a satisfactory way. Also, data on alimony are not available, which means that items 12 and 13 are not considered.

In conclusion, we opt for the secondary income, with the exclusion of income from wealth, deductions above the 4% rule for acquisition costs, received private pensions and alimony, as the income concept.

4.3 THE INCOME UNIT

The income unit can be defined as the individual or group of persons to which the income is linked. This linkage can be made in two ways. One point of departure is the income formation approach, in which persons receiving an income (from labour or entrepreneurship or social security) constitute the income unit. The other side is the spending of income. In that case, the group of persons who share income are treated as an income unit. Although the actual obtaining of income also often depends on decisions (on division of labour inside and outside the household) made within the household, the definition of the income unit along the income formation side or along the spending side, largely corresponds to the difference between individuals and households.

Our study refers to the redistributional aspects of one specific income component (social security) and in this, both the individual income characteristics and the income characteristics of possible other household members influence claims for a social security benefit. This means we have to know both the individual income and the household income in our model. The

komen') and spendable income ('*besteedbaar inkomen*'). The first one consists of income from primary sources (profits, wages, salaries – benefits paid by the employer for sickness, unemployment and disability included – and income from property) minus related fiscal deductions. This original income plus the received unbound transfers minus the contributions to social security and other paid transfers (taxes on wages, salaries, profits and property income excluded) gives the total income. Diminishing this with the taxes levied on this income gives us the spendable income. The taxation authorities again use other income concepts: gross income, premium income, taxable income and taxable sum. An overview of the relationships between the different income concepts can be found in Social and Cultural Planning Agency (1985: 87). Next, the Central Planning Agency uses disposable income. Its relation with primary income, original and total income is given in Ritzen, *et al.* (1977: 26–27) and NCBS (1983: 11–12).

individual has been used as the point of departure to determine each income. In this income formation process, his or her claims for a social security benefit (and also tax payments) are affected by the income of other household members. This implies that an individual's income position cannot be treated independently of the total household income. In our analysis, we therefore take the household income – being the sum of the income of all individuals in the household – as the relevant income. This also means that we assume that the total received income in the household is available for all members of the household. This implies that we assume that each household member benefits from the income of each of the other household members.

In order to compare the income of individuals belonging to different household types, we will standardize the income (see section 4.4). In this way the effect of the size and the structure of households on income spending is extracted.

We now have to define the notion of household. The choice for the household as the income unit implicitly assumes that the welfare position of individual household members does not differ, or is negligible, or not even relevant. The most important criteria for the distinction between households are [Social and Cultural Planning Agency (1981: 29 and further) and Ritzen (1979: 85–90)]:

- The extent to which one jointly consumes the income;
- The extent to which one is able to decide independently;
- The extent to which one is dependent on anybody's income.

Each choice implies a choice for weights among these criteria of 'spending dependence' (or income pooling), 'decision dependence' and 'income dependence'. The choice especially affects:

(a) Children living with their parents, being able to decide independently and receiving an income of their own;
(b) Children living with their parents, being able to decide independently and not receiving an income of their own;
(c) Children living by themselves, without an income of their own;
(d) Persons in institutions and remaining there for a long period;
(e) Partners with an income of their own;
(f) Partners without an income of their own.

All these groups form a household of their own according to at least one of the aforementioned criteria. Using spending dependency, partners with their own income form a household with their wife or husband. This partly holds for the first category, depending on the degree to which the children place their income at the disposal of joint household expenditures. A partner who does not have an income of his or her own is considered not to add (imputed) income – also not via housekeeping – but is considered (jointly) to spend the income. Children by themselves are assumed to manage a household of their own. Persons in institutions cannot be treated unequivocally. Depending on the kind of institution, we have to do with one or with a number of households in the institution. If one opts for the second criterion, only minor children and people in institutions cannot be considered as separate households.

The criterion of income dependency implies that only persons with no income are not considered as separate households. But a partner with an income of his or her own is treated as a separate household.

The optimal criterion appears to be the spending dependency. So, we define a household as the group of two or more persons who live together, who jointly consume the income and who jointly manage the household, as well as persons who manage a household of their own (single persons). This definition is also used by the Netherlands Central Bureau of Statistics [see *e.g.* NCBS (1983: 10)]. The most important advantage of this definition is that the household is considered a consumption unit and the consumption possibilities are probably the most important indicators of the welfare position of the household. The requirement that they share each income ensures that the welfare positions of the individual household members do not differ too much, and that an increase in the income of one household member will increase the welfare of each household member.

As a consequence, individuals jointly managing a household but not sharing an income – *e.g.* students in a 'student flat' or aged people living in an old age home are each considered as a separate household (together with their partner, if present).

4.4 INCOME STANDARDIZATION

The purpose of this study is to gain more insight into welfare distribution. This means that we have to take into account the consumption possibilities of households, and that we have to look at the welfare comparison between households which differ in size and composition. If we want to make comparable the welfare positions of different types of households, we have to standardize. Standardization can be defined as the transformation of household incomes in such a way that equal, standardized incomes reflect an equal welfare position, irrespective of household size and composition [Ritzen (1979: 91)].[10] The result is called equivalent household income.

[10] In recent years it has been debated whether the number of working persons in a household has also to be taken into account, see Hagenaars, *et al.* (1984). In view of the ongoing character of the discussion, we do not standardize according to this point. Another element is the limitation of the free consumption possibilities of households which are hit by special circumstances, like relatively high housing costs, home care costs, sickness costs, and so on. These elements are also not considered in our standardization. One reason for this is the fact that

Standardization is executed by standardization factors (or standardization amounts), also called equivalence factors. An equivalence or a standardization factor can be defined as the quotient of the income which a household requires to reach a fixed level of welfare and the income which a chosen standard household needs to reach the same level of welfare [Berends-Ballast, *et al.* (1980: 292)].

The chosen welfare concept determines the standardization method. The welfare notion can have as its point of departure the welfare which households are considered to enjoy in view of fixed norms, or the welfare which households enjoy in view of their actual consumption, or the welfare as experienced by the household itself. The standardization methods corresponding with these three notions [Berends-Ballast, *et al.* (1980) and Muellbauer (1980)] are sometimes called normative methods, empirical–objective methods and empirical–subjective methods, respectively.

Normative methods are, among others, the expenditure unit scales and the fiscal method. The expenditure unit scales express the nutrition of persons of different ages in the nutrition of an adult. Disadvantages of these methods are that account is taken only of nutrition needs and household size. The fiscal method is based on general deductions in the income tax system and on family allowances. The greatest advantage is that it is based on norms which are more or less accepted in society. In this way, it partly meets an important objection against standardization, namely that household formation is partly an expenditure decision, and as such forms part of the welfare notion. Disadvantages are the relatively rough standardization and the presence of considerations other than household size and composition in determining tax deductions and family allowances.

Empirical–objective methods are the arithmetical method, the Barten method and the Nicholson method. The arithmetical method divides the household expenditures into fixed and variable costs. Expenditures which do not depend on the household size and composition are treated as fixed costs. The variable costs are those expenditures which – by unchanging welfare – depend on the household size and composition. Next, these variable costs are distributed among parents and children using a (more or less) objective scheme of proportions. The Barten method [Barten (1964); an extensive treatment can also be found in Deaton and Muellbauer (1980: ch.8)] derives equivalence scales from an estimated econometric model, which describes the household expenditures on different categories of goods. The Nicholson method [Nicholson (1949)] assumes that households enjoy the same level of welfare if the typical parental expenditures are the same.

One major disadvantage is that it is not possible to derive equivalence scales for all household types, while data are not available for all these types to a sufficient extent. The chosen scheme of proportions or the chosen

some of these kinds of expenditures are – in whole or in part – freely chosen, which means that we have to know to which extent free choices are at work.

composition of representative goods can always be discussed. None of these methods takes into account the age composition of the household. Moreover, the methods do not take account of the fact that welfare is not an absolute but a relative element.

Therefore, we prefer the empirical–subjective methods. These methods ask people what income is sufficient to live on for themselves or for others. The answer can be related to the household composition, the actual household income, the average income of the household's reference group, and so on. Examples are the Leyden Poverty Line (LPL) and the Subjective Poverty Line (SPL); Goedhart, *et al.* (1976 and 1977). The method has been developed by Kapteyn and Van Praag (1976) and Van Herwaarden, Kapteyn and Van Praag (1977). We will use the results from the SPL-method [Kapteyn, *et al.* (1985)], in which households themselves are asked what income they need to reach a minimum level of welfare.[11] The SPL is operationalized with the aid of the regression result of the minimum income – as answered by the group with an income which more or less equals the benefit levels of the ABW – on the family size,[12] family size in the reference group,[13] family income and mean income in the reference group. The effect of household size and composition is estimated empirically in this way. It appears that the children's ages are hardly important. On the contrary, the parents' ages have a large impact.

A couple without children is chosen as the standard household. The resulting equivalence factors for some households are given in table 4.7.

Table 4.7 *Equivalence factors for several household types*[a)]

one adult	0.74	2A + 6	1.11
two adults	1	2A + 12	1.16
1A + 6	0.89	2A + 6,12	1.26
1A + 12	0.96	2A + 1,6,12	1.30
1A + 6,12	1.07	2A + 1,6,12,18	1.45
1A + 1,6,12	1.13	2A + 1,2,6,12	1.36
1A + 1,6,12,18	1.30	2A + 1,2,6,12,18	1.50
1A + 1,2,6,12	1.18	2A + 1,2,6,7,12	1.43
1A + 1,2,6,12,18	1.36	2A + 1,2,6,7,12,18	1.56
1A + 1,2,6,7,12	1.26	2A + 6,7,12,13,17,18	1.70
1A + 1,2,6,7,12,18	1.43		
1A + 6,7,12,13,17,18	1.59		

a) 1A + 6,12 means: a family with one adult and two children, aged 6 and 12 years old.
Source: Kapteyn, *et al.* (1985: 45)

[11] The LPL-method asks people what income would be considered as being very bad, which one as bad, and so on to which income is valued as very good.

[12] The variable family size (fs) has been determined by $\log fs = \sum_{i=s}^{n} \alpha_i . f(a_i)$. In this, n is the number of family members, a_i is the age of the i-th family member, $f(a_i)$ is an age function and α_i are weights. For persons of 19 years and older, $f(a_i)$ is one and for the younger ones $f(a_i) = 1 + \delta_1.(a_i - 18)^2 + \delta_2.(a_i - 18)^2.(a_i + 36)$, whereby δ_1 and δ_2 are estimated. The weights α_i follow a decreasing logarithmic pattern: $\alpha_1 = 1$, $\alpha_2 = \log 2$, $\alpha_3 = \log 3/2$, $\alpha_4 = \log 4/3$, and so on.

[13] Defined as the group of persons with the same education (5 levels) and age group (4 groups).

PART TWO

The Microsimulation Model

5

The demographic module[1]

5.1 INTRODUCTION

The demographic module contains the following submodules: immigration, emigration, mortality, marriage, cohabitation, divorce, dehabitation, flows into and out of old people's homes, splitting off of children and fertility. The way in which the demographic module is passed through is indicated in figure 5.1.

Each year starts with the determination of the number of 'new' immigrants. By new immigrants we mean people who have never before lived in the Netherlands. New immigrants lead to an increase in the number of personal records. Next, the individuals in our database who are still alive go through each of the following processes successively: family reunification of immigrants, emigration and return immigration. Then, a check on immigration takes place to ensure that all new immigrants have been dealt with.

Thereafter, the people of our database are subjected to the possibility of moving into or out of an old people's home, of death, of being a candidate for marriage, of divorce, of dehabitation and of being a candidate for cohabitation. When all persons are dealt with, the matching of persons takes place to complete the simulation of marriage and cohabitation.

The last steps in each year are the simulation of splitting off of children and fertility.

During the passage through the demographic module, different occurrence–exposure rates are calculated. First, the family reunion rates and return immigration rates are determined. After the addition of new immigrants, return emigration rates and first emigration rates are calculated. After the check on immigration, the rates for the flows into and out of the old people's homes, death rates, marriage rates, divorce rates, dehabitation rates and cohabitation rates are calculated. Rates for leaving the parental home and fertility are determined after the matching of persons in consensual

[1] For a performance test of the demographic module, see Nelissen (1991c).

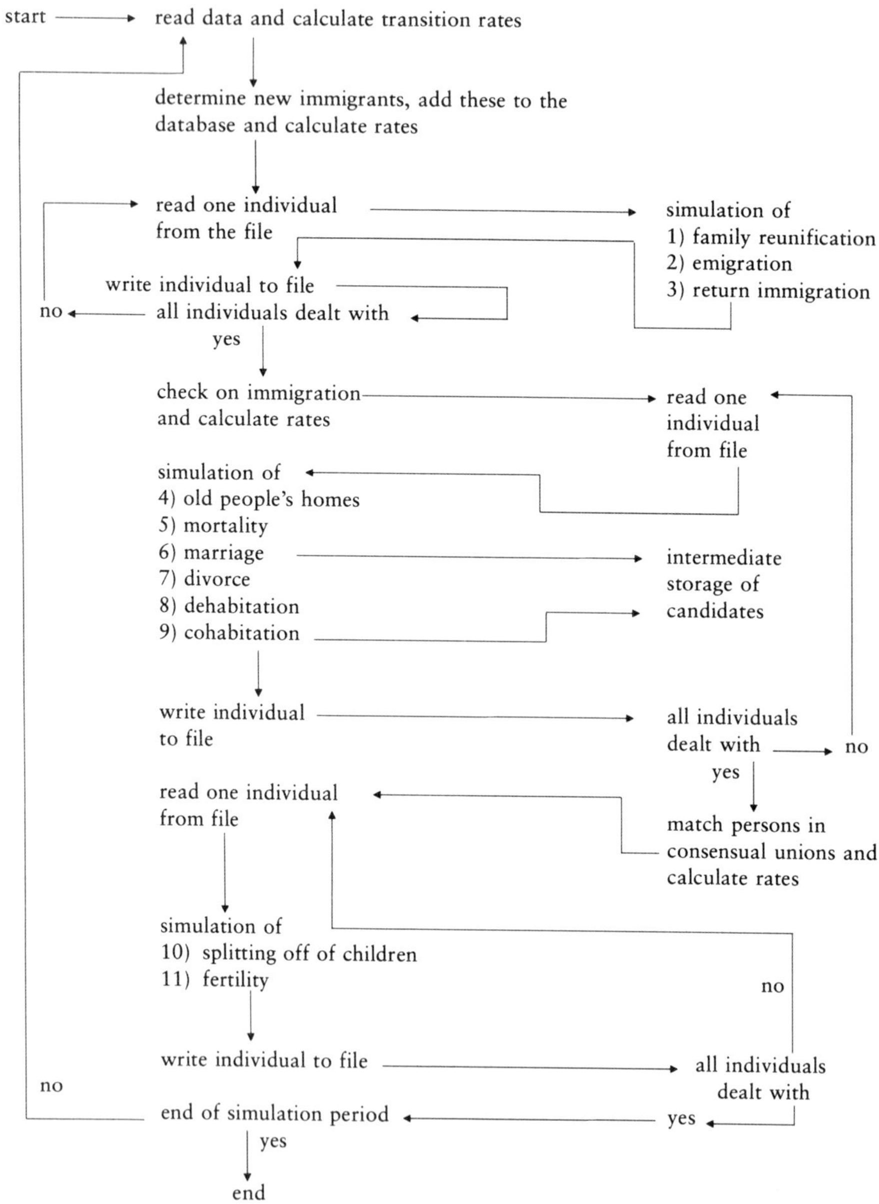

Figure 5.1 The demographic module.

unions has taken place. In calculating these rates, we used, among other, data as generated by the simulation model, NCBS data on the population by age, sex and marital status for the years 1947–1985[2] and the same forecast data from the NCBS 1984 forecast [also available from tables from NCBS, see also NCBS (1985a)]. From 2035, the rates are held constant at the 2034 level. The size of a number of simulated sub-populations is determined to calculate some of the above mentioned rates. This concerns the number of new male and female immigrants and emigrants by year of immigration and emigration, respectively; the female population, aged 15 up to 50 years, by parity, marital status and whether cohabiting or not; the number of dehabitations plus the number of cohabitations that ended through the death of one of the partners plus the number of cohabiting men emigrating without their family; the number of married men living abroad without their family; the number of immigrant married men living in the Netherlands without their family and the number of male and female persons, aged 15 to 40, still living with their parents.

All demographic events are assumed to take place on 1 July each year. Divorce and dehabitation do not occur in the year of marriage or cohabitation. And after a divorce or dehabitation, the possibility of remarrying or recohabiting does not exist until the next year. If a person dies, (s)he is, in spite of this, subjected to the other possible demographic events. However, the probability that these events will occur is halved. In the case of emigration, the person's record is maintained. In the year of emigration other possible demographic events also occur with a 50% chance. In the following years, no demographic changes are allowed until (s)he decides to return to the Netherlands, with the exception of mortality. This means that, in spite of the recursive nature of the model, competing risks are dealt with to a large extent. Only the occurrence of marriage, cohabitation, dehabitation and divorce in the same year are excluded. The resulting error, however, is very small.

Technically, the problem could be solved by introducing the possibility of remarriage or recohabitation in the year of divorce or dehabitation. Its disadvantage is that *e.g.* the remarriage rates are not specified by duration since divorce. Were we only to use an age specific rate then the remarriage probability would be strongly overestimated. The same holds for a divorce in the year of marriage. Therefore, the chosen option seems to be the optimal one in view of the absence of the required rates by duration.

In section 5.2 up to and including 5.11 we will describe these elements of the demographic module. The last section in this chapter, section 5.12, describes the construction of a representative initial population.

[2] These data were provided in the form of tables by the Netherlands Central Bureau of Statistics (NCBS). See also NCBS (1953b and 1970).

5.2 IMMIGRATION

Immigration is simulated in four steps. The first step is the determination of the number of new immigrants and the number of return immigrants. The starting point is the total number of immigrants. For 1947 we know the total number of male and female immigrants.[3] Using the 1949 distribution of immigrants by age group and the distinction between married and unmarried persons and using the distribution by sex, age and marital status in 1960, these figures are transformed into age, sex and marital status specific numbers. For 1948, we know the number of immigrants by sex, by six age groups and whether they are married or unmarried [NCBS (1950)]. These are transformed into sex, age and marital status specific numbers in the same way as those for 1947. For the years 1949 up to and including 1959 we know the total number of male and female immigrants for the age groups 0–14, 15–19, 20–24, 25–29, 30–34, 35–39, 40–49, 50–64, 65 and older, all – with the exception of the first age group – for married and unmarried people [NCBS (2)]. These numbers are transformed to age, sex and marital status specific numbers, using the distribution of immigrants by marital status and sex for the distinguished age groups in 1960 and the localization coefficients within these groups in the same year.

For the period 1960–1985 we obtained age, sex and marital status specific number of immigrants from the NCBS,[4] and from 1986 to 2010 we use the NCBS 1984 forecast. After 2010 the number of immigrants has been set equal to zero, in accordance with the aforementioned NCBS 1984 forecast.

The number of return immigrants has been calculated on the basis of the return immigration rates by number of years passed since the year of emigration and the number of emigrants in those years who are still living alive abroad. We used the return immigration rates for the years 1950 (covering the period all 1947–1952), 1955 (1953–1957), 1960 (1958–1962), 1965 (1963–1972), 1975 (1973–1977) and 1980 (covering the period from 1978); these rates can be derived from NCBS (1953a, 1958a, 1962, 1968b, 1977a and 1982b). In this, we limited ourselves to people who emigrated between the current year and six years earlier. However, we do not know the people who emigrated before 1947, in the sense that we do not know their personal attributes. They are not in our sample, because our initial population only contains people who were living in the Netherlands on 31 May 1947. For that reason, in 1947 we first determined only the number of return immigrants who had emigrated from the Netherlands, in the same year between 1 June and 31 December. Later, a proportion (based on the return immigration rates) of the new immigrants were called return immigrants and supposed to have emigrated between 1 January 1942 and

[3] Source: tables NCBS.
[4] Tables supplied by the NCBS.

31 May 1947. In 1948 this procedure was applied for the determination of return immigrants who had emigrated between 1 January 1943 and 31 May 1947 and so on. This procedure is necessary to know the real number of new immigrants, because return emigration only holds for new immigrants and does not apply to re-immigrated persons.

Subtracting the resulting number of return immigrants from the total number of immigrants, we get the number of new immigrants (by age, sex and marital status).

The second step is the addition of new immigrants to our sample. For that purpose the number of new immigrants is multiplied by the proportion of the sample population in the real population (the sampling ratio), in which rounding occurs by lot, using the uniform [0, 1] distribution. This resulting number of new immigrants is added to our sample. In this process, we distinguish six subgroups:

(a) Married women with or without children, who immigrate without a partner. We assume that these are cases of family reunification. The proportion of these women in the total number of immigrating married women is calculated using the probability that family reunification takes place with immigrated married men, living in the Netherlands without their family. These probabilities are derived [NCBS (1953a, 1958a, 1962, 1968b, 1974, 1977a and 1982b)] by assuming that married females, immigrating without their husbands are cases of family reunification. For the future, we assume that the proportion of married women involved in family reunification as a proportion of the total number of married women will equal the proportion in 1980 [being about 65%, see NCBS (1982b)]. The number of women in this subgroup is related to the number of immigrated married men living in the Netherlands without a partner [see (e)]. This gives us the probability of family reunification.

Using a Monte Carlo process, we determined for each married man, without a partner whether or not family reunification takes place. If this occurs, one female person is added to the sample. The number of persons in the database is raised by one and she gets this number as her personal identification number. The sex of this person is, of course, female, the marital status married. The pointer to her husband equals the identification number of the man in question and, conversely, the pointer of the man for his wife is set equal to the identification number of the female in question. Her year of immigration is the current year. The age of the wife is set equal to the male's one minus three, unless such a woman is not available in the set of immigrating married women. In the latter case the age difference between man and woman is minimalized. The age at which she is assumed to have left her parental home is put at the year in which she became 18. If she is younger than 18, she leaves the parental home in the current year. It is also assumed that she marries in the year in which she left the parental home. The number of new immigrating married women of this age is decreased by one. If family reunification did take place, the number of minor children involved in the reunion is simulated. For that purpose we use the distribution of immigrating family heads by number of minor children.

We assume that immigrating women aged 64 years and older do not have minor children in their households. The number of minor children is determined by a Monte Carlo process. The age of the children is dependent on the age of the woman and on the number of children by age in our population of new immigrants, if available. If a child is added to the immigrating female, the number of persons in the database grows by one and this number becomes the child's personal identification number. The sex of each child is assigned by lot, his or her marital status is unmarried, not cohabiting. The child gets a pointer for his father and mother, and *vice versa*. Also, the number of siblings is added to the child's attributes. The number of children of the father and mother is increased by one and the number of siblings of the other children is also increased by one. Every time a child is allocated to a woman, the number of children of that age and sex in the population of new immigrants is diminished by one. If no more children are available, no children are attached in the case of family reunification.

(b) Unmarried people older than 17. We assume that these persons immigrate as single persons, without children. The number of this kind of persons in the population of new immigrants is added to our sample. These persons get their personal attributes in the same way as the immigrating married women.

(c) The same applies for the group of widowed and divorced men.

(d) Widowed and divorced women: these groups are also added to our sample. In this case, children may be present. The presence of children is determined in the same way as under a., on the understanding that now the number of children is determined by a random draw from the distribution of female-headed immigrating households by number of children.

(e) Married men who immigrate without their family and consequently leave behind their wives and children, if present, in the country of origin. The probability that a married man will immigrate without his family is derived from NCBS (2). A Monte Carlo process determines whether this will happen. If this is the case, the man is added to the sample, otherwise we have to make do with a person of category (f).

(f) Married men, immigrating with their family. The probability that this will occur has been determined above. A wife is attached to him, analogously to women in category (a), if present. Children are attached in a similar manner.

When this has happened all unmarried men and women older than 17 years, all widowed and divorced persons, and all married men out of our population of new immigrants are added to our sample. However, we are not sure that this also holds for married women and for minor children. Now, the third step, if necessary, contains the addition of the remaining married women and minor children to the sample.

When the population of newly immigrated married women does not equal zero, first the remaining women are added to the sample and a husband is drawn from the set of married men living in the Netherlands without a partner. Both wife and husband get a pointer to their partner.

Analogously, if minor children are still present in our set of new immigrants, a father and/or mother are drawn for each child out of the immigrated married people in the current year and the child is added to his father and/or mother. Pointers are added and so on.

Now all new immigrants are inserted in our sample. The fourth and last step is the simulation of return immigration. Earlier, we fixed the number of return immigrants by year of emigration up to and including six years ago. Dividing these numbers by our sampling ratio and the number of emigrants (who have not yet re-immigrated or died) in the last seven years in our sample, gives us the probability of return migration. These probabilities are used to determine whether a person who emigrated during the last six years or the current year will return to the Netherlands. In this, we assume that married women immigrate with their husbands and that minor children immigrate with their mothers, or in case of divorce or widowhood, with their fathers. Adult children are assumed to decide independently whether they will immigrate or not. If parents decide to immigrate, whereas their children (older than 17 and living with their parents) do not, the consequence is that these children will decide to leave their parental home and form a one-person household. Analogously, if these children decide to immigrate, whereas their parents stay abroad, they will also decide to leave the parental home. Their personal attributes are then adjusted.

5.3 EMIGRATION

Emigration is largely simulated analogously to immigration. However, no persons are added to our sample population. As with immigration, the first step is the determination of return emigrants and 'new' emigrants. The starting point is the total number of emigrants. For 1947 we know the total number of male and female emigrants. Using the 1949 distribution of emigrants by age group and the distinction between married and unmarried persons, and using the distribution by sex, age and marital status in 1960, these figures are transformed into age, sex and marital status specific numbers. For 1948, we know the number of emigrants by sex, by six age groups and whether they are married or unmarried. These are transformed into sex, age and marital status specific numbers in the same way as those for 1947. For the year 1949 up to and including 1959 we know the total number of male and female emigrants for the age groups 0–14, 15–19, 20–24, 25–29, 30–34, 35–39, 40–49, 50–64, 65 and older, all – with the exception of the first age group – for married and unmarried people [NCBS (2)]. These number are transformed into age, sex and marital status specific numbers, using the distribution of emigrants by marital status and sex for the distinguished age groups in 1960 and the localization coefficients within these groups in the same year. For the period 1960–1985 we have age, sex and marital status specific numbers of emigrants[5] and from 1986 to 2010 we use the NCBS 1984 forecast. After 2010 the number of emigrants has been set equal to zero, in accordance with the NCBS 1984 forecast.

The number of return emigrants is calculated on the basis of the return emigration rates by number of years passed since the year of immigration and the number of immigrants in those years, still living in the Netherlands. We used the return emigration rates for the years 1955 (covering the period 1947–1957), 1960 (1958–1962), 1965 (1963–1967) and 1970 (covering the period from 1968 on); NCBS (1958a, 1962, 1968b, and 1974). We limited ourselves to people who had immigrated between the current year and five years earlier. However, we do not know the people who immigrated before 31 May 1947, in the sense that we do not know their personal attributes. They are in our sample, but our initial population does not contain information on this subject. For that reason, we determine – for 1947 (between 1 June and 31 December) – only the number of return emigrants, who had immigrated in the same year. Then, a proportion (based on the return emigration rates) of the new emigrants were called return emigrants, who are assumed to have immigrated between 1 January 1943 and 31 May 1947. In 1948 this procedure was applied for the determination of return emigrants who had immigrated between 1 January 1944 and 31 May 1947, and so on. This procedure must be applied to determine the true number of new emigrants, while return immigration only holds for new emigrants and does not apply to re-emigrated persons.

Subtracting the resulting number of return emigrants from the total number of emigrants, we get the number of new emigrants (by age, sex and marital status). On the basis of the populations at risk, the probability of return emigration and the new emigration rates are determined. It is assumed that the probability of return emigration is independent of age and household composition. Return emigration takes place as a family, with the exception of children older than 17 years. The latter decide for themselves whether they want to emigrate or not. Given the limited data, it is also assumed that return emigration differs from the emigration pattern of new emigrants only

[5] Also from tables from NCBS.

during the first five years of their residence in the Netherlands. The new emigration probability is dependent on age, sex and marital status. Cohabiting people are treated in the same way as married people. The whole emigration process is regulated by Monte Carlo decisions.

The process for new emigrating persons can be divided into four subprocesses:

(a) Married and cohabiting men, who emigrate on their own, *i.e.* without their family. The probability is derived from NCBS (1953a, 1958a, 1962, 1968b, 1974, 1977a and 1982b). For the years 1981 and later, we assume that this probability does not change. If it is decided (using a Monte Carlo process) that a married man emigrates without his family, a Boolean variable assigned to the wife (called 'empartner'), which stands for the question of whether her partner has emigrated alone, is put true. The variable year of emigration is put equal to the current year.
(b) Married and cohabiting men, who emigrate with their family. Again, it is assumed that children older than 17 years decide whether or not they want to emigrate, independent of their parents' choice. If a child, still living with his or her parent(s), decides not to emigrate, the consequence is that the child decides to live alone. So the year of leaving the parental home becomes the current year.
(c) Not cohabiting men and women older than 17 years. Minor children, if present, emigrate together with their father or mother.
(d) Cohabiting women, whose husbands have already emigrated in the past (the variable empartner is true, see under (a) and who emigrate for reasons of family reunification [NCBS (1953a, 1958a, 1962, 1968b, 1974, 1977a and 1982b)]. If minor children are present, these will accompany their mother.

If a person has emigrated (and (s)he had not immigrated before) (s)he is only subjected to return immigration and mortality. All other (demographic) transitions are ignored.

5.4 OLD PEOPLE'S HOMES

From the NCBS we know the probability of staying in an old people's home for the years 1950 and 1965 for the age groups younger than 65, 65–69, 70–74, 75–79, 80–84 and 85 years and older for both males and females. From 1965 we have yearly data on the number of people staying in an old people's home, the number of people who died in an old people's home, the number of discharges and the number of admissions for the same age groups with the exception of the oldest one, which has been split into the age groups 85–89 and older than 89 years. Using these data, occurrence-exposure rates were calculated for entering and leaving old people's homes for the years 1965, 1970, 1977 and 1984 [NCBS (1951a, 1968a, 1973, 1980b and 1987a)]. Between these years the rates were interpolated. From 1984 the rates were held constant, just as the departure rate before 1965 is held constant at the 1965 level. Between 1950 and 1965 we interpolated between the probability of remaining in an old people's home in 1950 and the entrance rate in 1965. For the years 1949 and earlier, the figures for 1950 were used. In all these rates and probabilities, a distinction was made between married and unmarried males and females.

Each year, a Monte Carlo process decides whether a married woman or an unmarried person enters an old people's home or not, if the person in question is 60 years or older and still living outside such a home. If the person decides to enter an old people's home, the person's attribute 'living in an old people's home' becomes true instead of false. If this person is a married woman, her partner – if he has not emigrated alone – also enters the old people's home and his attribute 'living in an old people's home' also becomes true. Analogously, it is determined whether people living in an old people's home will leave this home. If this occurs their attribute 'living in an old people's home' becomes false.

5.5 MORTALITY

Mortality is simulated by subjecting the individuals in the sample to age, sex and marital status, specific death occurrence-exposure rates. These rates are derived from NCBS data and forecasts. The number of deceased people by age, sex and marital status for the period 1947–1985 are known from NCBS. The numbers for the period 1986–2035 are derived from the NCBS 1984 forecast. The death rates were calculated using the population at risk. In this process, we distinguish between persons remaining in an old people's home and those living on their own. The death rates for people living in an old people's home and not living there respectively by age as a proportion of the death rate for the whole population by age, are derived from NCBS (1968a, 1973, 1980b and 1987a) and the death rates as calculated before.

Each year, a Monte Carlo process decides for each person whether (s)he will die. If this occurs, the individual's year of death is put equal to the current year. If the person in question is married, his or her partner becomes widowed and the year of widowhood is put equal to the current year. If the individual cohabits, the partner's marital status changes back into the status (s)he had before the start of the cohabitation with the deceased person. Also in this case, the attribute 'year of widowhood' is put equal to the current year. If a married man, who has emigrated without his family, has died, the attribute 'empartner' is set to false.

If the deceased person has children, the pointer to the father or mother (depending on who died) of these children becomes zero, whereas for each child the last (last but one) child's pointer of the identification numbers of children at the former partner is put equal to the pointer to the child's father (mother). If the other parent had already died before, the child has become an orphan.

5.6 MARRIAGE

From 1948 to 1985 we have the number of marrying persons by age, sex and (former) marital status for each year. The same (forecasted) data are available from the NCBS 1984 forecast for the period 1986–2035. For 1947 we have the total number of marrying persons by sex and (former) marital status for eight age groups. Using the localization coefficients in 1948, these numbers are transformed to age, sex and (former) marital status specific numbers. Marriage rates were calculated by dividing these numbers by the appropriate population at risk.

For each person in our database who is older than 14 years and younger than 85 years and not married, a Monte Carlo process decides each year whether or not (s)he will marry. If the decision is to marry, the person is stored in a file of potential marriage candidates. When all persons have passed through the marriage submodule, the matching process takes place (figure 5.1).

First, the number of marriages to be contracted is determined. It is put at half the sum of the number of male and female candidates, in which a Monte Carlo process decides in case of rounding off. The resulting number is indicated by N.

The next step in the matching process is contracting the marriages of cohabiting persons. The female is the starting point in this. Therefore, we take all women in our stock of candidates who live in a consensual union. They are said to marry their partner (even if this partner is not included in our stock of male candidates). These people get the marital status married and their year of marriage becomes the current year. It is possible that the wife or husband has died in the current year. In that case the marital status of the person still alive becomes widowed. If both partners have died during the current year, nothing has changed.

If all women in our stock of candidates who lived in a consensual union, have married their partners, then all men and women in this stock who cohabit are deleted. To get the intended total number of N marriages, we determine whether we have to draw extra candidates (not married, not cohabiting, aged 15 to 84 years), or delete candidates from the stock. In both cases, the localization coefficients for marriages are used as weights. In this way, we get an equal number of men and women who have to be coupled to each other.

Using the distribution of marriages by ages of both partners, the number of marriages still to be contracted after the aforementioned marriage process of cohabiting persons, and the RAS–method [Steger (1980: 147 and further)], we determined the number of marriages in our sample by age of the partners. This matrix is called M. The distribution of marriages by partners' age is available for 1960 and 1976 from unpublished data of the NCBS. We used eight age groups: 19 years and younger, 20–21 years, 22–23 years, 24–25 years, 26–29 years, 30–34 years, 35–44 years and 45 years and older. For 1960 and before we used the 1960 distribution, whereas for 1976 and later the 1976 distribution was the starting point for the RAS–procedure. Between 1960 and 1976 interpolations were used.

The matching process of the males and females, now left in our stock of candidates, is carried out in two steps. Again, the woman is the starting point. In the first step, a female candidate is taken from the stock and we look at whether the number of male candidates is still more than ten. If so, we draw ten male candidates using the distribution by age of the male partner, given the female's age, and under the condition that the concerning cell in the matrix M is positive.

In the second step the most suitable candidate out of these ten is determined on the basis of the female's level of education and the distribution of husbands by level of education conditional on the woman's level of education. This last distribution is known for the marriages existing on 28 February 1971 by period of contraction [NCBS (1981: 58 and 166–169)]. In this, the following periods are distinguished: 1949 and before, 1950–1954, 1955–1959, 1960–1964, 1965–1969 and 1970. For 1971 and after, we use the 1970 distribution.

If the remaining number of women is ten or less, then these women are coupled to a husband on the basis of the distribution by age only. When a wife has chosen her husband, the corresponding cell in the matrix M is diminished by one. Both the male's and female's year of marriage becomes the current year, their year of divorce (if positive) becomes zero, their marital status is now married. Each gets a pointer to his or her partner, which equals the partner's identification number. If one of the partners was still living with his or her parents, the year of leaving the parental home of this partner becomes the current year. If one of the partners already had children, these children are also assigned to the other partner. This means that the number of children of this last partner becomes positive, that (s)he gets pointers to these children and that the children concerned get a pointer to their new parent. If both partners already had children, these children are mutually assigned to both parents.

It is also possible that the wife or husband has died in the current year. In that case the marital status of the person still alive becomes widowed. If both partners died during the current year, nothing has changed.

5.7 DIVORCE

Divorce is carried out by subjecting the married women in our sample population to an age specific divorce occurrence-exposure rate. These rates are calculated from NCBS data and forecasts. For 1948–1985 we have the numbers of divorces by age of the women [tables from the NCBS; also NCBS (1958b and 1976)] at our disposal, whereas for 1986 and later, we use the numbers of divorces by age of the women as forecasted by the NCBS. For 1947 we know the number of divorces for seven age groups. Using the localization coefficients within these age groups in 1948, the number of divorces by age groups is transformed into the number of divorces by individual ages.

A Monte Carlo process decides whether or not a wife's marriage ends in divorce in the current year. If divorce occurs, the marital status of the woman and her husband are changed to divorced. The pointer to the partner becomes zero, whereas the pointer referring to the former partner is set equal to the corresponding personal identification numbers. For both individuals the year of divorce becomes positive (and equals the current year). If the husband has emigrated, the number of emigrated people without a partner is diminished by one.

If children live with their parents, we determined for each child whether the woman or her husband is granted custody of the child. Up to 1975 we assumed that the father had a five per cent chance of being granted custody. For 1980 and 2000 the probability amounts to 10 and 20%, respectively. Between these years an interpolation is made for the probability. If a child is allocated to the father (mother), the number of children allocated to the partner is increased by one for the mother (father) and the corresponding pointer of children allocated to the partner is set equal to the child's identification number.

5.8 DEHABITATION

Dehabitation is carried out by subjecting the cohabiting women in our sample population to an age specific dehabitation occurrence-exposure rate. These rates are derived from the age specific divorce rates, while data for the dehabitation process hardly exist. Here, we have to fall back on the scarce information from surveys held in the 1980s, especially as reported by the NCBS (1985c). From this source we have drawn information on the dehabitation of persons who cohabit for the first time between 1974 and 1979 and who were younger than 30 years when they started cohabiting. The data refer to the duration of their cohabitation. If we compare the resulting rates with the divorce rates by duration of marriage in the early 1980s, we can deduce that the dehabitation probability in the first six years of cohabitation is 3.13 times higher, on average, than the divorce probability of married people in the same period of six years. After about six years, however, the dehabitation rate approximates the divorce rate. Moreover, the older the persons in question, the smaller the difference between both rates. Therefore, we take the dehabitation rate as being 3.13 times the divorce rate, corresponding to the wife's age, if the duration of the cohabitation amounts to six years or less, and the wife is 35 years or younger. In all the other cases, the dehabitation rate is assumed to be equal to the divorce probability.

A Monte Carlo process decides whether or not a wife's cohabitation ends in a dehabitation in the current year. If dehabitation occurs, the marital status of the woman and her husband are changed into their marital status prior to the last cohabitation. The pointer to the partner becomes zero, whereas the pointer referring to the former partner is set equal to the corresponding personal identification numbers. For both individuals the year of dehabitation becomes positive (and equals the current year). If the husband has emigrated, the number of emigrated people without a partner is diminished by one.

If children lived with their parents, we determined for each child whether the woman or her husband was granted custody of the child. This was exactly the same as in the case of divorce.

5.9 COHABITATION

The process of (unmarried) cohabitation is largely analogous to the marriage process. The most important difference is the way in which we determine the transition rate for a first cohabitation. We assume that no cohabitations took place before 1965. From van 't Klooster–van Wingerden (1979: 35–37) we find 18 291 male headed non-family households with female non-relatives, 16 671 female headed non-family households with male non-relatives, 3126 male headed one-parent family households with other female non-relatives and 8294 female headed one-parent family households with other male non-relatives for 1971. This makes 46 382 unmarried cohabitations in 1971. It is assumed that 5000 cohabitations existed in 1965 and that there was an exponential growth between 1965 and 1971.

For 1982, we find about 205 000 cohabitations on the basis of the Netherlands Fertility Survey (*Onderzoek Gezinsvorming*)[6] and additional estimates for the persons older than 37 years. Between 1971 and 1982 we also interpolated exponentially. For 1983 and later, we assume that the percentage of people living together, married or unmarried, at every age, does not change.

[6] Personal communication with van der Giessen of the NCBS and own calculations.

Given the (expected) number of married people by age and sex, we can calculate the number of people cohabiting by age and sex. Using this number of cohabiting people, the number of people by age and sex cohabiting in the model population at the beginning of the year, the expected number of non-first cohabitations started in the current year and the expected number of dehabitations in the current year yields us the number of first cohabitations in the current year. Coupling these numbers to the population at risk gives the first cohabitation rate. On the basis of the Netherlands Fertility Survey it is also assumed that the non-first cohabitation rate equals the remarriage rate for divorced people for those 33 years or older and it equals twice this remarriage rate for those under 25 years. Between the two ages the multiplication rate is interpolated.

Using these cohabitation rates, a Monte Carlo process decides whether or not a non-cohabiting person will be a cohabitation candidate. If so, (s)he is temporarily stored. After all persons have gone through the cohabitation submodule, the candidates are matched. This process is analogous to the marriage process for non-cohabiting marriage candidates. Therefore, we can refer to the marriage process.

5.10 SPLITTING OFF

The next submodule in the demographic part of our model is the splitting off of children for reasons other than marriage or cohabitation. Only limited information is available on this subject. We use results from the 1971 Census and the 1977 and 1981 Housing Surveys (*Woningbehoefte-nonderzoek*); van Leeuwen (1980), Ploegmakers and van Leeuwen (1983) and Heida and Gordijn (1985). From these data we know the percentages of unmarried men and women by age, living with their parents in the years in question. Between 1971 and 1977 and 1977 and 1981 we interpolated these percentages. For 1982 and later, we assume that these percentages do not change, whereas before 1971 we take those of 1971, corrected for the relative participation rate in university education by persons between 18 and 25 years (1971 = 100) squared [derived from NCBS (1984a)]. This last factor is considered as a proxy for the developments in splitting off of children for reasons other than marriage or cohabitation in the 1950s and 1960s.

When marriage and cohabitation take place in our model, we can count the number of unmarried persons still living with their parents. Decreasing these numbers with the numbers resulting when applying the calculated percentages and dividing these differences by the counted numbers (being the population at risk), gives us the desired probability for splitting off for reasons other than marriage or cohabitation. Via a Monte Carlo procedure we determined whether an unmarried, non-cohabiting person living with his or her parents, will leave the parental home. If so, (s)he starts a one-person household. This procedure is only executed for persons younger than 40 years. If someone reaches the age of 40 and is still living with his or her parents, we decided that the person in question leaves the parental home in the current year.

5.11 FERTILITY

Births are based on marital status specific parity progression rates for the ages 15 to 50 years. In this parity, one, two, three and four and over are distinguished. The first step is the determination of the number of births within and outside marriage by the mother's age and parity.

The total number of births by the mother's age is known for the years 1947–1949 for the five-year age groups 15–19 up to and including 45–49 years [NCBS (1955: 47)]. Using the localization coefficients by individual age and parity for 1950, these numbers are transformed into number of births by mother's age and parity. The total number of births by mother's age and parity are available for the period 1950–1985 from NCBS. For the period 1986–2035, we use the resulting numbers from the NCBS 1984 forecast.

The number of extramarital births in 1947 and 1948 is known for five age groups: 15–19, 20–24, 25–29, 30–34 and 35–49 [NCBS (1975: 22)]. Using the distribution by parity 1 and 2^+ in 1950, the distribution of parity 2^+ by parity 2, 3 and 4^+ in 1968 and the localization coefficients by age in 1968, these numbers are transformed into numbers of extramarital births by mother's age and parity. For the period 1950–1967 the total number of extramarital births is known for the same age groups as for 1948 and 1949, but also by parity (1 and 2^+), [NCBS (1975: 23)]. Using the distribution of parity 2^+ by parity 2, 3 and 4^+ in 1968 and the localization coefficients by age in 1968, these numbers are transformed into numbers of extramarital births by mother's age and parity. The period 1968–1979 readily furnishes us the desired information: the number of extramarital births by mother's age and parity. For the period 1980–1984 we have the number of extramarital births for the age groups 15–24, 25–29, 30–34 and 35–49 [NCBS (1986: 13)]. Using the localization coefficients for 1979 and the distribution by parity in the same year, these numbers are also transformed into numbers of extramarital births by mother's age and parity. For the period 1985–2026 we use the total number of extramarital births from the low variant of the NCBS 1980 forecast [NCBS (1982a: 48)] and extrapolate this number for the period 2027–2035. Using the localization coefficients for 1979 and the distribution by parity in the same year, these numbers are again transformed into numbers of extramarital births by mother's age and parity.

With the aid of the distribution of extramarital births by mother's marital status (unmarried, widowed and divorced) for the age groups 15–19, 20–24,

25–29, 30–34, 35–39 and 40^+ in the years 1975–1985 [NCBS (1986)], these numbers are transformed into numbers of extramarital births by mother's age, marital status and parity. For the years before 1975 we use the 1975 distribution and for the years 1985 and later, we use the 1984 distribution. Subtracting these numbers of extramarital births from the total number of births, we get the number of marital births by mother's age and parity.

The next step is to transpose these numbers into age, parity and marital status specific birth rates. The population at risk is not known from vital statistics. Therefore, we use the simulated female population by age, marital status and parity, as population at risk. For females with four or more children, it is assumed that the parity progression rate for a fifth, a sixth, and so on, child equals the parity progression rate for a fourth child.

Within the category of unmarried persons, we distinguish between cohabiting and non-cohabiting women. It appears that the first group's probability of having an additional child is about twice the second group's probability [NCBS (1984c: 71)]. We assume that this also holds in the past and the future. Therefore, we adjust the parity progression rates for unmarried women in the following way.

For non-cohabiting unmarried women (with k children) the calculated parity progression rate (of age a) is multiplied by the quotient of the number of unmarried women of age a with k children on the one hand, and the sum of the number of non-cohabiting unmarried women of age a with k children and twice the number of cohabiting unmarried women of the same age and the same number of children on the other hand.

For cohabiting unmarried women the multiplication factor is twice that for non-cohabiting ones. The parity progression rates for cohabiting widowed and cohabiting divorced women are not adjusted for cohabitation, because too little information is available for this group.

Using these parity progression rates we determine whether a child is born or not for each year for every female aged 15 to 49 years. If this occurs, the number of children of the woman is raised by one, the number of personal records is also increased by one and this number becomes the child's identification number. The same number is used as the pointer of the mother for her newly born child. The child's pointer for its mother is set equal to the mother's identification number. The child's sex is assigned by lot and its year of birth becomes the current year. The number of children minus one is assigned to the newly born child as its number of brothers and sisters, and the same is done with its brothers and sisters. The same adjustments have been made for, and with reference to the partner, if present.

It is possible that the mother died in the remainder of the year. In that case, the pointer to the mother becomes zero and if no father was present, this means that the child becomes an orphan. Next, the child is subjected to the probability of death during the rest of the year. This procedure is analogous to the one reported in section 5.5.

5.12 CONSTRUCTION OF A REPRESENTATIVE INITIAL POPULATION

To start the simulation process we need a representative sample in the starting year 1947. The available data of the 1947 Census are, in part, suitable for the construction of our initial population [NCBS (1951b, 1951c and 1954)]. However, the data are not available at the micro level. Consequently, we must derive our microdata set from some macro tables. We have, among others, the following tables at our disposal:

(a) The distribution of all marriages, still existing on 31 May 1947, by eight age groups for both partners.
(b) The distribution of all marriages, still existing on 31 May 1947, by year of contraction of the marriage.
(c) The distribution of all marriages, still existing on 31 May 1947, by eight age groups for both partners at the moment of contraction of the marriage.
(d) The population by age, sex and marital status on 31 May 1947.
(e) The number of marriages by year of contraction of the marriage and the number of live born children in these marriages.
(f) The number of marriages with and without children by year of contraction of the marriage and woman's age at marriage.
(g) The number of households with children present at composition and number of children.
(h) The number of children born out of existing marriages by year of marriage and woman's age at marriage.

The simulation of the initial population starts with the simulation of married persons. It appears that the distribution of all marriages, existing on 31 May 1947, by age group of both partners, fits in very well with the marriages contracted in the period 1935–1940. This implies that this distribution has remained rather constant during the 1930s and 1940s and that between about 1900 and 1930 the number of marriages at higher ages (50^+) must have decreased. This decrease must be comparable with the loss of marriages as a consequence of death, which have occurred between the year of contraction and 31 May 1947. If this was not the case, the correspondence between all existing marriages and those contracted in the late 1930s should almost be impossible. Assuming this, we can state that the distribution of marriages by age of both partners on 31 May 1947 can be used for all existing marriages, independent of the year of contraction of the marriage.

We put the sampling ratio in our initial population at 1/n. We now draw 1/n part of the number of married men and women out of the table as mentioned under (d). Rounding off is executed by a Monte Carlo process. We look for an equal number of males and females, as described in section 5.6. Suppose, that m men and m women result. For each of the m women, for whom we have the exact age, we continue as follows:

1) With the aid of the distribution of all marriages, still existing on 31 May 1947, by age groups for both partners at the moment of contraction of the marriage, see under (c), we determine the probability for the age group in the year of her marriage. Thereafter the age group at marriage is assigned by lot.
2) The man's age group at marriage can also be determined using the distribution under (c). The exact man's age at marriage within this age group is fixed by lot.
3) The woman's age in 1947 and the age group at marriage gives us the marriage period. Using the distribution under (b) the exact year of marriage has been determined. The man's age in 1947 is also known. It is assumed that both partners left their parental home on marriage.
4) We now control whether a married man of that age is available in the group of m drawn married men. If a man with that age is available, the man is coupled to the woman. If not, a man is looked for in the nearest age (one year younger or older), and so on.
5) Next, we determine the number of children born into this marriage. The family parity progression rates for the different marriage generations can be derived from the data under (h). These are given in table 5.1.

Table 5.1 *Family parity progression rates for the marriage generations 1914–1946 (parity 1, a_0, up to and including parity 10, a_9)*

marriage generation	a_0	a_1	a_2	a_3	a_4	a_5	a_6	a_7	a_8	a_9
'44–'46	0.47	0.17	0.05	0	0	0	0	0	0	0
'39–'43	0.86	0.68	0.42	0.34	0.27	0.21	0.18	0.16	0.33	0
'34–'38	0.89	0.82	0.64	0.57	0.54	0.50	0.45	0.38	0.32	0.26
'29–'33	0.89	0.84	0.71	0.67	0.66	0.65	0.64	0.61	0.57	0.52
'24–'28	0.89	0.84	0.72	0.70	0.70	0.71	0.70	0.69	0.67	0.64
'19–'23	0.90	0.85	0.74	0.72	0.72	0.72	0.72	0.72	0.70	0.67
'14–'18	0.92	0.89	0.78	0.74	0.74	0.74	0.74	0.73	0.71	0.68

The family parity progression rates for the marriage generations 1913 and before are set equal to these for the generation 1914–1918. Of course, the woman's age at marriage is also an important determinant for the number of children born into that marriage. Correction factors for the age at marriage can also be deduced from the data under (h). We assume that these are independent of the year of marriage. We only distinguish between the parity progression rate for families with no children and that for families with at least one child. These correction factors are to be found in table 5.2.

Table 5.2 *Correction factors for the mother's age at marriage for the parity progression rates for families with no children (a_0) and at least one child (a_*)*

age at marriage	a_0	a_*
< 20	1.09	1.35
20–24	1.05	1.12
25–29	0.99	0.92
30–34	0.88	0.69
35–39	0.68	0.35
40–44	0.33	0.09
> 44	0.11	0.01

The number of children born into the marriage is assigned by lot, using a Monte Carlo procedure. We assume that a maximum of ten children are born. We do not distinguish between first and any subsequent marriages. Mortality has been neglected. In their totality, these three factors keep each other in equilibrium. The limitation to ten children at maximum underestimates the number of children by about 2–3%, the neglect of the difference between first and subsequent marriages overestimates the number of children by about 1% and the neglect of mortality results in an overestimation of the number of children by about 2%.

6) Hereafter, the woman's age at which the children are born is determined. The age is fixed by a Monte Carlo procedure. The localization coefficients for births by duration of the marriage in 1937 is our starting point. So, the duration since the contraction of the marriage is assigned by lot for the year of birth of each of the children. The year of marriage is known and thus we know the year of birth of each of the children. In this, we limit ourselves to children who are younger than 26 years in 1947. If the child is between 15 and 26 years whether the child has ever been married is assigned by lot. These children are considered as not living with their parents and are also not matched to their parents. All other children who are younger than 26 years are assumed to live with their parents. Next, the child's sex is assigned by lot. Now, we control whether a boy or girl is available from our set under (d), adjusted for the sample ratio. If no child of the appropriate age is available, a child is looked for in the nearest ages. If no children are present at all, the procedure for children is stopped.

7) All characteristics of the family are now assigned to the attributes of the family members: year of birth, year of marriage (which equals year of leaving parental home), number of children, identification numbers, pointers from parents to children and *vice versa*. These are put into our file of personal records.

The households headed by divorced and widowed women are now simulated. Given our limited data, it is impossible to find the former husband of divorced women. For this reason, step 1) up to and including step 4) for married women are not executed. We know the number of children younger than 21 years and living in female headed one-parent households. The number of divorced women with at least one child is also known, and the same holds for widowed women. We assume that only women younger than 65 years have children below the age of 21 years in their household. Dividing the number of widowed women (divorced women) younger than 65 years by the number of widowed women (divorced women) with at least one child in her household, we get the probability of having at least one child in a household headed by a widowed (divorced) woman. We also assume that only one or two children are present in such households. It is possible to determine the probability that two children are present in the household. The procedure is analogous to that for married people. Instead of the localization coefficients for births by duration of the marriage, we use the localization coefficients by age. Because we cannot determine the father, the children do not get a pointer to their father.

The same process is used for divorced and widowed men. The same localization coefficients by age are used. However, it is assumed that the father is two years older than the mother, which is about the mean age difference between husbands and wives.

We assume that unmarried people do not have children. Our data are too limited to reconstruct this element. As a consequence, children born out of wedlock and whose mother did not marry between the child's birth and 31 May 1947, have the 'wrong' mother in the simulation model. We do not know how many children are involved.

If, after all these assignments, some children are without a mother or father, these children are assigned by lot to a mother. We implicitly assumed that the mother or father is alive for all persons under 26 years. This means that we have no orphans under 26 years in our initial population. Another interpretation could be that if a child becomes an orphan, the child is adopted by another family as a foster child. Using the model of Goodman, *et al.* (1974), we can calculate the probability of being an orphan [Bartlema (1987)]. For a person aged 15 years, the probability amounts to 0.17%, for someone aged 21 the probability 0.46% and for a person aged 25 years 1.18%. So, the error involved is limited.

Of course, we also want to know who are whose parents, for those who are not living with their parents. These are unmarried persons older than 26 years, and all persons ever married. We use Bartlema's model [Bartlema (1987)] to determine whether no parent, or at least one parent, is alive. The average probability of having a mother and a father still alive, respectively, is given in table 5.3.

Table 5.3 *The average probability that the mother and father, respectively, are still alive for some ages of a child, based on the life table for the period 1931–1940*

Age child	Probability mother lives	Probability father lives
15	0.9598	0.9560
20	0.9327	0.9247
25	0.8917	0.8817
30	0.8301	0.8005
35	0.7407	0.6920
40	0.6193	0.5516
45	0.4718	0.3851
50	0.3167	0.2248
55	0.1796	0.0994
60	0.0819	0.0311
65	0.0283	0.0071
70	0.0068	0.0005
75	0.0010	0
80	0.0001	0
85^+	0	0

For each of the persons concerned, we assign by lot the mother's age at the birth of the person in question (using the localization coefficients for births in 1937 by mother's age). The person's age and the mother's age at the birth of that person gives the mother's age in 1947. Using Bartlema's data it is determined by chance whether the mother is still alive or not. If she is still alive, her marital status is assigned by lot. So, we have determined the mother, and a woman with these characteristics is drawn from our database. The woman's partner, if present, is considered to be the father of the person in question. Next, pointers are interchanged. If the mother was dead, it is determined whether the father is still alive. This father then has to be either divorced or widowed. If the father is still alive, we apply an analogous procedure to find the father. If it is decided that he has also died, the person in question is an orphan and does not have pointers to his or her parents.

6

The labour market and income formation module[1]

6.1 INTRODUCTION

The labour market and income formation module contains the following submodules: education, scholarship, the determination of the income percentile, labour income, taxes and the transitions between the several possible economic activities (employed, unemployed, disabled, houseman/housewife, conscript, retired).

The way in which the labour market and income formation module is passed through is shown in figure 6.1. When all persons have gone through the demographic module, the labour market and income formation module is entered. At first, educational decisions are made (section 6.2). If an individual is six years old, it is decided whether (s)he enters school at that age or at the age of seven. If (s)he is already at school, it is decided whether (s)he repeats, moves up, goes to another type of school or ends education. When all six- or seven-year-old children and all students have gone through this part of the model, the re-entering of school is simulated (part-time or full-time).

Next, scholarship is simulated if the individual is at a vocational college or at university (see also section 6.2). The income percentile of people who have already finished the education process and are not yet 65 years or who are part-time students, is adapted (section 6.4.4) and there is an investigation into whether changes in his or her economic activity take place (section 6.3). If the year under consideration is 1988 or before, the number of simulated employed and unemployed men and women is compared with the numbers in reality and adjustments, if any, are executed (see section 6.3.7).

Now, the exogeneous variables in the equation for the mean and variance of labour income for the various cohorts are known, and wage income can be determined for each employed person (section 6.4). The last element in

[1] For a performance test of this module, see Nelissen (1991c and 1993).

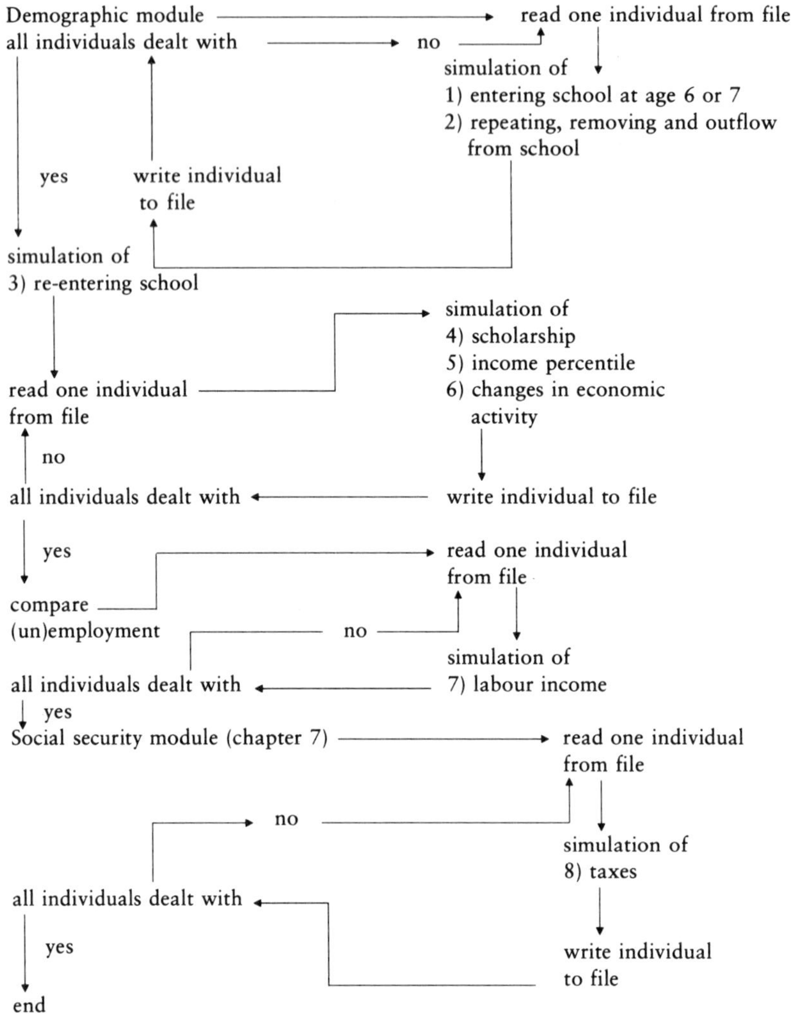

Figure 6.1 The labour market and income formation module.

the module under consideration is the determination of taxes (section 6.5). This is executed after the benefits from and contributions to social security have taken place.

6.2 EDUCATION

When an individual has passed through the demographic module and is six years or older, (s)he enters the education submodule. This submodule aims to simulate each individual's passage through the grades (year by year) and through the different fields of education. The input of the required data and the determination of the enrolment probabilities occur at the same moment as the demographic module (figure 6.1). If the person is six years old, a decision is made whether or not (s)he will enter primary (from 1986 the third group of the so-called basic education) or special education. If the decision is negative, the person will enter the education process when (s)he reaches the age of seven. Then, (s)he gets the economic activity student. The choice between special and primary education is also subject to chance.

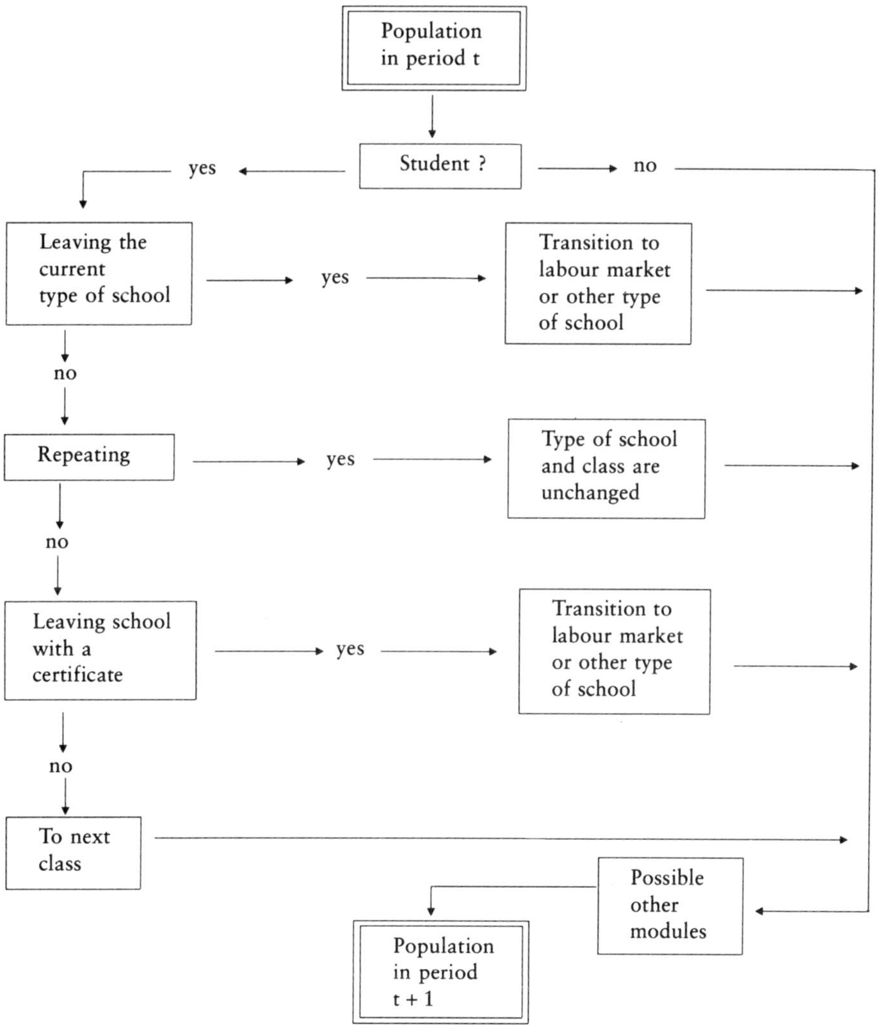

Figure 6.2 Enrolment through the education submodule.

If one enters primary education, one's level of education becomes 1 and if one enters special education this level of education becomes 11.

Table 6.1 *The types of education distinguished in the education submodule and the corresponding levels of education*[2]

type of education	level of education
*primary education	1–6
– continued primary education (*vglo*)	111–112
*special education	11–16
*secondary general education (*avo*)	
– elementary secondary education (*lavo*)	51–53
– first form of secondary school (*brugklas*)	61–63
– junior secondary schools (*mavo/mulo*)	141–144
– senior secondary schools (*havo*)	151–155
– pre-university education	
– hbs/gymnasium/lyceum (*vhmo*, old style)	131–136
– vwo	161–166
*junior vocational training (*lbo*)	
– junior technical training (*lto*)	21–24
– junior agricultural training (*lao*)	31–34
– junior domestic science training (*lhno*)	41–44
– junior economic and administrative training (*leao*)	51–54
– junior nautical training (*lno*)	71–74
– junior training for the retail trade (*lmo*)	81–84
*senior vocational training (*mbo*)	
– senior general/vocational training (*havo/mbo*)	151–155
– senior technical training (*mto*)	221–224
– senior agricultural training (*mao*)	231–233
– senior service and health care training (*mdgo*)	241–242
– senior domestic science training (*mhno*)	241–242
– senior economic and administrative training (*meao*)	251–253
– nursery school teachers' training (*klos*)	261–263
– senior nautical training (*mno*)	271–272
– senior training for the retail trade (*mmo*)	281–283
– short senior vocational training (*kmbo*)	291–292
*vocational colleges	
– technical and nautical colleges (*htno*)	321–324
– agricultural colleges (*hao*)	331–334
– health care colleges (*hgzo*)	341–344
– economic colleges (*heo*)	351–354
– social studies colleges (*hsao*)	361–364
– fine arts colleges (*hko*)	371–374
– teachers training colleges (*hpo*)	381–384
– domestic science colleges (*hhno*)	391–394
*university education	401–406

[2] Between parentheses are the Dutch abbreviations.

For each year the person is in the education process, it is assigned by lot whether the individual is moved up (the level of education is increased by one), has to repeat (the level of education does not change) or has left the type of school in question (with or without a certificate, in which case the level of education ends at 8 and 7, respectively). When (s)he leaves a particular type of school, a decision is made whether the pupil leaves education entirely or not, and if not, then it is decided which type of education the person will enter. After a pupil has left school (s)he gets another economic activity (see section 6.3.1) and (s)he may return to school after some time, and thus re-enter the education submodule. In that case, the probability of part-time education is also considered. If a student returns to school full-time, that person again gets the economic activity student. If part-time education is entered, the economic activity does not change, but the attribute part-time education is set equal to true. The enrolment and flow probabilities are assumed to be equal for part-time and full-time students. The process is sketched in figure 6.2.

The education submodule contains the following routines:

(a) Entering school at age six or seven (primary or special education);
(b) Repeating, moving up and outflow from primary and special education;
(c) Repeating, moving up and outflow from secondary general education;
(d) Repeating, moving up and outflow from junior vocational training;
(e) Repeating, moving up and outflow from senior vocational training;
(f) Repeating, moving up and outflow vocational colleges;
(g) Repeating, moving up and outflow university education; and
(h) Re-entering of the education module (part-time or full-time).

Within the aforementioned fields of education different types of schools are distinguished. These are given in table 6.1. The possible transitions between the different fields of education are given in figure 6.3.

Children in primary education may only move up, leave the education process, repeat or switch to special education in the first four classes.

The following possibilities exist in the fifth class (with between parentheses the level of education): to repeat (5), to move up into class six (6), to leave the education process (7) or to go over to special education (15), to class one of junior technical training (21), to junior agricultural training (31), to junior domestic science training (41), to elementary secondary education (51), to junior economic and administrative training (also 51) or to junior secondary school (121).

In class six of primary education, one can repeat (6), leave the educational process (7) or go over to special education (16) or to class one of the continued primary education (111), junior secondary school (121), pre-university education (161 or 131), senior secondary school (151), first form of secondary school (61), junior technical training (21), junior agricultural training (31), junior domestic science training (41), elementary secondary education (51), junior economic and administrative training (51), junior nautical training (71) or junior training for the retail trade (81). The transition probabilities are derived from NCBS (1, 2, 3 and 4).

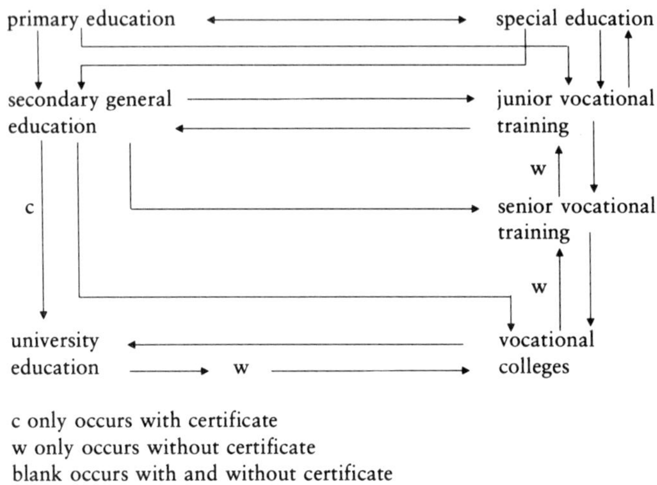

Figure 6.3 The fields of education and possible transitions.

Special education has the following possibilities during the first five classes: to repeat the same class, to move up to the next class, to go up to primary education and to leave full-time education. In class six of this type of school the pupil may repeat, leave full-time education or go to primary education, continued primary education, junior secondary school, junior technical training (21), junior agricultural training (31), junior domestic science training (41), elementary secondary education (51), junior economic and administrative training (51) or junior training for the retail trade (81). The data and the transition probabilities are derived from NCBS (1, 2, 5 and 6).

A pupil in junior vocational training is allowed to repeat the same class, to move up to the next class (with the exception of the last class), to leave full-time education or to choose another school type. If another school type is selected, the possibilities and transition probabilities differ for people with and without a certificate from the school just left. The choices are between special education, another type of junior vocational training, senior vocational training and secondary general education. Whether or not a certificate of the junior vocational training has been obtained determines the class into which one moves. The type of junior or senior vocational training entered depends on the type of junior vocational training left. The transition probabilities *etc.* are based on NCBS (1, 2, 12, 13, 17, 18, 21, 22 and 23).

Analogously, a student in secondary vocational training is allowed to repeat the same class, to move up to the next class (with the exception of the last class), to leave full-time education or to choose another school type. If another school type is selected, the possibilities and transition probabilities differ for people with and without a certificate from the type of school left. A student can enter junior vocational training, another type of senior vocational training or vocational colleges. The class into which a student goes is determined by whether a certificate of senior vocational training has been obtained. The type of junior or senior vocational training or vocational colleges entered depends on the type of junior vocational training left. The transition probabilities *etc.* are based on NCBS (1, 2, 12, 13, 14, 15, 16, 17, 18, 21, 22 and 23).

In vocational colleges the process is analogous to that in senior vocational training, on the understanding that in case of leaving a vocational college, the possibilities are: senior vocational training, another type of vocational college and university education, whereas the transition probabilities are derived from NCBS (1, 2, 10, 11, 12, 13, 17, 18, 20, 21, 22, 23 and 25).

In secondary general education it is again determined whether the student repeats the class in question, moves up to the next class or leaves (with or without a certificate) this form of education. After this type of school, a student may go into junior and senior vocational training, vocational colleges, university and other types of general secondary education. The enrolment and flow probabilities are derived from NCBS (1, 2, 7, 8 and 9).

If a student enters university education, then it is assigned by lot whether a degree is obtained, and according to this decision it is determined how many years a student remains at university. A student obtaining a degree is assumed to leave full-time education or else to start another study at a university or a vocational college. The transition probabilities are from NCBS (1, 2, 24 and 25).

The enrolment and outflow probabilities in the model differ between classes in primary and special education since 1950 and for secondary general education since 1968. In other cases we do not distinguish between classes. The same holds for the outflow probabilities and the distribution of people leaving a type of school without a certificate. The class into which a student goes depends on the class just left.

Educational attributes are adjusted for each year in schooling (part-time or full-time), unless a class is repeated. The level of education is adjusted and if a student leaves school, the Boolean for part-time education is set equal to false and end of education is set equal to the current year.

If the individual has left the education process, (s)he enters the module of changes in economic activity, which is the subject of section 6.3 (especially section 6.3.1 for school leavers) and (s)he can be considered a candidate for a re-entrance in education, full-time or part-time. Using the observed numbers of re-entrances in the past [NCBS (1 up to and including 25)], and assuming that the re-entrance probabilities do not change in the future, it is assigned by lot who re-enters the education process. The probability of being drawn is dependent of the level of education, age and sex. If a person is assigned by lot to re-enter full-time education, the attribute 'end of education' is set equal to zero, the level of education becomes the new type of school entered and the attribute 'economic activity' becomes student. If a school is re-entered part-time, the last attribute is not adjusted, but the Boolean standing for part-time education becomes true.

Unfortunately, we do not know the level of education at the start of our simulation in 1947. The first available information on the level of education of the Dutch population was provided by the 1971 Census [NCBS (1980d)]. The transition and enrolment probabilities are generally known from about 1967. For the period 1947–1966 we have some information from publications of the Netherlands Central Bureau of Statistics. The required transition and enrolment probabilities for the other years are determined by interpolation and extrapolation. In that way it was possible to derive the level of education of the initial population in 1947 by means of simulation. For the period 1985–2000 we use the probabilities for 1984. The flow probabilities (out of education) are calculated taking account of mortality and emigration.

Up to and including 1985, the level of a grant influenced claims for family allowances. Therefore, we also have to simulate grants. That has been done in a rather crude way. It is assumed that one can receive a grant for, at most, six years. It is also assumed that for 60% of the students who can claim a grant, the amount of the grant is such that these students count for one child for the family allowances, whereas the other 40% receive a limited amount, such that these students can claim family allowances for two children (under the condition that they are not living with their parents). The probability of getting a scholarship is determined using NCBS (29 and 1965), the inflow into vocational colleges and university education, parental income and the number of persons in the model population who already receive a grant.

6.3 CHANGES IN ECONOMIC ACTIVITY

As we saw in chapter 3, 16 positions are distinguished as economic activity, namely: employee, self-employed, civil servant, retired, unemployed employee, unemployed civil servant, unemployed others, conscript, disabled employee, disabled civil servant, disabled others, student, housewife or houseman, unemployed ex-disabled employee, unemployed ex-disabled civil servant and unemployed ex-disabled others.

The 1977 Labour Force Survey (*Arbeidskrachtentelling*), NCBS (1980c), is the starting point for the determination of the transition probabilities between the different states of economic activity. This contains information on economic activity in 1976 and 1977 for men and women of all ages between 14 and 66 years. We have transformed the states used in the Labour Force Survey into six states: disabled, employed, unemployed, conscript, student and retired or working in own household (housemen and housewives). Using these data, it is determined for each year for each individual whether his or her economic activity changes. In this process, additional data are used, *e.g.* data that refer to unemployment.

In this process, the determination of the labour supply is an important element. Labour supply is determined with a labour supply equation, modelled by Van Soest, Woittiez and Kapteyn (1990), which explicitly takes account of demand-side restrictions. The labour supply of individual household members is considered in a neo-classical framework, in which after-tax wages, unearned income, the social security and tax system and the household composition are taken into account.

The starting point is a modified version of the model introduced by Hausman (1981), in which the random preferences are included in the constant term rather than in the income coefficient. Instead of the error term that represents among other things the deviations from preferred number of hours due to demand-side restrictions, the demand-side restrictions are modelled via distributional assumptions about job offers. Moreover, the number of hours of work is not a continuous variable, but a discrete one. The authors use four-hour intervals (0, 4, 8 and so on). It is assumed that employers offer jobs with fixed numbers of hours and workers face the market distribution of these employment opportunities. This market distribution of job offers does not differ between workers. The number of job offers for an individual (called N) is a drawing from a binomial distribution $B(10, P_{offer})$. So, the labour supply decision is a discrete choice between those N job offers and the decision not to work. '. . . The main idea of the model is that an individual is only observed to work h_k (> 0) hours if (s)he received at least one job offer h_k and prefers this job offer to all different job offers which were received and to unemployment. The individual is unemployed if (s)he prefers zero hours of work to all job offers received or if (s)he received zero offers . . .' [Van Soest, Woittiez and Kapteyn (1990: 533)]. For an extended description and the estimation results, see Van Soest, *et al.* (1990: 532–537). Here, we only indicate the way in which those results were used in NEDYMAS.

For each individual whose labour supply has to be determined, we calculate for which labour supply the utility was highest. For that purpose, utility is calculated when an individual does not work, and the N numbers of hours belonging to the job offers. For each of these numbers, we have to calculate his or her after-tax wage rate. Therefore, pre-tax wage is determined as indicated in section 6.4. Then, we investigate which benefits (s)he receives from social security (see chapter 7) taking into account the partner's income, if present. Lastly, the resulting tax (see section 6.5) and social security payments (see also chapter 7) are calculated. When the after-tax wage rate is known, the individual's utility can be calculated using the estimated coefficients.[3] In this, we keep in mind the stochastic nature of the process.

We now deal with the possible transitions in the various states of economic activity. Transitions to the state of student are not considered here. These transitions take place in the education submodule and are described in section 6.2. Transitions are only considered up to the age of 65 years. From that age on, we assume that people are retired, do not work and consequently do not receive labour income.

6.3.1 Transitions from the state student

If an individual leaves full-time education, his or her new state is assigned by lot. In the first step one becomes disabled, unemployed, houseman/housewife or a conscript. In this process, we use the transition probabilities, given one's age and sex, from the 1977 Labour Force Survey. This means that we assume that the transition probabilities into the states conscript, houseman/housewife and disabled are constant during the period under consideration.

If someone becomes disabled (which implies state 11, 'disabled others') the degree of disability is determined. For that goal the distribution of WAO- or AAW-receiving persons by degree of disability has been used [Social and Cultural Planning Agency (1984b: 48)]. The attribute disabled becomes true and the year of disablement becomes the current year.

If someone becomes a conscript or houseman/housewife, we have to fix the date at which that happens. If someone leaves the education process without a certificate, a randomly chosen date in the current year has been taken. In the other case, we limit ourselves to a randomly chosen date in the second half of the year.

If the individual is unemployed (s)he becomes 'unemployed others' (state 4) and labour supply has been determined. It is assumed that (s)he has been looking for a job since 1 May of the current year and that (s)he starts working not before 1 August. So, the month of unemployment becomes 5 (May) and the year of unemployment is the current year. If and when the individual finds a job, is determined in section 6.3.5.

For people leaving part-time education, the state (which had not changed as a consequence of entrance of part-time education) remains the same. Only their percentile is again determined (section 6.4).

[3] The coefficients that refer to prices (*e.g.* wages) are deflated by the price index number for the gross national income. See NCBS (26).

6.3.2 Transitions from the state disabled

Using the transition probabilities derived from the 1977 Labour Force Survey for age and sex, we determine for disabled persons, whether they stay disabled or not. If we determine that the individual is no longer disabled, we have to determine whether (s)he becomes unemployed (state 14, 15 or 16) or becomes a houseman/housewife (state 13).

If the individual becomes a houseman or housewife then (s)he becomes state 13 or labour supply has been determined and (s)he becomes state 14 if (s)he was an employee, before one became disabled, (s)he becomes state 15 if civil servant was the socio-economic state before becoming disabled and (s)he becomes state 16 in all other cases. The point at which disability ends, and unemployment or working in own household starts is also assigned by lot. In the case of becoming unemployed, the month drawn becomes the month of unemployment, whereas the year of unemployment becomes the current year. The attribute 'disabled' is now false and the 'percentage disabled' becomes zero. If the individual could claim an AAW or a WAO benefit (section 7.5 and 7.6), these benefits are paid until the moment of leaving the disablement state.

6.3.3 Transitions from the state conscript

First, the duration of being a liable military servant is fixed. For the period up to 1964, it is assumed that conscription lasts 18 months. Between 1964 and 1975 a duration of 16 months is assumed, and from 1976 on 14 months. Persons who become an officer stay three more months and non-commissioned officers two months longer. The probability of becoming an officer is about 0.5% and the probability of becoming a non-commissioned officer is 5%.

If the period of conscription ends in the current year, we determine whether the individual becomes disabled, houseman or unemployed. Again, we use the transition probabilities derived from the 1977 Labour Force Survey.

If someone becomes disabled – state 11 (disabled others) – the percentage of disability is assigned by lot, the year of disability becomes the current year and the attribute 'disabled' becomes true. The month of disability has been drawn randomly.

If someone becomes a houseman, the date at which that happens equals the month in which conscription ends.

If an individual becomes unemployed, (s)he becomes 'unemployed others' (state 4) and labour supply has been determined. The month of unemployment is set equal to the month in which conscription ends. It is also assumed that he is already looking for a job during the last three months of his conscription, but the job does not start before the end of the conscription period. If and when he finds a job is again determined in section 6.3.5.

Finally, we state that the conscript's salary is not considered to be a source of income in determining lifetime income.

6.3.4 Transitions from the state employed

First, we decide, using the transition probabilities from 1977 the Labour Force Survey, whether one becomes disabled (self-employed persons only), housewife/houseman or conscript. The transition rates for the state housewife/houseman in 1977 and years after are adjusted using Theeuwes, *et al.* (1988: 45).

If an individual becomes disabled, (s)he becomes state 11, disabled others. Employees and civil servants only flow into the state disabled via the Sickness Benefit Law (ZW).[4] It is assumed that (s)he becomes disabled on 1 July of the current year. This means that (s)he receives (labour) income during half a year. The attribute 'disabled' becomes true, the percentage of disablement is assigned by lot and the year of disablement becomes the current year.

If he is conscripted, the date of conscription is assigned by lot. Economic activity becomes conscript (state 8) and the wage is paid up to the date of conscription.

If the individual becomes a houseman or housewife (s)he becomes state 13. Until the date of which (s)he is assigned this economic activity by lot, labour income has been paid.

If labour supply remains positive we investigate whether or not individuals become unemployed. For that purpose we have to determine the unemployment probability from the state employed. The starting point is the corresponding probability by age and sex in 1977, which can be determined from the Labour Force Survey of that year. In view of the probability of becoming employed again by duration of unemployment (next section) in 1977 and the number of persons at work in 1976, but unemployed in 1977 [51 000 men and 21 000 women according to the Labour Force Survey, Corpeleijn (1979: 651)] we calculated that 220 000 men and 74 000 women lost their jobs. The number of persons who are laid off in the current year, is determined up to 1988 by the 1977 number, the change in the unemployment rate, the change in the probability of finding a job and a correction factor for the size of the labour force. For the period 1988–2020 we assume that unemployment declines by an annual growth in employment of 0.5% [Departementale Werkgroep SZW (1984)]. After 2020, the number of lost jobs is assumed not to change: 130 000 men and 130 000 women.

So, the probability of becoming unemployed for wo(men) by age in the current year is determined as the probability in 1977, multiplied by the number of wo(men) who lost their jobs in the current year and the size of

[4] When sickness lasts one year (section 7.7).

the fe(male) labour force in 1977 (3 478 000 men and 1 191 000 women, respectively) and divided by the number of wo(men) dismissed in 1977 (220 000 men and 74 000, women respectively) and the size of the fe(male) labour force in the current year.

This probability is adjusted for being a civil servant or not. Civil servants have a lower probability of being laid off. The correction factor is derived from Meesters (1983). Until 1956, a female civil servant is dismissed if she marries.

The probability of becoming unemployed is also corrected for the level of education. The effect of the level of education on the probability of losing one's job is derived from Spannenburg (1981). On both last adjustments, a correction is executed for changes in the structure of the level of education of the labour force and the proportion of persons working as a civil servant, respectively, to guarantee consistency.

Next, we decide by lot whether a person is laid off or not. If (s)he becomes unemployed, (s)he becomes the economic activity 'unemployed employee' (state 6), 'unemployed civil servant' (state 7) or 'unemployed others' (state 4), depending on the former state. We again assigned by lot at which date (s)he is dismissed. That date becomes the 'month of unemployment' and up to that date labour income has been paid. The 'year of unemployment' becomes the current year.

6.3.5 Transitions from the state unemployed

If a person is unemployed, we first decide whether (s)he remains unemployed or not. For that goal the exit probabilities out of the state unemployed are calculated for both men and women. For the period 1953–1986 we know the number of new registrations at the labour exchange [for the period 1953–1977, Hartog (1980) and for later years NCBS (27)]. From NCBS (27), we have the number of registered unemployed persons, unemployed for less than three months, on 1 February, on 1 May, on 1 August and on 1 November, of each year. Using these figures, we can calculate the exit probability out of the unemployed state during the first three months of being unemployed. These two sources give us the proportion of people who became unemployed between two of the aforementioned dates and were no longer unemployed at the end of that period. Suppose that this is x%. Let 100 * exp(q) be the probability of being still unemployed after one day and assume that this probability does not change during the first three months and that the inflow is distributed uniformly over time. Let d be the number of days between two dates. Then we see that:

$$x = \frac{1}{d}\int_0^d e^{(d-t)*q}\,dt = \frac{e^{d.q} - 1}{q * d} \qquad (6.3.1)$$

From (6.3.1.) we can determine q numerically. The monthly exit probability during the first three months of being unemployed (p) is now:

$$p = 1 - e^{q * d} \tag{6.3.2}$$

Using the data from NCBS (27) we can also derive the probability of flowing out of the state of being unemployed between three and six months and the exit probability in the second half year of unemployment. Up to 1978, this last exit probability is also applied to persons who are unemployed for one year, one and a half years, and so on. For 1978 and after, the yearly exit probabilities are also known for persons who are unemployed for one year, two years and three years [for example, Social and Cultural Planning Agency (1986: 311)].

While data before 1953 are lacking, the 1953 probabilities are also applied to the years 1947 up to and including 1952. For 1987 and after, we assume that the exit probabilities remain constant at the 1986 level.

These general exit probabilities are corrected for individuals for their level of education. The correction factors are determined on the basis of the 1977 and 1985 Labour Force Surveys [NCBS (1980c and 1987b)]. Between these two years, the correction factors are interpolated. For 1976 and before, the correction factor for 1977 is the starting point. The figures for 1977 are adjusted for the changes of the level of education of the unemployed in comparison with 1977. For 1986 and after the procedure is analogous, with 1985 as the year of departure.

From 1973 on, we also adjusted the exit probability if the person is disabled before becoming unemployed (so, one now has state 14, 15 or 16). The Labour Force Surveys show that the exit probabilities of disabled persons have decreased relatively since that year.

On the basis of this exit probability, whether an individual will leave unemployment in the current year is assigned by lot. If (s)he leaves unemployment, the date (between the datum dates in question) at which this happens is also assigned by lot. Until this date, any possible unemployment benefit (chapter 7) will be paid.

Using the transition probabilities as derived from the 1977 Labour Force Survey, we again investigate whether the person becomes disabled (only for persons in state 4 or 16), becomes houseman/housewife (state 13) or enters the state of conscript. If (s)he becomes disabled his or her state becomes 11, the year of disablement becomes the current year, the attribute 'disabled' is now true and the percentage of disablement is assigned by lot. If he is conscripted, the assigned date is the date of conscription.

If the person does not become disabled, houseman/housewife or a conscript, his or her labour supply is determined. We assume that (s)he finds a job, for the number of hours that follows from the optimalization of the labour supply. The year and month of employment are given by the aforementioned date. Next, the state the individual becomes – civil servant, employee or self-employed – is assigned by lot. This depends on the income percentile in which (s)he is classified (section 6.4.4.). The distribution of self-employed persons, employees and civil servants over the different percentiles is based on the income distribution for 1979 [NCBS (1984b)]. For the period 1947–1965, it is corrected for the fact that married women are not considered for jobs as civil servants. Again, a correction is made for the relative size of the three groups [NCBS (26)], in which we assume that no changes take place in this distribution after 1986.

6.3.6 Transitions from the state houseman/housewife

If an individual is in state 13, houseman or housewife, we decide for each year, using the transition probabilities from the 1977 Labour Force Survey, whether (s)he becomes disabled (self-employed persons only) or conscript.

If (s)he becomes disabled, (s)he becomes state 11, disabled others. It is assumed that the person becomes disabled on 1 July of the current year. The attribute 'disabled' becomes true, the percentage of disablement is assigned by lot and the year becomes the current year. If the individual has to do military service, the date of conscription is assigned by lot. Economic activity becomes conscript (state 8).

6.3.7 Adjustments in the economic activity of the population

When the aforementioned transitions have taken place, the simulated number of employed and unemployed persons will generally differ from the actual or predicted number of employed and unemployed persons. We carry out this correction, while the estimation of the parameters of the labour supply function is executed with data referring to 1985. It is debatable whether people in, for example, the 1950s show the same behaviour patterns. Therefore, we confront the simulated numbers of those with the actual or predicted figures. For the period 1990–2029 we use the forecasts of Departementale Werkgroep SZW (1984). For 2030 and beyond we assume that the number of unemployed persons remains constant and that labour force participation rates remain constant at the 2029 level.

We are now in a position to compare the simulated numbers (corrected for the sample size) with the realized numbers and to adjust the economic activity of the population if the aforementioned numbers differ substantially. First, the simulated and the true numbers of unemployed men and women are compared. If the simulated number is less than the true one, the simulated number is raised by giving the unemployed state to those who are houseman/housewife or employed. Labour supply is tested if this concerns a housewife or a houseman. They are only added to the unemployed if labour supply is positive. This process continues until the simulated number of unemployed persons equals the true one.

If the simulated number is larger than the true number of unemployed persons, the simulated number is diminished by giving the corresponding number of unemployed persons in the sample, the state houseman/housewife. This also happens in a random way.

Next, the simulated and actual numbers of employed men and women are compared. The procedure is similar to that described above. If the simulated number is less than the true one, the simulated number is raised by randomly giving persons who are houseman or housewife, the state employed if their labour supply is positive. If, after this operation, the simulated number is still less than the true number, persons are randomly drawn from those who are disabled. Using the labour supply function, we determine whether their labour supply is positive and, if so, they are added to the employed population. This process continues until the simulated number of employed persons equals the true one.

If the simulated number is larger than the true number of employed persons, the simulated number is diminished by giving the corresponding number of employed persons in the sample, the state houseman/housewife. This happens in a random way.

Finally, we test whether the employed population is correctly subdivided into the categories employees, civil servants and self-employed persons. If this is not the case, economic status has been adjusted to get the right numbers.

6.3.8 The economic activity of the initial population

If a person has left his education before 1947, the income percentile is fixed as described in section 6.4.4. Then, the required number of conscripts is drawn from the population. For the remaining persons, it is simulated whether or not they are in the labour force. For that goal the participation rates from the 1947 Census [NCBS (1952)] are used. We differentiate by age, sex and marital status. The unemployment rate by sex in 1947 is used to simulate whether (s)he has a job or not. If it is decided that a person is unemployed, the status becomes unemployed, others (state 4), the year of unemployment is 1946 and the month of unemployment is assigned by lot. If the individual has a job, (using his or her income percentile) whether (s)he is an employee, civil servant or self-employed is assigned by lot. If a person is not in the labour force, (s)he becomes state 13, houseman or housewife. This means that we do not consider the state disabled. While the disablement benefits start in 1967, this is no problem in view of our goal.

6.4 LABOUR INCOME

Generally, the distribution of lifetime earnings is derived from panel data or a pooling of cohort and cross-sectional data, covering only a relatively small part of the period when a person earns money. In the most favourable cases, the period under investigation spans about ten years [*e.g.* Creedy and Hart (1979) and Fase (1969)]. This means that the age-earnings profile does not relate to the complete lifetime earnings of any one individual. Generally, research starts from the widely accepted assumption that, at a particular age, earnings are distributed lognormally, the evolution of the mean of the logarithms of earnings to age has been assumed to follow a quadratic function in the variable age, whereas the variance is assumed to follow a linear function in the variable age [for example, Fase (1969)].[5] Sometimes other variables are added. For example, Creedy and Hart (1979) use dummies for the different birth cohorts. The functions are estimated, and thus the distribution of lifetime earnings has been determined. In a similar way, it is possible to describe the distribution of earnings in a particular year.

Apart from the fact that the functions for different cohorts are based on a (too) limited period, there is another important drawback. It is hardly possible to derive the distribution of earnings for the future or for the past, because the parameters of the aforementioned quadratic and linear functions for the mean μ_t and variance σ_t^2 differ between generations and years. This is, of course, the result of the fact that these functions are not based on theoretical arguments, but only on empirical insight.[6] Therefore, it is hardly possible to derive the distribution of lifetime earnings. Fase (1972) claims that his model can be used for this purpose. However, in practice he can only provide us with the geometric mean. His method also only holds for homogeneous educational or occupational categories, so that the method cannot be applied to the total population of a country. This severely limits its application. The foundation of this kind of stochastic models is also weakened by the result of Thatcher (1976) and especially Taubman (1976) tests. Sahota's conclusion in his 1978 survey on personal income distribution theories is clear: '. . . The old stochastic theory of distribution is apparently in disrepute . . .' [Sahota (1978: 9)].

The course of lifetime earnings can be explained in two ways. On the one hand, we can work in a completely descriptive manner. On the other hand, we can select an appropriate function on the basis of income-formation theories. The first approach has the disadvantage that the user does not know what determines the course of the income curve, so that the forecast

[5] This immediately follows from the assumption that logincome at age t equals logincome at age t–1 plus a systematic term and an additive random shock.

[6] Human capital theory also gives an inverted U-shaped profile for μ_t. The statistical model for μ_t can also be interpreted in this way. See Fase (1971).

of the future course becomes speculative. However, if one wants to know the real course of the age-earnings profile of, for example, the birth generation of 1950, knowledge concerning the future is of vital importance. On the other hand, the method has the advantage that (part of) the course of the profile can be determined in a simple way using only relatively few data. This does not hold for the second method, in which microdata are preferred.

These data, however, are not available for a sufficiently long period for most countries. The USA and the UK are probably the only exceptions; Atkinson, Bourguignon and Morrisson (1988 and 1992). From this viewpoint it is not an obvious choice to follow this method. In the light of the available data for the Netherlands, we opted for a pragmatic approach in which we estimate μ_t and σ_t^2 using macrodata and extending the model used by *e.g.* Creedy and Hart (1979). We drop the assumption that logincome in the current year equals logincome in the foregoing year plus a systematic term and an additive random shock. This means that the limitation to homogeneous categories does not hold, whereas it will be possible to derive the income distribution.

Following a description of the data in section 6.4.1, we discuss the model in section 6.4.2. In the next section we estimate the course of the mean male full-time income and variance by age. Lastly, we show how we use these results to simulate the age–income profile for individuals.

6.4.1 The data

Since 1962, the Netherlands Central Bureau of Statistics (NCBS) has published (aggregated) earnings data for individuals. Before 1962, the household was the income unit, so that in the case of married people, each individual's income, and thus the mean (aggregated) income, was not available. We use the '*kerninkomen*', which gives the sum of the income components which are characteristic for each socio-economic category. As a consequence, the same income elements are included in the *kerninkomen* of self-employed persons, civil servants, employees, and managers of private and limited liability companies and corporations. The *kerninkomen* can be considered as the primary income excluding income from capital. This will be our income concept. This means that we use the income from **labour** of the self-employed, employees, and managers of private and limited liability companies and corporations.[7] From the NCBS we have received data for different age groups for both males and females for 1967, 1970, 1975, 1983 and 1985. Available data for other years are not used because these are not completely comparable. In the data used some changes in definitions have also taken place, [NCBS (1967a and b, 1972a and b, 1977b, 1979, 1980a, 1982c, 1984b and 1985b)]. From these pooled cross-sectional data, we can

[7] Some benefits for the unemployed are included and cannot be isolated. However, their impact during the period under investigation was limited.

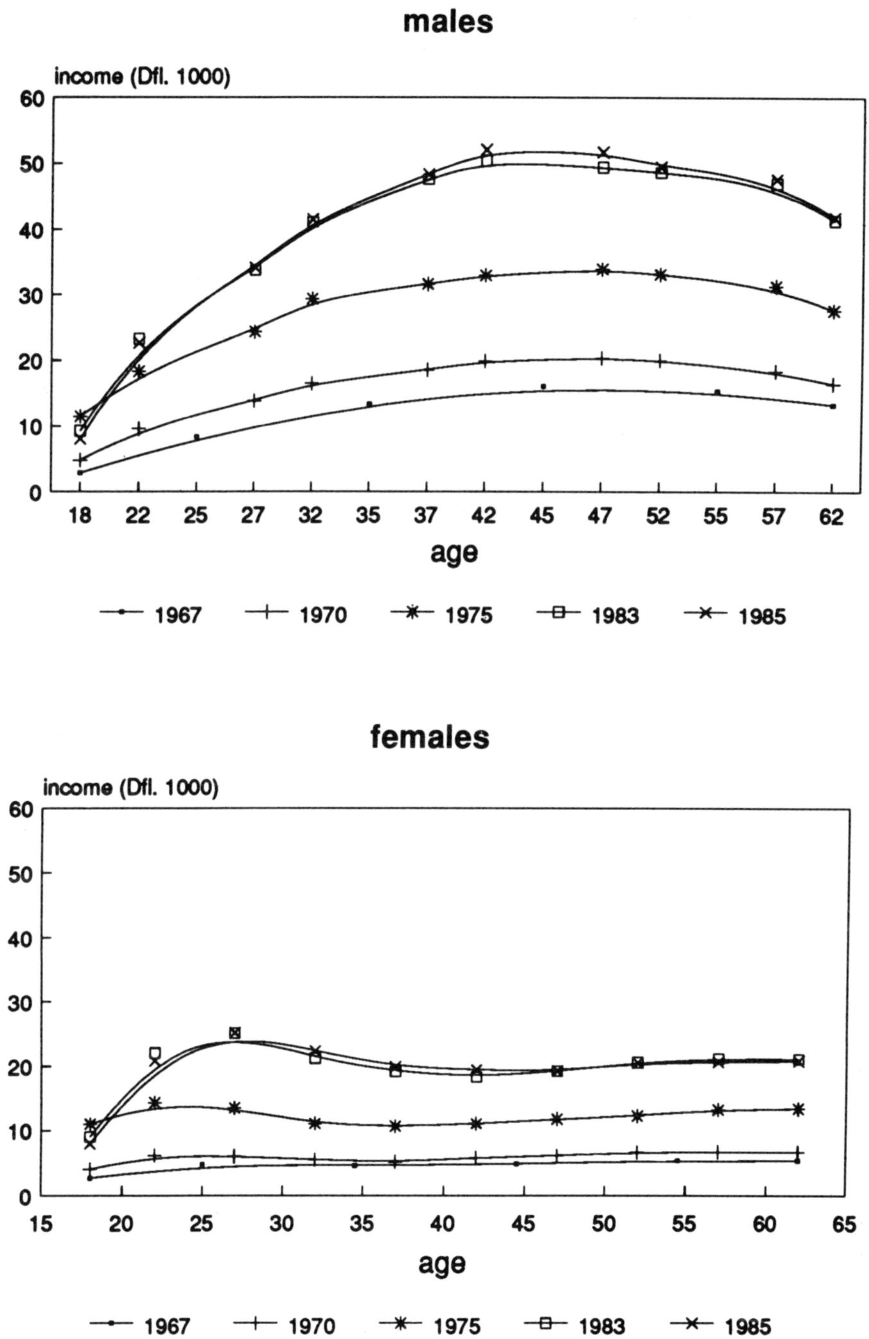

Figure 6.4 The age–income profile, the Netherlands; 1967, 1970, 1975, 1983 and 1985.

derive 46 observations for the mean income and the variance: six age groups in 1967 and ten age groups in the other years.

Because we are using pooled cross-sectional data, the individuals aged about 17.5 years in 1970, for example, who earned on average about 4800 guilders, are not the same people as those aged 22.5 years in 1975 who earned, on average, 18 300 guilders in that year. No doubt, many of these people were the same, but because some people left the labour force, and others of the same age entered the labour force between these two years, these data do not measure exactly the earnings of the cohort born around 1939–1940 in this example. In interpreting our results, we must realize that they only hold for those people who are in the labour force at the moment under investigation. The mean labour income by age is given in figure 6.4.

The graph shows a continuous increase of mean labour income by age between 1967 and 1983, whereas this income in 1985 for most age groups does not differ from that in 1983. Within a year, the males' income increases up to about 45 years. Thereafter it declines. The picture for the females' mean labour income is quite different. In 1967 and 1970 females' mean income is stable over the different ages. In 1975 we see a real top for the first time and this picture becomes clear in 1983 and 1985: a top at the age of about 25–30 years, next a decline in income (until about 40 years), whereafter income rises again. This picture is, of course, the result of the large number of part-time jobs held by females. The data are not corrected for part-time labour participation. While part-time labour participation strongly influences the development in females' mean income and its coefficient of variation we will limit our estimations to male income.

The variance is based on grouped data. The number of income brackets varies between 13 and 32. This means that the true inequality is underestimated, while the inequality within brackets is neglected. The degree of underestimation depends on the number of income brackets. Empirical studies show that the underestimation is limited to a few per cent when ten or more income brackets are used [*e.g.* Gastwirth (1972), and more specifically for the Netherlands, Odink and van Imhoff (1984)]. The coefficients of variation for the different male age groups decline up to about the age of 22–27 years, and thereafter generally increase. For women, the picture is again different. Here, a clear top is present at about the age of 55 years. The level of the coefficient of variation is generally larger for females than for males. Here, the differences in participation rates and the extent of part-time jobs will also influence the picture.

6.4.2 The model

Our point of departure is the statistical model, adapted from Aitchison and Brown (1957) and Fase (1969), which describes the distribution of individual income by age. Individual income has been considered as a random variable related to age. The individual is assumed to start his or her career at age s, at which (s)he receives an annual income equal to y_s. This variable y_s is assumed to follow a two-parameter lognormal distribution and age is considered to be a discrete variable. This implies:

$$P(\underline{y}_s \leqslant y_s) = \wedge(y_s;\, \mu_s,\, \sigma_s^2) \tag{6.4.1}$$

with

$$\wedge(y_s;\, \mu_s,\, \sigma_s^2) = \int_0^{y_s} \left(y.\sigma_s.\sqrt{2\pi}\right)^{-1} * e^{-1/2((\log y-\mu_s)/\sigma_s)^2} dy$$

If we also assume that the distribution of proportional changes in income with increasing age is a normal one, which is a realistic assumption, income follows a lognormal distribution for all ages [Hart (1973)].
Thus,

$$P(\underline{y}_t \leqslant y_t | t) = \wedge(y_t;\, \mu_t,\, \sigma_t^2) \tag{6.4.2}$$

with

$$\wedge(y_t;\, \mu_t,\, \sigma_t^2) = \int_0^{y_t} \left(y.\sigma_t.\sqrt{2\pi}\right)^{-1} * e^{-1/2((\log y-\mu_t)/\sigma_t)^2} dy$$

Using $\underline{x}_t = \log \underline{y}_t$ equation (6.4.2) can be transformed into the normal distribution, so that for all ages:

$$\mathrm{F}(x|t) = \mathrm{N}(x_t;\, \mu_t,\, \sigma_t^2) \tag{6.4.3}$$

This model has been extensively tested by Creedy (1974). As mentioned before, the usual procedure is to determine the distribution of the complete age–income profile by introducing a quadratic function in the variable age for μ_t and a linear one for σ_t^2 [*e.g.* Fase (1969) and Creedy (1975)], whereby in some cases dummy variables for different cohorts are also used [for example, Creedy and Hart (1979)]. Although this approach gives a fairly good description for the age–earnings profile within a year, or for (part of) a generation, the problem is that the parameters of the aforementioned quadratic and linear functions are, of course, not constant over time and differ between generations. So, this method can hardly be used to describe the future profile, unless we are able to predict and explain the parameters. In that case, however, it would be preferable to look for a better model. We will follow this method by introducing theoretically interpretable variables.

The foregoing only implies that labour income at every age follows a lognormal distribution. No assumptions have been made concerning the distribution of labour income over a range of years.[8]

[8] Generally, this last distribution is not the normal one and probably it will be leptokurtic; see Hill (1959).

While μ_t, being the mean of the logarithm of the income at age t, cannot be calculated from the data, we will estimate the logarithm of the mean income (called $\log\alpha_t$). For the same reason we will estimate the variance of the income (β_t^2) instead of the variance of the logarithm of the income (σ_t^2). Then, μ_t and σ_t^2 can be determined via $\mu_t = \log\alpha_t - 1/2 * \sigma_t^2$ and $\beta_t^2 = \alpha_t^2 * [(\exp(\sigma_t^2)) - 1]$; Aitchison and Brown (1957: 8).

6.4.3 The estimation of α and β

A general model for $\log \alpha$ is:

$$\log \underline{\alpha}_t = X_t \cdot \beta + Z_t \cdot \tau + \underline{\varepsilon}_t \qquad (6.4.4)$$

where $X_t = (X_{t1}, \dots, X_{tm})'$ a vector of m explanatory variables, which represent individual attributes which are fixed over time (such as sex, formal education),
$Z_t = (Z_{t1}, \dots, Z_{tk})'$ a vector of k explanatory variables, which represent individual attributes, which vary over time (such as family status and job-related characteristics)
$\beta = (\beta_1, \dots, \beta_m)'$ a vector of parameters and
$\tau = (\tau_1, \dots, \tau_k)'$ a vector of parameters and
$\underline{\varepsilon}_t$ an error term, representing unobserved characteristics.

We now have two problems. First, what explanatory variables have to be included in equation (6.4.4)? A review of theories can be found in Sahota (1978). An all-embracing general theory, however, is not available. Theories of primary income formation can be divided into four categories [*e.g.* Hagenaars and Wunderink-Van Veen (1990)]:

a) Theories based on free choices, in which consumers try to maximize their utility. This implies, among others, the following explanatory variables: education, age, household composition and type of job;
b) Theories in which characteristics of the parents explain the income profile: inheritance of genetic characteristics, upbringing and social environment;
c) Theories based on chance mechanisms; and
d) Theories based on imperfect markets, for example segregated labour markets.

Some theories combine these four types. According to Sahota these are 'more complete theories'. They seem to be the most appropriate ones for our purpose.

Our second problem now becomes clear: we must limit ourselves to macrodata and this means that we have to use explanatory variables that are aggregate approximations of elements that are at work at the micro level. Besides, data are not available for all variables that should be included.

We limit ourselves to the following variables:

1) The evolution in the logarithm of the income per head of the working population, **NI**.
2) Age minus 15 years, **AGE15**, and its square, **AGE152**.
3) The unemployment rate for each age group as a proportion of the average unemployment rate by age, **UN**.
4) The proportion of people with primary or secondary education by cohort, **EDL**.

Because evolution in mean income depends on the growth in national income, and on the size of the earning population, given by the proportion of the working population in the total population, the inclusion of the variable NI is self-evident. This variable, like the dependent variable, is measured in constant 1980 prices. We expect, of course, a positive effect of NI on the mean income by age.

According to human capital theory, one would prefer an inverted U-shaped profile in the variable age. Therefore, the variables AGE15 and AGE152 are inserted.

UN is inserted because a relatively high unemployment, indicative of a larger gap between labour supply and labour demand, could put pressure on labour income.

Lastly, we have the variable EDL. It is assumed that a higher level of education means a larger marginal productivity and, thus, a higher income per worker. Studies in the field of the effect of schooling on earnings, affirm this picture. Human capital theory also leads to this conclusion; for a review, see *e.g.* Freeman (1986). We assume therefore that a lowering of the proportion of persons with only a primary education has a positive effect on the mean income.

Because the income profiles of individual females are heavily affected by strong fluctuations in labour supply, while changes in male income profiles are limited, we restrict ourselves to an explanation of the mean income of males and its dispersion. In this, we use full-time income for males aged 20 and older.

The estimated results can be found in table 6.2. The goodness-of-fit as measured by the adjusted R^2 is very high. All variables have the expected sign. The coefficients of the age variables imply that income increases up to about the age of 48. Thereafter, it declines. If the logarithm of the national income, corrected for the proportion of the working population in the total population, increases by one percentage point, this means that the logarithm of the mean income rises by 0.908 in each age group. The relative unemployment rate is not significant. An increase in the variable EDL by one percentage point results in a decline in the logarithm of mean income of 0.168.

Table 6.2 *LS estimation results for* log α *and* β/α

equation variable	log α coeff.	log α t-value	β/α coeff.	β/α t-value
intercept	− 0.122	− 0.27	2.070	2.85
NI	0.908	27.01	− 0.255	− 4.63
UN	− 0.011	− 0.34	0.210	3.18
AGE15	0.069	15.27	0.043	5.21
AGE152	− 0.104E − 2	− 12.70	− .057E − 2	− 3.55
EDL	− 0.168	− 1.63	0.387	1.57
$R^2_{adj} = 0.990$			$R^2_{adj} = 0.899$	
$\sigma_\varepsilon = 0.050$			$\sigma_\varepsilon = 0.077$	
mean log α = 10.24			mean β/α = 0.702	
observations = 41			observations = 41	

In a similar way a regression equation for the logarithm coefficient of variation β_t/α_t has been estimated. Here, the same explanatory variables are inserted. It is assumed that income inequality decreases if the level of education increases. The variable EDL has been used to measure this impact on income inequality. The sign should be positive: a decrease in the proportion of lower educated persons diminishes inequality. For the variable NI we assume an analogous mechanism: an increase in NI decreases income inequality. To cover the impact of changes in the distribution of productivity as age increases (for example, as a consequence of a larger inequality in health) the variables AGE15 and AGE152 are also incorporated. The effect of differences in unemployment rates between age groups is measured by the variable UN. We expect a positive sign: the larger the unemployment rate, the larger the income inequality. The regression result is also given in table 6.2.

Again, the variables have the expected sign, and are all – with exception of EDL – significant. A decrease of 1% in the proportion of persons with lower levels of education results in a decrease in income inequality, as measured by β/α, by 0.387%. A rise in the logarithm of the national income, corrected for the proportion of the working population in the total population (NI), also lowers income inequality. If relative unemployment is large in an age group, the resulting income inequality will be relatively larger. The coefficients of the variables AGE15 and AGE152 show that income inequality increases as people become older. Maximum inequality is reached at about the age of 63.

We have now implicitly derived the age-income profile for the period 1967–1983 (the estimation period for both equations). For the past, the observations for the different variables were used. For the future, we assume the following. National income will grow by 2% a year, whereas employment rises by 0.5% up to 2020 (see also section 6.3.4). The other variables are obtained from the NEDYMAS results. We will use these results to simulate the income course of individuals, which is the subject of the next section.

6.4.4 Individual age–income profile

The distribution of the age–income profile, determined in the foregoing, is a distribution at the macro level. For every year we can indicate the mean income and its variance for each age. For that purpose, the working population, EDL and UN are calculated each year. Using the evolution in the national income, we can derive NI.

If we now know in which quantile of the distribution an individual is, we are able to say what his or her income will be. Let υ_q be the q-th quantile of the normal distribution, with mean zero and variance one, then there holds for τ_q, being the q-th quantile of the lognormal distribution with mean μ and variance σ^2 (parameters which are determined in section 6.4.3):

$$\tau_q = \exp(\mu + \upsilon_q.\sigma) \qquad (6.4.5)$$

The implication for our model NEDYMAS is that, if we know for each age in which quantile an individual is, we also know his or her lifetime income profile.

If an individual leaves school, it is assigned by lot in percentile (s)he arrives. The drawn percentile depends on his or her sex and level of education. The probabilities are based on Corpeleijn (1987), which contains the mean full-time labour income and its variance for persons, aged 23 and 24 years, by age and level of education for 1979 and 1985. Using these data, we simulated the distribution by percentiles for different levels of education for both men and women. A procedure maintains consistency, if the distribution of persons leaving school, by level of education, changes. With the help of this distribution, and the level of education, the percentile is assigned by lot in the year in which the person leaves the educational process.

Income mobility has been modelled using Alessie, Camphuis and Kapteyn (1990). These authors used microdata from the first four waves of the Socio Economic Panel, collected by the NCBS, held in April 1984, October 1984, April 1985 and October 1985. In this panel only after-tax wages are investigated. These after-tax wages were transformed to taxable income. Next, Alessie, *et al.* estimate the taxable income of people who have a paid job. Although this income concept differs from ours (primary income; for the differences, see table 4.6 and footnote 9 in chapter 4), we will use their results because for our goal these are the only available ones using microdata.[9] While our model is based on full-time annual income, we only use

[9] The Socio Economic Panel data are not available for this study in view of its costs. If it had been available we could have transformed the after tax wages into before tax wages.

their results for heads of households. In this group, the majority works full-time.

Alessie, Camphuis and Kapteyn adopt the following model:

$$\underline{Y}_{it} = X'_{it} \cdot \beta + \underline{\phi}_i + \underline{\varepsilon}_{it} \tag{6.4.6}$$

in which Y_{it} is the logarithm of individual i's income in year t; X'_{it} is a vector of explanatory variables; β is a vector of parameters; ϕ_i is a normally distributed error term with mean zero and variance σ^2_ϕ; ε_{it} is a normally distributed error term with mean zero and variance σ^2_ε. The error terms ϕ_i and ε_{it} are independent. This specification implies a stochastic part composed of an individual effect (ϕ_i) and a time-independent effect (ε_{it}). The first part stands for differences between persons, which are not incorporated in the systematic part of equation (6.4.6), $X'_{it} \cdot \beta$, such as differences in natural ability and in labour ethos, and which do not differ over time. The second part stands for other elements which are not incorporated in the systematic part. These factors are allowed to vary over individuals as well as over time. The first part of the stochastic specification can be considered to be implicitly incorporated in our assignment of the percentile an individual belongs to after leaving school.

Alessie, Camphuis and Kapteyn (1990) use the following explanatory variables: the natural logarithm of age, its square, dummy variables for level of education and dummy variables for type of education. This results for σ^2_ε in an estimated value of 0.11. We use this value to determine income mobility in our model. The starting point is the percentile the individual is assigned. Each year, the income belonging to this percentile is determined using the results for the mean income and its variance for the individual's birth cohort (using table 6.2). This income is adjusted for the evolution in ε_{it}, according to:

$$Y_{it} = \exp(\mu_{it} + v_{it} \cdot \sigma_{it} + \varepsilon_{it}) \tag{6.4.7}$$

in which Y_{it} is the income of individual i in year t, μ_{it} is the mean of logincome of i's birth cohort in year t; v_{it} is i's percentile assigned for year t; σ_{it} is the variance of logincome of i's birth cohort in year t; ε_{it} is a draw from the normal distribution with mean zero and variance 0.11. When each person has passed through the labour income submodule, each person's percentile is again determined.

Given the percentile in which the individual is classified, his or her age, the calculated NI, UN, EDL, and the random draws from the normal distribution, his or her full-time labour income for the current year is determined. Multiplying this full-time labour income by the participation rate and the number of months worked in the current year divided by 12 gives the earned labour income.

6.5 TAXES[10]

Because we have limited ourselves to labour income, only income taxes have to be considered. In the Dutch income tax system, the taxes to be paid are determined by the tax group in which one is classified and the tax rate (which differs among tax groups up to 1973).

Between 1947 and 1972 the Dutch income tax system consisted of three tax groups. Tax group III applied to persons who were entitled to family allowances. The tax rate within this group also depended on the number of children for whom one received family allowances. Tax group II applied to married persons who could not claim family allowances, for divorced and widowed persons, who were 65 years or older or had been married for at least five years, and for unmarried persons who had reached the age of 65 years. All other persons came within tax group I. Each of these tax groups had a different personal tax allowance. From 1955, disabled (but younger than 65 years) and aged people received an extra income tax deduction. Married women were not taxable. Their income was added to the husband's income and tax was levied on this combined income.

Separate tax tables existed for all tax groups. The tax to be paid was fixed in these tables for different income groups. The distinguished number of income groups was very large. For example, tax group I contained 1507 income groups in 1972! For practical reasons, we approximated this tax system by a derived graded system of income brackets for tax assessment, one for tax group I and another for the other tax groups. It appeared that the marginal income tax rates hardly differed between tax groups II and III, and within the last group, if we took account of the personal tax allowances. So we could limit ourselves to a number of income groups that range from 16 income groups for tax groups II and III in 1947 to 34 income groups for tax group I in 1948, 1949 and 1950.

The Dutch labour income tax system was revised in 1973. Since then, four tax groups are distinguished, which determine the personal tax allowance. One tax rate system is applied to the taxable income, independent of the tax group. The number of income groups is also limited: eight in 1973 and 1974 and nine from 1975. Up to and including 1982 the aged were allowed an extra income deduction. The deduction differed between married and non-married[11] persons. Up to and including 1982, disabled persons also received an extra deduction, if they were younger than 65 years and at least 45% disabled.[12] Since 1973, self-employed people received an extra deduction if their income was below a certain level. Up to 1978, a tax deduction for children existed. The deduction depended on the number of children

[10] All data used in this submodule are derived from NCBS (28).

[11] Non-married refers to single, divorced, separated and widowed persons.

[12] In 1981 two groups were distinguished: those with a degree of disability of more than 80% and those whose disability was less.

and on whether or not one could claim family allowances pursuant to the 'Family Allowance Act for Wage-Earners' (section 7.4).

For 1973 and to and including 1983, the classification into tax groups was as follows:

I Working married women;
II Unmarried persons up to 34 years old;
III a) Unmarried persons older than 34 years;
b) Unmarried persons up to 34 years old, who could claim family allowances;
c) Widowed and divorced persons;
IV Married men.

In 1984, the classification changed. The possibility of transfer of tax allowances between partners and an extra allowance for one-parent families were also introduced. The possibility of transfer of tax allowances implied that if the income was lower than the personal tax allowance, the difference between both could be added to the partner's personal tax allowance. The extra allowance for one-parent families only held for persons belonging to tax group IV. The extra allowance amounted to 25% of his or her income, up to a maximum. The classification for tax groups became:

I All persons not belonging to tax groups II, III or IV;
II 1) Non-married, non-cohabiting people older than 33 years, who run a one-person household;
2) Non-married, not cohabiting with a partner, who run a household with children younger than 27 years, for whom one cannot claim family allowances;
3) Cohabiting people, 27 years or older, and married persons, whose partner is also 27 years or older, and whose partner has an income of his or her own between a certain lower and upper limit;
4) Cohabiting people, who can claim family allowances;
III Cohabiting people, 27 years or older, whose partner is also 27 years or older, and where the partner's income amounts to less than the lower limit under II b);
IV Non-married non-cohabiting persons, who can claim family allowances for at least one child, younger than 27 years, and belonging to his or her household.

In 1985, the tax group classification changed again, as did the requirements for receiving the extra allowance for one-parent families. An allowance for working persons and an extra allowance for specific working persons were introduced. The allowance for self-employed persons remained unchanged.

Those working outside the home, are entitled to claim the allowance for working persons. This extra allowance can be claimed if:

1) (s)he can claim the (normal) allowance for working persons, belongs to tax group I, and has a child younger than 12 years in his or her household, or
2) (s)he is self-employed, receives an allowance for working persons, belongs to tax group III, and his or her partner works in his or her firm.

In the latter case, the partner can also claim the extra allowance. The extra allowance for one-parent families can now be claimed if one belongs to tax group IV, works outside the home, if at least one child aged 13 years or younger belongs to his or her household, and if there is no child, aged 16 to 27 years old, who runs the household.

The tax group classification between 1985 and 1989 was:

- I All persons not belonging to tax groups II, III or IV;
- II 1) Single persons, aged 27 years or older, who cannot claim family allowances;
  - 2) Non-married, non-cohabiting persons, aged 27 years or older, with children up to 27 years belonging to the household, for whom no claims on family allowances exist;
- III 1) Married persons, whose partner has no income;
  - 2) Cohabiting, non-married persons, aged 27 years or older, whose partner has no income and is 18 years or older;
- IV Non-cohabiting, non-married persons, who can claim family allowances for children belonging to their household.

In 1990 the proposals of the so-called Oort Committee came into operation. These proposals [Ministerie van Sociale Zaken en Werkgelegenheld (1989: 46–47) and Directoraat-Generaal der Belastingen (1989)] have resulted in relatively radical changes, both in the tax system and in the way in which premiums for general insurances are levied. Labour income taxes and the premiums for AOW, AWW, AAW and AWBZ[13] are combined in one levy.[14] This also implies a transfer of the AAW and AWBZ premiums from employers to employees. Employees are compensated for this transfer by an extra allowance on the labour income. From now on, the maximum premium income (*e.g.* section 7.2) equals the first income tax group. The nine income tax rates are replaced by only three rates, and the premiums for the general insurances are no longer deductable. Six tax groups are now used:

[13] The AKW premium was terminated in 1988. It is now paid by the state.

[14] With the exception of persons older than 64 years. These people do not pay AOW and AWW premiums.

I Married or cohabiting persons who transfer their tax allowance to their partner. The tax allowance for the person in this group becomes zero;
  1) Married or cohabiting persons in a household in which both partners earn an income above the tax allowance (Dfl. 4568 in 1990);
  2) Single persons, who are not classified in group VI;

II 3) Persons, who are head of a one-parent family, but who are not classified in groups IV, V or VI; the tax allowance amounts to Dfl. 4568 in 1990;

III Married and cohabiting persons who received the tax allowance of their partner. Their tax allowance now is Dfl. 9112 in 1990;

IV Non-married, non-cohabiting people who run a household with at least one child younger than 27 years and no children over 26 years. The tax allowance amounts to Dfl. 8222 in 1990;

V Non-married, non-cohabiting people who have a paid job and who run a household with at least one child younger than 12 years. The tax allowance amounts to Dfl. 8222 plus 6% of the labour income (up to a maximum of Dfl. 3654) in 1990;

VI Single persons, aged 27 to 65 years, with an income below Dfl. 35 000 (in 1990). The tax allowance amounts to Dfl. 5695 (in 1990).

Contrary to the past (when a partial transfer was possible), the complete tax allowance is now transferred to the partner. The extra allowances for working persons and the extra one for specific working persons have been abolished.

The aforementioned tax group classifications, the tax rates (for the period 1947–1972 in an approximate manner) and the allowances, have been built in to NEDYMAS. When a person has passed the social security module (chapter 7), his or her tax group is determined for the current year.[15] Taxes can only be determined at this point, because his or her taxable income is not known until this stage. With reference to the other tax-deductible items (such as extraordinary charges, deduction of costs above the so-called 4% acquisition costs rule,[16] commuting costs above the minimum deduction, various specific costs and gains for self-employed persons) we only consider the 4% acquisition costs rule[17] and a fixed amount for commuting costs

[15] With the exclusion of married women up to 1973. Their income has been added to their husbands' income.

[16] Generally speaking, working people can always claim a reduction for costs which are necessary for the acquisition of an income on their taxable income. The reduction is 4% of the gross wage after deduction of the private pension premium and the deduction for civil servants (see chapter 7), at minimum. But the minimum deductible amount is limited downwards and upwards (Dfl. 200 and Dfl. 800, respectively, in 1988). This regular 4% deduction is called the 4% acquisition costs rule. If real acquisition costs are larger than these 4% or Dfl. 800 (in 1988) one can claim the real costs.

[17] In this way, most employees have been treated in the right way. From NCBS (1985b: 144) it is known that 94% of the employees apply the 4% rule and consequently 6% claim more than 4%.

(Dfl. 200 in 1988). An example of the determination of an employee's taxable income is shown in table 6.3.[18]

Table 6.3 *Derivation of the taxable income for an employee in 1986 (Dfl.)*

a.	gross wage	40 000
b.	private pension premium (5.1% of the gross wage after deduction of the franchise of Dfl. 25,640)	732
c.	income on which the employee insurances are levied (a–b)	39 268
d.	premium ZFW, employers' part (4.8% of c)	1 885
e.	premium WW (1.75% of c)	687
f.	premium ZW (1% of c)	393
g.	premium WAO (15.05% of c, after deduction of the franchise of 23,751)	2 335
h.	deductions–commuting costs	200
	– 4% acquisition costs rule (upper limit)	800
i.	income on which the general insurances are levied (c + d – e – f – g – h)	36 738
j.	premiums AOW and AWW (12.7% of i)	4 666
k.	**taxable income** (i – j)	32 072

Until 1990 this taxable income is reduced by claims on disablement allowances, allowances for the aged, tax deduction for children, the allowance for one-parent families, the allowance for working people, the extra allowance for working people and the allowance for self-employed persons. If the resulting amount is less than the tax group allowance, no tax is levied since 1984 and the difference between both amounts is transferred to the partner, if present. If this amount is larger than the tax group allowance, this amount is reduced by the tax group allowance, and the tax rates are applied to this. From 1990, taxable income equals the income on which general insurances are levied (in both cases item i. in table 6.3 minus the tax allowances).

6.6 INITIAL LEVEL OF EDUCATION AND ECONOMIC ACTIVITY OF IMMIGRANTS

If a person has immigrated in the current year and (s)he has already reached school age, his or her level of education is simulated up to the year in question. If we are dealing with a 'new' immigrant, (s)he flows through the education process twice and is assigned the lowest level of education. This procedure results in a level of education that is reasonably near the actual level.

If education was completed before the current year and the person is younger than 65 years (in the other case one becomes state 3, retired), then economic activity is determined. First, it is decided (using the probabilities

[18] The example is taken from Bolhuis (1987: 133).

derived from the 1977 Labour Force Survey) whether (s)he is disabled or not. If so, the pointer 'disabled' becomes true, the state becomes 'disabled, others' (state 11) and the percentage of disablement is assigned by lot.

If the person is not disabled, his or her labour supply is determined, using the labour supply function in section 6.3. If this labour supply is zero or negative, (s)he becomes a houseman or housewife (state 13). If it is positive, the person becomes state 'unemployed, others' (state 4). It is assumed that people start looking for a job three months before they immigrate. This determines the year and month of unemployment. Next, we follow the procedure as described in section 6.3.5, on the understanding that the start of a job cannot take place before the date of immigration.

7

The social security module[1]

7.1 INTRODUCTION

After the determination of labour income, the social security module starts. This process is shown in figure 7.1. First, the premiums for private and civil servant pensions and the deduction for civil servants are determined. This gives us the gross wage. If this has been executed for all workers and we are in 1993 or later, via the net–net and gross–gross coupling, the level of the different benefits, the maximum premium income for the general insurances and the maximum premium income for the employee insurances are calculated (see section 7.20). For 1987 and earlier, these amounts are known from NCBS (30).[2] Next, the claims for the General Old Age Pensions Act, the General Widows and Orphans Pensions Act, the widows and orphans pensions of the Civil Servants Pensions Fund, the family allowances, the General Disablement Benefits Act, the Sickness Benefit Act, the Disablement Insurance Act, the disablement pensions of the Civil Servants Pensions Fund, the old age pensions of the Civil Servants Pensions Fund, the unemployment benefits for civil servants, the Unemployment Insurance Act, the Unemployment Provisions Act and the New Unemployment Insurance Act are determined. If this is executed for all persons, we can calculate the claims that also depend on the income of other household members: the Provision for Older and Partly Disabled Unemployed Employees, the Supplementary Benefits Act and the General Social Assistance Act. If we are in 1993 or later, we have to calculate the premium percentages. Lastly, we can determine the premium payments for the Health Insurance Fund Act, the Sickness Benefit Act, the Disablement Insurance Act, the Unemployment Insurance Act, the New Unemployment Insurance Act, the General Old Age Pensions Act, the General Widows and Orphans Pensions Act, the family allowances, the General Disablement Benefits Act and the General Exceptional Medical Expenses Act. At this point, all calculations for the social

[1] For a performance test of this module, Nelissen (1993).
[2] Like all other data, unless mentioned otherwise.

security module are executed and we go back to the labour market and income formation module to calculate the taxes.

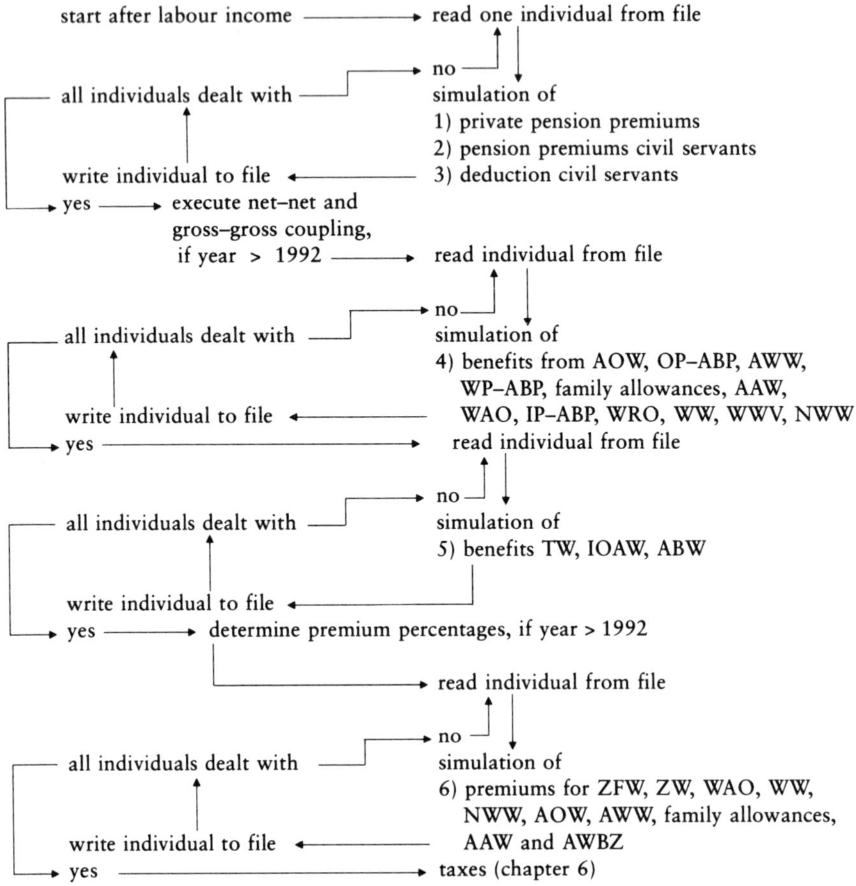

Figure 7.1 An overview of the social security module.

7.2 THE GENERAL OLD AGE PENSIONS ACT (AOW)[3]

The AOW came into force on 1 January 1957. The law provides for a compulsory insurance against the financial consequences of old age on reaching 65 years. All residents in the Netherlands aged 15 to 65 years are

[3] The description is derived from NCBS (30) and Elseviers (1983: 117–123).

insured.[4] An individual can claim an AOW benefit if s(he) is 65 years or older and has been insured. Until 1 April 1985, married women generally could not claim a benefit. Their benefit was linked to that of their husbands. The husband's claim started on the first day of the month in which he turned 65 years. Since 1 April 1985, both married women and men are independently entitled to an AOW benefit.

Initially, the AOW benefit was a relatively small amount. It was raised to a social minimum on 1 January 1965, so that a fixed minimum standard of living was guaranteed. In the early 1970s further structural increments took place and holiday allowances were added to the benefit. From 1976, the (net) AOW benefit for a married couple equals the net minimum wage. An unmarried individual now receives a benefit which amounts to 70% of the benefit which a couple receives.

Since 1 January 1987, new cases of unmarried cohabiting people are treated in the same way as married persons. Relatives in the first degree (for example a parent and a child) are treated as non-cohabiting persons. As from the aforementioned date, a married person receives 50% of the total benefit for married couples, when (s)he reaches 65 years. On this same date, a special AOW benefit for one-parent families, receiving family allowances, was introduced. This benefit amounts to 90% of the (100%) benefit for married couples.

Between 1 January 1987 and 1 April 1988, an extra allowance – which is independent of the income of the younger partner – is paid if one of the partners receives an AOW benefit, even if the other partner has not yet reached the age of 65 years. Since 1 April 1988, a pension of 70% of the net minimum wage is paid to a person eligible for the AOW, if his or her partner is younger than 65 years. The amount of the extra allowance depends on the partner's income if this partner is 59 years or younger. The extra allowance is made up to a maximum of 100% of the AOW benefit for married couples. This income dependancy does not hold if (s)he was eligible for the AOW benefit before 1 April 1988.

The AOW benefit is based on an insurance duration of 50 years (between the ages of 15 and 65 years). A number of temporary provisions relate to persons who were already 15 years or older on 1 January 1957, when the AOW was introduced. Temporary provisions for immigrants and emigrants also apply. If one has not been insured for a year, or did not pay the AOW premium because of carelessness, the AOW benefit is reduced. In the case of death, the AOW benefit is paid up to and including two months after the month of death for married persons, and up to and including the month of death in the case of an unmarried person.

[4] Non-residents who are governed by Dutch tax laws while they are employed in the Netherlands, are also insured for the AOW. However, residents who are insured for a foreign old age pension, because they are employed abroad, are not insured for the AOW. Persons who are no longer insured, have the possibility of continuing the AOW insurance – which is only possible in combination with a voluntary AWW insurance – by voluntary premium payments.

The AOW premium is levied on the so-called premium income for the general insurances (see point i. in table 6.3) up to 1990. From 1990 onwards, the premium is based on the taxable income. The premium is a percentage, up to the maximum premium income, which from 1990 is equal to the upper limit of the first income tax group. Self-employed persons with an income below a fixed amount receive an integral or a partial reduction. This reduction is financed by the government.

Until 1 April 1985, the wife's income was added to her husband's income and the AOW premium was levied on this sum (up to the maximum premium income). If the woman's income was larger than her husband's, it was possible to take the woman's income as the starting point. Generally, this has fiscal advantages. Since then, the AOW premium is levied on each income separately and the maximum premium income also holds for both incomes separately.

Almost all of the foregoing has been built into NEDYMAS. The only exceptions are:

- The exceptions for residents and non-residents as mentioned in foot note 4. Residents are considered to be insured; non-residents are not insured.
- The provisions for immigrants are only partly taken into account.
- The voluntary premium payments by emigrants are not taken into account.
- The provision, existing up to 1 January 1987, that married females who were the breadwinners and whose husbands were disabled and had not yet reached the age of 65 years could claim an AOW benefit when they are 65 years or older, has not been modelled.

7.3 THE GENERAL WIDOWS AND ORPHANS PENSIONS ACT (AWW)[5]

The AWW came into force on 1 October 1959. It is a compulsory general insurance against the financial consequences of death of the insured husband (the widows pension) or both wife and husband (the orphans pension). Recently, the *Centrale Raad van Beroep* (Court of Appeal) decided that men can – under the same conditions as women – also claim an AWW benefit when their (insured) wife dies. As a consequence, widowers have been able to claim an AWW benefit since 1 January 1988. What follows, therefore, is also applicable to men.

The group of insured persons is exactly the same as for the AOW. Analogous temporary provisions are at work and a voluntary insurance is also

[5] NCBS (30) and Elseviers (1983: 107–111).

possible here (but only in combination with a voluntary insurance for the AOW). Specific groups of widows and orphans living abroad are also entitled to claim an AWW benefit.

The AWW has four types of benefits. First, we have the **high widows pension** for widows with at least one unmarried child younger than 18 years living at home. The benefit equals the amount a married couple receives from the AOW (and thus equals the net minimum wage since 1976). The high widows pension ends if the widow no longer meets the conditions. If she meets the conditions for the low widows pension, then her pension is transformed into this type of pension. If this is not the case, she can claim a temporary widows pension.

Second, we have the **low widows pension**. If the widow cannot claim a high widows pension, she may have the right to this type of widows pension. This pension holds for widows who have at least one unmarried child, but no unmarried child younger than 18 years living at home; for widows who were 40 years or older or were disabled at the time of the death of their husband; and for other widows who were 35 years or older, but not yet 40 years on the last day of the month in which their husband died and have or have had a child who was married or had died before her husband died, assuming that the widow was already 35 years at the time the child married or died. The benefit amounts to 70% of the AOW benefit for married couples. The low widows pension ends when the widow no longer meets the conditions, unless she was already at least 40 years when her disablement ended, or at least 35 years when her last child married or died. In these last two cases, her low widows pension continues. If it ends, she can claim the temporary widows benefit.

In all other cases, the widow can claim the third type when her husband dies, the **temporary widows benefit**. The duration is for a maximum of 19 months and depends on her age. The benefit is paid for six months at least. If the widow is 27 years or older, then the benefit period is increased by one month for each year she is older than 27 years at the moment of becoming a widow, taking into account the maximum period of 19 months. The amount of the benefit is also 70% of the AOW benefit for married couples.

These three types of widows benefits are always terminated in the month the widow reaches the age of 65 years. From that moment on, she can claim an AOW benefit. If the widow remarries, the widows benefit is terminated.

The fourth and last type of AWW benefit is the **orphans pension**. It is paid to full orphans up to and including the age of 15 years (without any limitation), to disabled full orphans aged 16 and 17 years, to full orphans aged 16 up to 27 years, who are studying, and to full orphans in the same age category who run the household in which at least one other child can claim an orphans pension. The amount depends on the orphan's age.

The AWW premium is levied in the same way as the AOW premium.

The foregoing is inserted in NEDYMAS, with the exception of:

- A number of specific provisions for widows and orphans living abroad;
- The settlements for residents and non-residents and the provisions for immigrants are treated in the same way as in section 7.2;
- The voluntary premium payments by emigrants are not taken into account.

7.4 FAMILY ALLOWANCES (KW/KWL/KWR/KKZ/KTO/AKW)[6]

The purpose of the various family allowances is to provide additional income to ensure the standard of living of children up to a certain age. Until January 1979 family allowances were received without further conditions (on the understanding that one was insured) for children up to 16 years. Since then, the age limit is 18 years. If a child is older, but disabled or running the household or a student (up to 1 October 1986) one receives family allowances if the child is younger than 27 years and the child is largely supported by his or her parents. From 1963 on, twice or even three times a family allowances benefit may be received for one child under certain conditions; it is then said that the child counts for two and three children, respectively. A child counts for two children if the s(he) is younger than 16 years, lives outside the parental home for reasons of education or sickness and is largely supported by his or her parents (that is to say for 50% or more), or if the child is 16 or 17 years, lives alone and is largely supported by his or her parents, or if the child is aged between 18 and 27 years, is studying (up to 1 October 1986) or running the household, and is largely supported by the parents. Up to 1 October 1986, children living outside the parental home, who were studying, aged between 18 and 27 years, counted for three children if they were supported completely or almost completely (that is to say, for 90% or more) by their parents. From 1 January 1983, unemployed school leavers aged 21 years or younger can claim family allowances for six months.

As was outlined in the Introduction, the following family allowances acts are incorporated in NEDYMAS: the Family Allowances Act (KW) and the Benefit Receiving Persons Family Allowances Act (KWR), which both apply in the period 1947–1962, the Wage Earners Family Allowances Act (KWL) and the Self-Employed Persons Family Allowances Act (KKZ), both of which operated between 1963 and 1979, the Civil Servants Family Allowances Provision (KTO), which applied between 1947 and 1979 and the General Family Allowances Act (AKW) which has been in force since 1963.

[6] NCBS (30) and Elseviers (1983: 102–105).

From January 1980 the AKW provides family allowances from the first child onwards. Before that date, the AKW provided only family allowances for the third child and any subsequent children, and civil servants and teachers were excluded. These last two groups received no family allowances from the AKW. Following the extension in 1980, the KWL, KKZ and KTO were abolished.

From 1 January 1979, family allowances for the first child, if born after that date, were halved. Since 1 January 1983, the allowance is only halved if no other children are present in the household. From 1982, all family allowances are adjusted every six months to take account of the change in the price index figure of the consumption of employee families with two children. Since 1983, the benefit structure has been increasingly specified. Among other things, the child's age, for example, now also determines the benefit.

All residents who have reached the age of 15 years are insured. Besides this, some groups of non-residents are insured. Insured persons have to pay premiums up to of 65 years. For employees, the premium was paid by the employer up to 1 July 1988, and afterwards the premium was financed from public funds. Self-employed people have to pay their own premiums. Deductions similar to the payment for AOW and AWW hold for this group. Women who are 45 years or older, and who do not have children, are exempt from premium payments on their non-labour income.

The KKZ and KWL provided some groups of family allowances for the first two children between 1 January 1963 and 1 January 1980. Self-employed persons received family allowances from the KKZ for their first two children, if their income was less than a certain level. The income level for the second child was somewhat above that for the first child. Up to 1 July 1978 the benefit equalled the KWL benefit. While the tax deduction for children continued to exist for self-employed persons, whereas this deduction was abolished for other persons, the KKZ benefits have been below the KWL benefits since that date. The KKZ benefits were financed by public funds.

The KWL provided family allowances for the first and second child of employees and those who were treated as if they were employees. The last category almost coincides with persons who received a benefit from the ZW, the WAO, the AAW, the WWV, the WW, the AOW or the AWW. The employee premiums were paid by employers and, for the other group, the premiums were financed from public funds. The same maximum premium income as for the AKW applied.

Civil servants and teachers were covered by the KTO. Benefits and premium payments were in accordance with the KWL and AKW. The premiums were financed from public funds.

The group of insured persons for the KW is about the same as for the ZW (section 7.7). However, no income limit was in force. Civil servants, again, were excluded. The possibility of counting one child for two or three children did not yet exist. Also, no benefits were paid for children aged 16 years or older, who were running the household. Family allowances were provided for each employee's working day and for each day not worked for which the employee received a benefit under a social security act. The premium was paid by the employer and amounted to a percentage of the daily wage (up to a maximum, which equals the maximum premium income for the ZFW).

The KWR provided family allowances to persons receiving a benefit under the Disablement Act, the AOW or the AWW. The regulation was in accordance with the KW. Benefits were, however, paid for each month instead of each working day.

The settlements described above are almost all included in NEDYMAS. While the Disablement Act is not an element of NEDYMAS, it is not possible to determine the family allowances for people receiving a benefit from the Disablement Act. For student children, aged 16 years and older, only grants were considered as income (chapter 6) and this determines the extent to which these children are supported by their parents. It is also assumed that children running the household have no income, whereas disabled children only receive an AAW benefit (from 1 October 1976 onwards). The group of non-residents who are insured for the AKW are not included.

7.5 THE GENERAL DISABLEMENT BENEFITS ACT (AAW)[7]

The AAW took effect on 1 October 1976. It is an insurance against the financial consequences of long-lasting disability. All residents up to the age of 65 years and some groups of non-residents are compulsorily insured for the AAW.

One can receive a benefit from the age of 17. To receive a benefit at that age, one has to be disabled for at least one year and to be insured. If an individual becomes disabled after his or her 17th birthday, (s)he receives a benefit if (s)he is insured, if his or her disability has already existed at least one year and if, at the moment of becoming disabled, (s)he earned an income from or relating to labour, which exceeded a fixed minimal amount.[8] In all cases (s)he has to be at least 25% disabled. Married women have an independent right to a benefit from 1 January 1980, provided that they became disabled on or after 1 October 1975. Before that time, married women could only claim a benefit if they were breadwinners.[9]

[7] NCBS (30), Elseviers (1983: 40 and 56–68) and Ministerie van Sociale Zaken en Werkgelegenheid (1986: 19).

[8] On this last condition, several exceptions exist, among others for students, unmarried persons and self-employed persons.

[9] A verdict of the *Centrale Raad van Beroep* has laid these limitations for married women open to criticism. The consequences are not fully clear at the moment. In any event, women who were already disabled before 1979 can claim a benefit, even if they were not the breadwinner.

The level of the AAW benefit is determined on a certain amount, which we shall call the AAW–basis. Up to 1980 two bases existed:

(a) A high AAW–basis for married men and for unmarried persons who had to support at least one child, aged 17 or under;
(b) A low AAW–basis (which amounts to about 70% of the high AAW–basis, and as a consequence, from 1978 onwards, 70% of the net minimum wage) for all other rightful claimants.

From 1980 up to and including 1986, four AAW–bases existed. The general AAW–basis equals 70% of the net minimum wage, with the exception of persons up to the age of 21 years, for whom, in accordance with minimum youth wages, lower amounts apply. This general AAW–basis applies to everybody, unless another AAW–basis has been declared.

The middle AAW–basis applies to both married and unmarried persons who take care of children younger than 18 years, on condition that the insured person's income, augmented with his or her partner's income (if present), amounts to at least 15% and at most 30% of the maximum AAW–basis on the first day on which the AAW benefit may be claimed. In this case, the AAW–benefit amounts to 85% of the net minimum wage.

If the aforementioned sum of incomes amounts to less than 15% of the maximum AAW–basis, then one receives the maximum AAW–basis, which equals the net minimum wage.

Lastly, there is an individual AAW–basis. This applies to persons who worked part-time during the year preceding the day they became disabled and whose benefit would amount to more than 80% of their income during that year. They receive 80% of this income.

Since 1 January 1987 only one AAW–basis has been in operation: the general AAW–basis. Everyone receives 70% of the net minimum wage. If necessary, one can appeal under the provisions of Supplementary Benefits Act. A temporary provision applies to one-parent families. If they received a higher benefit on 31 December 1986, a supplementary benefit is paid of up to 100% of the net minimum wage. For persons up to of 23 years, the amounts in accordance with the minimum youth wages remain in force.

In addition to the AAW–basis, the AAW benefit is determined by the degree of disablement. The AAW benefit amounts to the AAW–basis times a proportion, which depends on the degree of disablement. The benefit is terminated if the degree of disability drops below 25%, or when one reaches the age of 65 years, or dies, or – being a widow – if she can claim an AWW benefit. If a person who receives an AAW benefit dies, his or her next of kin receives a death benefit under certain conditions. The death benefit equals the AAW benefit during the remaining part of the month in which the person died, plus two extra months.

The AAW also has the possibility of creating provisions which serve for maintenance, recuperation or benefit of one's disability, or for improvement of one's living conditions. Those who do not receive a benefit, but are insured, can also claim this kind of provision.

Premiums had to be paid by all insured persons aged between 15 and 65 years up to 1990. In the case of an employee, premiums were paid by the employer up to 1990. Since 1990 the AAW premium has to be paid by the employee. The employee receives a compensation for this amount from his or her employer. Up to 1990, the premium was a percentage of the so-called premium income for the general insurances, and from 1990 it is levied on the taxable income. Analogous to the AOW and AWW, a maximum premium income exists, which is the same for all general insurances. For self-employed persons, the same procedure holds as for the AOW, AWW and AKW.

The NEDYMAS model does not take into account the category of non-resident persons who are insured for the AAW and the additional provisions. The same applies to the minimum income condition for persons who become disabled after the age of 17 years. In practice, the impact of this is limited. The individual AAW–basis has not been included in the model. All other elements are included in NEDYMAS. An additional problem is related to the way in which the inflow is modelled. Inflow into the AAW (and also WAO) goes via the ZW for employees and via the DSO for civil servants (section 7.7), whereas others flow in via state transitions (section 6.3).

7.6 THE DISABLEMENT INSURANCE ACT (WAO)[10]

The WAO came into operation 1 July 1967. The law provided for the financial consequences of long-lasting disablement for employees up to the moment at which the AAW came into force. Since that time – 1 October 1976 – both the AAW and the WAO provide for the financial consequences of long-lasting disablement. For employees who became disabled after 1 October 1976, the WAO is a supplementary benefit.

All those who are insured for the ZW and persons who receive a WWV benefit are insured. Employees above 65 years are not insured. This also holds for members of the Civil Servants Pensions Fund.

All employees who have been disabled for 52 weeks and whose degree of disablement is at least 15% can claim a WAO benefit. The level of the benefit depends on the degree of disablement and on the daily wage. This is the wage earned on average each day in the profession practised in the year before becoming disabled. The level of the benefit is maximized by the fact that a maximum daily wage exists for the WAO. Nowadays, the benefit is at most 70% of the daily wage. Between 1969 and 1987 breadwinners

[10] NCBS (30), Elseviers (1983: 68–70) and Ministerie van Sociale Zaken en Werkgelegenheld (1986: 20–22).

with a degree of disability of more than 80% also had a minimum benefit. From 1987, the minimum daily wage for this group is guaranteed by the Supplementary Benefits Act (section 7.12). The benefit is index-linked to wages.

The benefit ends if the degree of disablement drops below 15%, if the recipient becomes 65 years or if (s)he dies. The revision of the social security system in 1987 also involved a re-examination of disabled persons aged 35 or less. Persons who became disabled after 1 January 1987, and are less than 80% disabled, are considered to be unemployed for the proportion for which they are not disabled. Before 1987 there was a possibility of enlarging the degree of disability if labour market conditions were weak, the so-called '*verdiscontering*'. This also holds for those re-examined disabled persons whose degree of disablement is readjusted downwards. On that account, one can claim an NWW benefit if one worked for at least six months before becoming disabled. For any additional claims after that period, see section 7.10. There is then a right to a partial Continued Benefit in view of the NWW, for a maximum of one year. Later, one can claim an additional benefit from the IOAW (section 7.11). The level of the partial Continued Benefit from the NWW and the AAW/WAO benefit amounts to 70% of the last earned wage income (which is index-linked). There is also the possibility of claiming an additional benefit from the TW (see section 7.12).

Until the AAW became operative, the WAO also had provisions which served for maintenance, recuperation or benefit of one's disability or for improvement of one's living conditions. If a person who receives a WAO benefit dies, his or her next of kin receives a death benefit under certain conditions. The death benefit equals the WAO benefit during the remainder of the month in which the person died, plus two extra months.

WAO premiums are paid by both employer and employee. Since 1981, employees have paid the largest share. Before then, employers paid the largest part. Premiums are levied proportional up to a maximum income, which is the same as for the ZW (next section). As a consequence of the introduction of the AAW, which governs the lower benefit part for employees, a part (the franchise) has been free of payment since 1977.

NEDYMAS contains all the foregoing elements with the exception of the provisions and the re-examination of disabled persons in 1987.[11]

7.7 THE SICKNESS BENEFIT ACT (ZW) AND SICKNESS PAYMENTS FOR CIVIL SERVANTS (DSO)[12]

The ZW came into operation in 1930 and is the oldest settlement treated in this chapter. Its goal is to insure employees up to 65 years against the

[11] The impact of the re-examination appears to be very limited.
[12] NCBS (30) and Elseviers (1983: 49–56).

financial consequences of not being able to work as a result of disability, accident (from 1 July, 1967[13]) or sickness, including pregnancy and childbirth. For the concept of the employee, see Elseviers (1983: 16). As a consequence, unemployed persons who receive a WW or an NWW benefit have to claim a ZW benefit in case of sickness. Civil servants cannot claim a ZW benefit. They are covered by the DSO. Before 1 July 1967, a ZW benefit could only be claimed if income was below a fixed upper limit, the so-called maximum wage limit.

The benefit amounted to 80% of the daily wage up to 1 May 1985, 75% between 1 May 1985 and 1 January 1986, and 70% afterwards. Between 1969 and 1987 a minimum wage guarantee existed during the first six weeks of sickness, on condition that the individual was married or took care of a child aged 17 years or younger and his or her income, augmented with the partner's income, amounted to less than 93.75% of the minimum wage. From 1 January 1987, one has to claim a benefit from the TW in this case. The benefit is limited by the maximum premium income. The benefit starts from the third day after the day the sickness (or disablement or accident) took place. The maximum benefit duration is one year. After that year one flows into the WAO or AAW or the disablement pension of the Civil Servants Pensions Fund. Before the introduction of the WAO, the Disablement Act or the Temporary Act for Disablement Pension Receivers applied.

Employers are allowed to give a supplement to the ZW benefit of up to 100% of the daily wage and to pay the first two days which are not paid by the ZW. This supplement is called the supplementary benefit. The ZW has the possibility of part-time resumption of work. The ZW benefit is accordingly reduced for that part.

If a person who receives a ZW benefit dies, his or her next of kin receives a death benefit from the ZW under certain conditions. The death benefit amounts to 100% of the daily wage during the remainder of the month in which the person died, plus two extra months.

The ZW considers pregnancy and childbirth benefits to be a specific element of the sickness benefit. Generally, a benefit which equals the daily wage is paid during six weeks before and six weeks after childbirth.

The ZW premium is a percentage of the wage, up to a maximum (the maximum premium income). The premium differs between branches of industry and depends on the risk of sickness in the various branches. The employer pays the premium, but is allowed to deduct half the premium, up to 1% at most, from the employee's wage. If the employer has provided supplementary benefits, the Ministry of Social Affairs can agree to deduct more than 1%.

[13] Before 1 July 1967, the financial consequences of accidents were covered by the Accident Insurance Act and those of disablement by the Disablement Act or the Temporary Act for Disablement Pension Receivers. We will not report on these acts for lack of sufficient data.

As we have seen, civil servants have a settlement of their own: the DSO. The DSO is more or less in accordance with the ZW. However, the benefit is 100%, the first two days of sickness are also paid and it is financed from public funds.

NEDYMAS assumes that the ZW benefit is supplied by the employer up to 100% and that the employer also pays the first two days.[14] The model does not take account of the possibility of a part-time resumption of work. Also, no distinction can be made between disability (before one year has expired), sickness and accidents, so that the financial consequences of accidents up to a duration of one year are included in the ZW before 1967. These belong to the Accident Insurance Act (footnote 13). Further, no differentiation has been made in premiums between various branches of industry. The average premium percentage has been used.

The inflow into the ZW and DSO is based on the number of sicknesses by age, sex and duration in firms for which the trade association[15] takes care of the ZW benefits [NCBS (31)]. These numbers are transformed into the probability of becoming ill for i days (i = 1, 2,..., 365).

The effect of socio-economic characteristics on the absence from work for illness has been incorporated by distinguishing duration of sickness by level of education (primary school, junior (vocational) training, secondary (vocational) training, vocational colleges and university), in which a correction was made for age and sex composition. The figures are derived from Van den Brekel (1986, table 5). It is assumed that an individual only receives a ZW or DSO benefit once a year.

7.8 THE UNEMPLOYMENT INSURANCE ACT (WW)[16]

The WW, which came into force on 1 July 1952, insured employees against the financial consequences of involuntary unemployment. On 1 January 1987, the WW was incorporated into the NWW (section 7.10). All employees up to 65 years were insured. Before 1957 people aged 65 and older were also insured. Civil servants were excluded. Separate settlements existed for this category (section 7.17). Until 1965 a maximum wage limit existed, which was identical to the maximum wage limit for the ZW.

The WW consisted of three parts: the unemployment insurance for persons belonging to a particular branch of industry (‘*wachtgeldverzekering*’), the general unemployment insurance for employees, and the insurance against the risk of unemployment due to weather conditions.

In the case of employees belonging to a given branch of industry, during their unemployment period they were included in the labour pool of that

[14] Nowadays, this holds for about 90 per cent of all employees.

[15] Private industrial executive body for social insurance in the Netherlands.

[16] NCBS (30) and Elseviers (1983: 77–91).

branch. A person was entitled to a benefit from this type of insurance if (s)he had been employed by employers who were members of the trade association in question for at least 130 days during the previous 12 months. The maximum benefit period was eight weeks in a period of 12 months. Until 1 January 1985 the level of the benefit was 80% of the employee's daily wage. From that date on, the benefit amounted to 70% of the daily wage. As was the case for the WAO and ZW, a maximum benefit existed, which was determined by the benefit percentage and the maximum premium income. Since 1969 a minimum benefit level has existed for breadwinners. The premium was fixed for each branch of industry by the trade association, which carried the insurance risk. Both employers and employees paid half the premium.

The second insurance, the general unemployment insurance for employees, held for those employees who were not eligible for the first type of unemployment insurance (because they did not belong to the labour pool of that branch), and for those unemployed persons whose maximum period for the first type of unemployment insurance had expired, or who had already used their eight weeks during a preceding period of unemployment. Here also, the employee had to be employed during at least 130 days during the previous 12 months. The maximum duration was 26 weeks a year, which was reduced by the period the first type of insurance benefit was received. The level equalled that for the first type. The premium did not differ between branches; it was a uniform rate. Both employers and employees had to pay a part of the premium.

Unemployment due to weather conditions was a particular type of unemployment, which, of course, differed between branches of industry. One had to have paid a premium for at least 120 days during the previous 12 months in order to receive a benefit. The benefit amounted to 110% of the hourly wage rate. The premium was paid by the employer.

Recipients of a WW benefit were insured for the ZW. In case of sickness, the unemployment benefit was replaced by a ZW benefit. If a person who received a WW benefit died, his or her next of kin received a death benefit under certain conditions from the ZW. The death benefit equalled the WW benefit during the remainder of the month in which the person died, plus two extra months.

In March 1974 a settlement for supplementary payments to wage income was introduced. If one accepted a job with a lower income, one received a supplementary payment to this income.

NEDYMAS does not distinguish between the unemployment insurance for persons belonging to a branch of industry and the general unemployment insurance for employees. The conditions for a benefit and the level of the benefit do not differ. The difference is in the premium payment. However, in NEDYMAS the branch of occupation is not modelled. Therefore, we use an average premium percentage for the first type of insurance. Unemployment due to weather conditions has not been incorporated, because there is not sufficient data. The settlement for supplementary payments has also not been incorporated.

The inflow into and the outflow out of the state unemployed is simulated by the submodule for state transitions (section 6.3). It is assumed that an individual loses his job once a year at most.

7.9 THE UNEMPLOYMENT PROVISIONS ACT (WWV)[17]

The WWV was in force between 1965 and 1987. When an employee (no longer) had a claim to the WW, (s)he could be eligible for a WWV benefit. To claim a WWV benefit one had to be employed at least during the last six weeks before being unemployed or during 130 days in the year previous to becoming unemployed. The benefit duration was two years in the first instance. If one had reached the age of 60 years after these two years, the WWV benefit was prolonged up to the retirement age of 65 years.

From 22 June 1983, young people up to the age of 23 years had to have been employed for at least 130 weeks in the three years preceding their unemployment. Their benefit duration was limited to a maximum of one year.

Since 1 May 1985 the benefit duration has depended on age. Persons up to 23 years could claim a benefit for six months at most, persons aged 23 to 30 years for one year, persons aged 30 to 35 years for 18 months and older people for two years. If one had been employed for 4.5 years during the previous six years, six months were added to the aforementioned period. If one had reached the age of 60 years at the end of the benefit period, the WWV benefit was prolonged up to the age of 65 years, but the level of the benefit was limited to the net minimum wage for breadwinners and to 70% of the net minimum wage for others.

The benefit amounted to 75% of the daily wage until 1 January 1985 and 70% after that year up to the maximum premium income. From 3 November 1969, a minimum daily wage was in force for breadwinners. The settlement for supplementary payments to wage income – if one accepted a job with a lower income – was also applied in the WWV. Married women could only claim a benefit from 1 October 1976. Up to 24 December 1984, married women only received a benefit if they were breadwinners. If a person died, his or her next of kin received a death benefit from the ZW under certain conditions. The death benefit equalled the WWV benefit during the remainder of the month in which the person died, plus two extra months. The WWV was financed from public funds and, thus, no premium levies were applicable.

[17] NCBS (30) and Elseviers (1983: 91–101).

NEDYMAS contains all the above elements, with the exception of the settlement for supplementary payments and the possibility of partial unemployment in combination with being employed for part of the time.

7.10 THE NEW UNEMPLOYMENT INSURANCE ACT (NWW)[18]

On 1 January 1987, the WW and the WWV were replaced by the NWW. The group of insured persons did not change. The main difference between the NWW and its predecessors is the dependence of the duration of the benefit on the number of years one has worked before becoming unemployed. Besides, the NWW has the possibility of voluntary insurance for, among others, development workers, employees who are employed abroad by a Dutch employer and housekeepers who are not insured compulsorily. The minimum benefit for breadwinners was also abolished and replaced by the TW (section 7.12).

The level of the benefit amounts to 70% of the daily wage and is limited by the maximum premium income. Premiums have to be paid by both the employer and the employee. The premiums are a percentage of the income and are also limited by the premium income.

Persons who become unemployed on or after 1 January 1987 are entitled to an NWW benefit if they were employed for at least 26 weeks in the preceding year. In that case one can claim a benefit over a six-month period. To be eligible for a benefit over a longer period, one has to have been employed during three years in the five years preceding becoming unemployed. If one was not employed for reasons of taking care of children up to the age of six years these years are considered as years worked; if the children are aged between six and 12 years, half of these years count as years worked.

Persons up to the age of 23 years can only receive a benefit for longer than six months if they have been employed for five years without interruption before becoming unemployed. In that case, their benefit is prolonged by three months.

The extra duration of the NWW benefit for persons aged 23 years and older (who were employed for three years during the previous five years) depends on their labour history. This has been defined as the individual's age minus 23 years plus the number of years (s)he was employed during the previous five years. If the labour history is between five and ten years, the benefit duration is prolonged by three months. Consequently, the total duration is nine months. If the labour history is ten to 15 years, the extra duration is six months. In case of a labour history of 15 to 20 years, 20 to 25 years, 25 to 30 years and 35 to 40 years, the extra duration amounts to one year, 18 months, two years, two and a half years and three and a half years, respectively. If the labour history is longer than 40 years, the extra duration is four and a half years.

[18] Ministerie van Sociale Zaken en Werkgelegenheid (1986: 4–5, 8–11 and 13–18).

When the NWW benefit ends and an individual meets the requirement of having been employed for three years (five years for persons up to the age of 23 years) during the previous five years before unemployment, and is still unemployed, there is an entitlement to a Continued Benefit for one year under the NWW. The Continued Benefit amounts to 70% of the minimum wage. The partner's income, if present, does not affect the benefit. If one is 57.5 years or older when the Continued Benefit starts, this can be claimed up to the age of 65 years.

If the Continued Benefit under the NWW ends and the individual is still unemployed, (s)he is normally entitled to the Governmental Group Provision for the Unemployed, the RWW (section 7.13). This does not hold for persons who received a Continued Benefit and are already 50 years or older when they become unemployed and for persons who do not receive a Continued Benefit, but are already 57.5 years or older when they become unemployed. These two groups can claim an IOAW benefit (section 7.11).

A number of temporary provisions hold for persons who received a WW or WWV benefit on 31 December 1986.

If a person who receives an NWW benefit dies, his or her next of kin receives a death benefit from the ZW under certain conditions. The death benefit equals the NWW benefit during the remainder of the month in which the person died, plus two extra months.

All these elements are incorporated in NEDYMAS, with the exception of the voluntary insurance and the possibility of part-time unemployment in combination with a part-time job. The claims for an NWW benefit for partly disabled persons are also included in the model. Inflow into and outflow out of the state unemployed takes place in the submodule for state transitions (section 6.3).

7.11 THE PROVISIONS FOR OLDER AND PARTLY DISABLED UNEMPLOYED EMPLOYEES (IOAW)[19]

The IOAW came into effect on 1 January 1987 and is financed from public funds. This provision is aimed at two groups of former employees. Firstly, it is an extra provision for older long-lasting unemployed persons, who have already received an NWW benefit (the Continued Benefits included) during the maximum period and who are at least 50 years old on their first day of unemployment. If an individual is aged 57.5 years or older, (s)he will only receive an IOAW benefit if (s)he is employed for less than three years during the five years before (s)he becomes unemployed. If (s)he is employed for three years or more during these five years, (s)he keeps the Continued Benefits under the NWW until (s)he reaches the age of 65 years. Those aged between 50 and

[19] Ministerie van Sociale Zaken en Werkgelegenheid (1986: 8, 10, 16 and 25–26).

57.5 years when they become unemployed enter the IOAW when the Continued Benefits ends. As a temporary provision, those who are aged between 47.5 and 50 years on 31 December 1986 and have a WW or WWV benefit will receive an IOAW benefit when their NWW benefit expires. Secondly, the IOAW refers to partly disabled employees who are unemployed for the non-disabled part, irrespective of age. These persons will receive an IOAW benefit when the NWW benefit (the Continued Benefits included) has ended.

Under the IOAW one is entitled to a(n) (additional) benefit up to the level of the social minimum. An individual only receives the benefit if the sum of his or her labour income plus the partner's labour income is below the social minimum. During the first two years, 30% of his or her own labour income and the partner's labour income is exempt, but the exempted amount is limited to 15% of the social minimum. The advantage of the IOAW in comparison with the ABW – under which other long-lasting employed persons fall – is that property is not taken into account.

These elements are incorporated in NEDYMAS. However, the model does not generate own labour income for unemployed and disabled persons. So, the exemption has not been modelled.

7.12 THE SUPPLEMENTARY BENEFITS ACT (TW)[20]

The TW supplements the NWW benefit, the WAO benefit, the AAW benefit and the ZW benefit to the social minimum, but never above the last earned wage. All additional income, including the partner's income, are taken into consideration, but not property. Part of the labour income is exempt for two years, unless one is 57.5 years or older when unemployment starts. In the latter case, the exemption has no maximum period. The exemption is 100% for incomes up to a sum of 5% of the minimum wage. Between 5 and 15% of the minimum wage, 30% of the income is exempt. If one dies, a death benefit under the ZW is received by the heir, analogous to, for example, the NWW. The TW is financed by public funds. For this reason, no premium levying takes place.

The foregoing is included in NEDYMAS. However, the exemption is not modelled for the same reason as mentioned for the IOAW.

7.13 THE GENERAL SOCIAL ASSISTANCE ACT (ABW)[21]

The ABW, which took effect on 1 January 1965, obliges the state to provide financial support to every resident with insufficient means to meet the

[20] Ministerie van Sociale Zaken en Werkgelegenheid (1986: 26).
[21] NCBS (30) and Elseviers (1983: 203–215).

necessary costs of living. An ABW benefit is only received as a last resort. In this way, the ABW has to be considered as the final element of the Dutch social security system.

Conditions for a benefit do exist. It is assumed that each individual is responsible for his or her own livelihood. Unemployed persons and school-leavers, therefore, have an obligation to look for an appropriate job in order to be eligible for an ABW benefit, unless medical, social or other reasons make it impossible for them to do so. As a consequence, one has to be registered at the Regional Labour Exchange. If this is not the case, the ABW benefit can be reduced or even be terminated.

The level of the ABW benefit is determined by the concept of 'necessary costs of living'. The benefit is fixed for individuals or for specific groups. The recipients may be grouped into three: the National Group Regulations, assistance for persons living at home and assistance for persons not living at home.

The group-oriented treatment of benefit recipients is regulated in the National Group Regulations. At present, the following National Group Regulations apply:

- The National Group Regulation War Victims 1940–1945;
- The National Group Regulation Repatriates;
- The National Group Regulation Amboinese;
- The National Group Regulation Unemployed Persons;
- The National Group Regulation Self-Employed Persons;
- The National Group Regulation Homeless Persons;
- The National Group Regulation Deduction Old Age Provisions for Special Groups;
- The National Group Regulation Elderly Self-Employed Persons.

Two further settlements have an additional purpose and cannot be fully considered as National Group Regulations: the Decree to Employers of Inland Navigation and the Decree to Caravan-Dwellers.

From 1 July 1974, general rules for the determination of the level of the benefit are given on the basis of the Decree National Standards Public Assistance. Before that time, no unequivocal interpretation of the concept of necessary costs of living existed and the level of the benefit differed from place to place. The decree does not hold for the National Group Regulation War Victims 1940–1945, the National Group Regulation Amboinese and the National Group Regulation Homeless Persons. A specific benefit structure applies for these groups. The benefits, fixed under the terms of the Decree National Standards Public Assistance, also hold for the assistance for persons living at home. The net minimum wage is the standard. Married and cohabiting couples receive 100% of the net minimum wage. One-parent families receive 90% and singles above the age of 22 years receive 70%.

Singles up to the age of 23 years receive 70% of the minimum youth wage. If one is 20 years or younger and living in the parental home, one receives an adjusted (lower) benefit. Singles who share a household, without living in a consensual union ('*voordeurdelers*'), receive a reduced benefit.

The Decree also rules the extent to which the benefit is reduced by own income and property. For this, the household is the central unit, not the person who receives the benefit. The ABW has the possibility of providing in-costs which exceed the current costs of living. This is called Incidental Assistance.

The benefits for persons not living at home are a way of indirect financing of institutions providing social or medical services. The benefit has three components: the costs for necessary nursing and medical attendance, the premium for the health insurances and an amount for personal expenditures.

The ABW is financed by public funds.

NEDYMAS does not distinguish between the different National Group Regulations. The Incidental Assistance and the assistance for persons not living at home (in so far as it exceeds the regular benefit) are not included. For each individual we investigate each year whether (s)he has an income below the social minimum. If this is the case, then it is assumed that one can claim an ABW benefit. The reduction for singles living together in one household is not considered. Also, no reductions are made for the presence of property.

7.14 THE HEALTH INSURANCE ACT (ZFW)[22]

The ZFW replaces the Decree on the Health Insurance and the Health Insurance Act for the Aged. The ZFW came into operation on 1 January 1966. As a consequence, the compulsory sickness fund insurance, the voluntary sickness fund insurance and the sickness fund insurance for the aged, were combined in one act. The ZFW regulates the provision of medical and surgical treatment (or its compensation). Compulsorily insured persons are insured by law. Until 1987, the ZFW distinguished between four types of insurance: the aforementioned three types and the additional insurance. The voluntary insurance and the insurance for the aged were abolished in 1987. About 65% of the Dutch population is covered by the ZFW.

Compulsorily insured persons for the ZW and a number of persons who are put on the same footing – such as those who receive a WAO benefit – are also compulsorily insured for the ZFW, on condition that their income is below the maximum wage threshold that holds for the ZFW. The comparable income for those receiving a WW benefit and for disabled persons is the income on the basis of which their benefit has been determined. The

[22] NCBS (30) and Elseviers (1983: 129–145). The conversion to a national health insurance – via the AWBZ – is not included in the simulation model.

compulsory insurance also holds for people receiving a WWV benefit or a benefit from the National Group Regulation Unemployed Persons. The ZFW also insures family members under certain conditions: spouses and children up to 16 years (27 years if disabled or – until 1987 – student) and living in the same household as the directly insured person. From 1 January 1988, unmarried cohabiting persons are treated as married couples. From 1987, one remains compulsory insured if one reaches the age of 65 years, whereas before 1987 this was not the case.

Up to 1987, if one was not compulsorily insured and one's income was below the wage threshold, one could insure oneself voluntarily for the ZFW.

The insurance for the aged offers aged persons the possibility of joining the ZFW if their income is below a certain income limit (which is considerably lower than the aforementioned wage threshold), for a limited premium. Aged persons with an income between the two limits are allowed to enter the voluntary insurance.

The additional insurance offers the possibility of insuring oneself against risks which are not (completely) covered by the sickness fund.

Until 1989, the ZFW premium for the compulsory insurance was a percentage of the wage income up to the ZFW premium income limit. Since 1989, the ZFW premium has been, in part, a fixed amount for each household member (for each adult and two children at most), with the remainder a percentage of the wage income up to the ZFW premium income limit. Employers and employees each paid half the amount until 1989. Since then, employers pay about 1.5 times the amount paid by employees.

The other insurances have fixed amounts as a premium. Reductions are possible in the voluntary insurance, whereas the premium in the insurance for the aged also depends on income.

NEDYMAS only includes the premium levying for the compulsory sickness fund insurance. There is not sufficient and differentiated data to model medical consumption or the premiums for the other types of insurance.

7.15 THE GENERAL EXCEPTIONAL MEDICAL EXPENSES ACT (AWBZ)[23]

The AWBZ, which came into operation in 1968, is an insurance against the financial consequences of special health costs, caused by long-lasting medical condition which generally are not covered by the ZFW and private health insurances. The AWBZ is a general, nationwide, insurance. All residents are insured and no age limits are in force. Like the ZFW, the AWBZ is characterized by provisions in kind – for example, long-lasting care in a nursing home, or a home for mentally or physically handicapped persons.

[23] NCBS (30) and Elseviers (1983: 145–153). Also footnote 22.

Subsequently, other types of care, with a less severe financial burden, such as aid by the Regional Institutions for Ambulant Mental Health Services, are included in the AWBZ.

The AWBZ can be considered to be complementary to the ZFW. Generally, the costs for maintenance in hospitals, institutions and so on are reimbursed by the ZFW or private health insurance companies during the first year, after which the costs are borne by the AWBZ. One has to pay a part of the costs for some facilities. These contributions have depended on income since 1 January 1983.

Up to 1990, premiums were paid by all insured persons aged between 15 and 65. If one was an employee, premiums were paid by the employer. Since 1990, the AWBZ premium has to be paid by the employee. However, the employee receives a compensation for this amount from his or her employer. From 1990, persons older than 64 also have to pay AWBZ premiums, for which their income is adjusted. Up to 1990, the premium was a percentage of the so-called premium income for the general insurances, and since 1990 it has been levied on the taxable income. Analogous to the AOW and AWW, a maximum premium income exists, which is the same for all general insurances. For self-employed persons, the same procedure holds as for the AOW, AWW and AKW.

The premiums are modelled in NEDYMAS. As with the ZFW, there is no data on medical consumption.

7.16 PRIVATE PENSIONS FOR EMPLOYEES[24]

The Netherlands has many arrangements which offer employees the possibility of retiring at a given age. It has not been possible to include all these in the model. Therefore, we must limit ourselves to modelling a more or less average pension premium. This is necessary because the private pension premium also determines the income on which the social security premiums are levied. We do not consider the benefits, because the model does not take account of employees' labour mobility. The necessary information on pension claims is also lacking at the macro level.

The pension premium is levied as a percentage of income, up to a fixed maximum amount. A franchise has been built in to cover the AOW claims.

7.17 THE CIVIL SERVANTS UNEMPLOYMENT BENEFIT (WRO)

A number of benefits exist for the civil servant who is dismissed and, therefore, becomes unemployed. The kind of benefit one receives depends

[24] Elseviers (1983: 116).

on the nature and the length of the contract, the reason for the dismissal and so on. We limit ourselves to the central issues of the Decree Civil Servants Unemployment Benefits 1959 and the Civil Servants Unemployment Benefit Provision 1966 ('*Rijkswachtgeldbesluit 1959*' and '*Uitkeringsregeling 1966*', respectively).

Persons working under a contract for six months or less are not considered as civil servants, but as employees. They receive a WW, a WWV or an NWW benefit.

A civil servant with a permanent appointment can claim a benefit from the Decree Civil Servants Unemployment Benefits 1959 if (s)he has been dismissed for any of the following reasons: discontinuance of the position, reorganization, strong objections against a transfer, apparent impossibility of replacement after returning from fixed types of special leave with a long duration or non-activity, or incapacity to occupy the position on grounds other than medical ones.

If the civil servant only has a temporary appointment, (s)he can also claim a benefit from the Decree Civil Servants Unemployment Benefits 1959, if (s)he has been dismissed for the aforementioned reasons, with the exclusion of the last. If (s)he has been dismissed for other reasons, the civil servant can claim a benefit from the Civil Servants Unemployment Benefit Provision 1966.

The duration of the benefit under the Decree Civil Servants Unemployment Benefits 1959 depends on the age and the term of service on and up to the day of dismissal. The duration is for a minimum of three months. Up to the age of 21, these three months are increased by 18% of the term of service. Next, the percentage is increased by 1.5% for each year of age above 20 years. If age plus term of service amounts to more than 60 years and the term of service is a minimum of 10 years, the benefit lasts until the month one reaches the age of 65 years.

Until 1 January 1985, the benefit during the first three months, amounted to 100% of the salary on the day of dismissal. After the first three months the benefit was reduced to 90% during nine months and thereafter to 80%. From 1985, the percentages decreased by ten percentage points. As a consequence of the pre-tax decline of salaries by 3% on 1 January 1984, an extra allowance of 3% was added to the benefit for a further five years.

The Civil Servants Unemployment Benefit Provision 1966 distinguishes between long- and short-term benefits. A civil servant can claim a long-term benefit if his or her term of service has been for at least three years. If the term of service has been interrupted for one month or longer, the claim becomes invalid. Also, if a term of service has been used for a benefit claim, the term of requirement has to start again. The duration of the benefit is one sixth part of the term of service, for a maximum of six months. The period benefit is prolonged by six months if the term of service is extended to more than 10 years and the sum of age and term of service amounts to at least 60 years. During the first two months, the level of the benefit equals 90% of the last earned salary, the following two months amounts to 80% and during the rest of the period 70%.

The short-term benefit under the Civil Servants Unemployment Benefit Provision 1966 has a duration of six months and amounts to 70% of the last earned salary.

In both types of benefit under the Civil Servants Unemployment Benefit Provision 1966, an extra allowance of 3% is also given from 1 January 1984.

For all benefits under the Decree Civil Servants Unemployment Benefits 1959 and the Civil Servants Unemployment Benefit Provision 1966, if an individual receives income from sources which come about after s(he) was dismissed, the benefit is diminished for that part of the income which – together with the benefit – exceeds the former salary. The benefits are financed from public funds.

The foregoing is incorporated in NEDYMAS with the exception of the reduction of the benefit in the case of new, additional income. The model does not generate this kind of income. It is assumed that civil servants with a term of service which is three years or less receive a short-term benefit under the Civil Servants Unemployment Benefit Provision 1966, that those with a term of service between three to six years receive a long-term benefit under this Provision and that those with a term of service which exceeds six years receive a benefit under the Decree Civil Servants Unemployment Benefits 1959.

7.18 PENSION PROVISIONS FOR CIVIL SERVANTS

Civil servants receive additional provisions for pensions such as those for old age, disability, widowhood, widowerhood and orphanhood. All these pensions are executed by the Civil Servants Pensions Fund (ABP). Those who became civil servants after 1965 have to earn a fixed minimum salary before they are included in the ABP. If people receive a benefit under the settlements treated in section 7.17, the benefit period counts for the pension rights. In the case of advanced retirement, this period counts for one half, whereas in the case of disability the period counts for the proportion for which one is disabled.

A person receives an old age pension (ABP–OP) on reaching 65 years. The level of the old age pension is determined by the term of service, the rate and the so-called middle sum. For the calculation of the pension, 40 years of service is the maximum which is taken into consideration. The rate is the proportion by which the term of service is multiplied. Generally, the rate is 1.75%. So, a term of service of 40 years or more generates an old age pension of 70%. The resulting percentage is multiplied by the middle sum. By and large, the middle sum equals the average salary during the two last but one calendar years before retirement or discharge. The middle sum is index linked. While civil servants also receive an AOW benefit, this benefit is built into the civil servant's pension. For each year of the term of service, 2% of the AOW benefit is built in. After a term of service of 40 years, this implies that 80% of the AOW benefit is considered to form part of the civil servant's pension and (s)he receives, on top of the ABP pension, 20% of the AOW benefit.

The civil servant who is fired for reasons of continual sickness or incapacity can claim a disability pension under the ABP (ABP–IP). The calculation of the level of the benefit is analogous to the old age pension: the term of service times the rate times the middle sum. This amount is compared with the amount which results from multiplying the middle sum with a proportion which depends on the degree of disability. The largest of the amounts will be paid as a disability pension. In view of the salary reduction on 1 January 1984, an extra allowance is now paid. For those who became disabled after 1 October 1976, the ABP–IP is a supplementary pension (to the AAW).

The widow of a civil servant, a former civil servant or a retired civil servant is entitled to a widows pension under the ABP (WP–ABP). The pension amounts to five-sevenths of the husband's pension or the pension he could have claimed. If the husband dies before he reaches 65 years, the widows pension is calculated on the basis of the term of service her husband would have served, had he reached the age of 65 years. If the widow remarries, the widows pension continues, but only includes the actual term of service. The divorced wife of a deceased civil servant can only claim a benefit if the divorce took place after 1 October 1971. Her pension is based on the term of service up to the day of the divorce. If the civil servant had remarried, the second wife's benefit is reduced by the amount the former wife receives.

A widowers pension (also ABP–WP) is paid if the widower's wife was a civil servant, a former civil servant or a retired civil servant, and if she was the breadwinner and the widower is at least 50% disabled. The level of the benefit is determined in the same way as for the widows pension. The orphans pension is similarly calculated. It amounts to one-seventh for semi-orphans and two-sevenths of the civil servant's pension for full orphans. Orphans pensions for a widower's children can only be claimed if the widower receives a widowers pension. The total amount of the widows, widowers and orphans pensions is never allowed to exceed the old age pension from which it is derived. An AWW or AOW benefit is built into the widows, widowers and orphans pension.

The pension premium is paid by employer and employee. The employee pays a fixed percentage of his or her salary diminished by a franchise. The premium payment, however, has to be at least a certain percentage of the salary.

With the exclusion of the widows pension for divorced women, the foregoing is completely incorporated in NEDYMAS.

7.19 THE CIVIL SERVANTS DEDUCTION ACT (IW)

The IW became operative in 1981. The IW aims at an equal treatment of civil servants and private employees for social security premiums. Civil servants do not pay premiums for the ZW, the WAO, the WW and the NWW and their benefits are financed from public funds. The IW corrects civil servants' income developments for changes in the premiums for these social security provisions to the extent that they are paid by the employees. The IW is completely included in NEDYMAS.

7.20 FUTURE PREMIUMS AND BENEFITS

In so far as the benefits are not based on the (former) income, we assume that the present legal regulations do not change. The gross–gross linking determines the gross minimum wage. It is assumed that the gross minimum wage changes according to the average wages. The net minimum wage is subsequently determined by reducing the gross minimum wage by the premiums for the different general and employee insurances and taxes. Next, this net minimum wage is translated into gross benefits. For example, for the AOW this means that the net amount is raised by the payable tax plus a part in the reimbursement of the costs of the health insurance [Huijser and Van Loo (1986: 52–55)].

Past premium percentages are known from NCBS (30). For the future, we have endogenized the premium percentages, with the exclusion of the ABP contribution rate, which has been held constant at the 1993 level. The sum of the benefits is determined by the model. Dividing this sum for each of the social insurances, plus a rise for administration expenses and mutual payments, by the sum of the concerning premium income, gives us the premium percentage. The rise for administration expenses and mutual payments between the several social insurances is based on the 1988 figures. These can be found in table 7.1. We also assume that the partial public funding of the AAW, AWW and AKW remains constant at the 1990 level.

Table 7.1 *Rise percentage for administration expenses and mutual payments*

Social insurance	Rise percentage
AOW	0.88
AWW	7.24
AAW	9.72
WAO	28.26
WW	22.34
ZW	14.04

Source: calculated from NCBS (1989)

In this, we assume that the maximum premium income and other income limits for the different insurances, the franchise for the WAO and the gross minimum wage change according to the average wages. This implies that we assume that the minimum wage and the benefits are indexed in the long run. It is also assumed that the state contribution does not change and that the division of the premiums between employers and employees remains unchanged. The premiums for the ZFW and AWBZ are held constant at the 1993 level.

PART THREE
Simulation Results

8

Lifetime income redistribution by social security

8.1 INTRODUCTION

In this chapter we look at the redistributive impact of the social security system on lifetime income in the Netherlands. The redistributional effects of the social security system are shown by looking at:

(a) The average lifetime wage and the average benefits from and contributions to the various social security schemes;
(b) The effect of the various premiums and benefits on the Theil coefficient;
(c) The contribution of the various social security benefits and premiums towards income per decile;

and

(d) The benefit–tax ratio per decile.

These four elements are given for the cohorts born in the years 1930–1935 (indicated by *cohort 1930*), 1936–1945 (indicated by *cohort 1940*), 1946–1955 (indicated by *cohort 1950*), 1956–1965 (indicated by *cohort 1960*), and for all persons living during 1970 (indicated by *year 1970*).

Before presenting the results, we repeat that income has been standardized using the equivalence factors in table 4.7. This implies, for example, that a one-year-old child in a household with two adults is assigned the same income as both adults.[1] Next, the resulting amounts have been transformed in 1990 guilders and discounted to 1990, using a discount rate of 2%. Moreover, persons who were involved in migration are not included in our calculations.

Further, we do not consider the results for the TW, IOAW and, to a lesser extent, the WRO and WWV, because the amounts involved are negligible in comparison with the other schemes.

[1] If one of these adults has an income of Dfl. 10 000, each of the household members is assigned an income of Dfl. 10 000 / 1.135 (the equivalence factor) = Dfl. 8810.57.

The calculations are based on ten runs with a different set of random numbers, all starting with a micro database of 10 000 persons in 1947. This resulted in the average number of persons belonging to each of the cohorts and the year studied, as given in table 8.1 (including the standard deviation).

Table 8.1 *The average number of persons (and its standard deviation) involved in the simulation*

	Average	Standard deviation
Cohort 1930	923	10.8
Cohort 1940	1 667	15.9
Cohort 1950	2 297	35.3
Cohort 1960	2 363	66.5
Year 1970	12 879	78.8

First, we look at the vertical redistribution. Then, section 8.3 considers the horizontal redistribution aspects. Finally, section 8.4 shows the effects of our choice of the income unit and the discount rate.

8.2 VERTICAL REDISTRIBUTION

8.2.1 The average lifetime income

Lifetime wages and social security benefits from and contributions to social security schemes are given in table 8.2. Lifetime gross wages (excluding employers' contributions) were on average Dfl. 2 903 600 for the cohort 1930, Dfl. 3 206 100 for 1940, Dfl. 3 445 500 for 1950 and Dfl. 3 460 300 for 1960. All persons living during 1970 had a lifetime wages income of on average Dfl. 2 927 300.

The foregoing implies that discounted gross lifetime wages for cohort 1940 were 10.4% higher than those for cohort 1940, that these wages for cohort 1950 were 7.5% higher than those for cohort 1940, whereas discounted gross lifetime wages for the youngest two cohorts hardly differed, the wages for the youngest cohort being only 0.4% larger. The average for those alive in 1970 is somewhat above the average for the cohort 1930 (about 1% more). We can consider employers' contributions to social security as a part of the employees' wages. So, we assume that the burden of employees and employers is shifted forward to household income. Therefore, we add these employers' contributions to the gross wage of employees. And this so-called employer's gross wage ('*super bruto loon*') will be used in the following as the starting point of our analysis.

Table 8.2 *Lifetime wages and social security benefits and premiums (in Dfl. 1000)*

	Cohort 1930 mean	s.d.	Cohort 1940 mean	s.d.	Cohort 1950 mean	s.d.	Cohort 1960 mean	s.d.	Year 1970 mean	s.d.
Gross wages	2903.6	89.2	3206.1	54.4	3445.5	44.8	3460.3	70.2	2927.3	36.3
Wages incl. Employers' contributions	3148.5	93.3	3466.7	56.0	3721.7	49.9	3719.3	76.8	3146.5	39.2
Employers' contributions	244.9	5.0	260.6	4.0	276.2	7.8	259.0	12.9	219.2	12.4
ABP	61.3	4.5	62.6	1.9	73.0	5.9	69.9	1.8	57.5	0.9
AKW	16.2	0.4	16.8	0.4	15.9	0.3	13.9	0.3	12.5	0.5
KW/KWL/KWBL	17.1	0.3	14.9	0.3	11.5	0.5	3.9	0.0	12.0	0.0
AAW	23.2	0.3	23.1	0.5	23.2	0.4	19.6	0.5	16.4	0.5
WAO	22.4	0.5	23.5	0.7	20.3	0.5	17.1	0.5	17.3	0.5
ZW	48.8	0.9	56.8	1.0	61.9	1.2	64.8	1.6	50.1	0.5
(N)WW	7.8	0.1	10.7	0.5	12.7	0.5	14.1	0.5	9.2	0.2
ZFW	19.2	0.6	23.6	0.5	29.6	0.8	31.8	0.4	22.3	0.5
AWBZ	29.2	0.6	28.7	0.5	28.2	0.4	23.9	0.3	21.9	0.3
Employees' contributions	337.1	7.7	446.5	10.5	573.6	5.0	705.7	26.4	440.6	13.5
AOW	166.5	3.3	209.2	3.1	261.0	3.3	326.1	4.3	206.6	2.5
AWW	24.0	1.1	31.0	1.1	38.2	1.9	45.6	2.0	29.0	1.3
AKW	3.7	0.2	3.3	0.2	2.9	0.1	3.0	0.1	2.9	0.1
AAW	10.4	0.4	19.0	0.5	30.2	0.7	44.2	0.9	22.4	0.4
WAO	35.7	1.1	53.7	1.5	72.5	1.3	86.5	2.2	51.2	0.7
ZW	10.0	0.0	12.6	0.5	15.0	0.0	17.3	0.5	12.0	0.0
(N)WW	11.6	0.5	16.0	0.4	19.7	0.5	21.0	0.6	13.8	0.4
ZFW	17.9	0.9	20.4	1.1	23.4	1.7	22.1	2.9	17.9	1.4
AWBZ	24.7	0.6	47.0	1.7	73.3	2.1	102.5	2.4	52.3	1.6
ABP	33.3	3.4	34.3	0.9	37.4	1.5	37.4	1.3	32.5	0.8

Table 8.2 (*Contd.*)

	Cohort 1930 mean	s.d.	Cohort 1940 mean	s.d.	Cohort 1950 mean	s.d.	Cohort 1960 mean	s.d.	Year 1970 mean	s.d.
Benefits	1012.3	23.7	1125.5	18.6	1177.8	16.3	1262.4	19.5	1021.7	0.8
AOW	369.0	9.9	365.0	6.8	341.7	8.0	344.1	9.6	367.8	5.5
AWW	29.9	3.9	33.2	3.3	39.2	2.4	38.1	2.9	29.5	1.9
AKW	70.0	2.8	59.9	1.4	57.1	1.1	100.9	2.7	56.6	1.3
AAW	94.9	3.8	110.8	5.3	119.4	2.1	133.5	5.0	90.7	1.8
KW/KWL/KBWL/KKZ/KTO	52.6	0.8	71.6	1.1	56.4	0.7	39.7	0.6	43.3	0.5
WAO	77.3	5.2	80.4	3.9	79.2	2.8	86.1	4.6	68.3	1.8
ZW/DSO	62.3	1.5	74.9	1.6	85.4	1.5	92.2	1.2	66.5	0.5
(N)WW	30.9	2.3	49.7	5.5	59.8	3.7	58.2	2.4	41.7	2.9
WWV	8.8	1.1	10.1	0.5	10.7	0.6	9.5	0.5	7.9	0.1
WRO	2.0	0.6	2.4	0.6	3.6	0.4	4.2	0.7	2.4	0.3
ABP-OP	72.6	12.2	73.8	4.4	89.2	6.1	102.4	6.3	76.8	2.1
ABP-WP	18.9	4.0	15.8	3.2	17.8	2.2	19.8	2.8	15.4	1.4
ABP-IP	57.0	10.5	66.8	5.3	84.2	4.9	90.0	5.1	60.3	1.9
ABW	65.8	11.1	107.4	7.6	134.8	8.3	142.7	8.8	94.1	2.2
Before tax lifetime income	3578.8	99.9	3885.1	52.5	4049.7	46.0	4017.0	70.7	3508.4	35.5
Taxes	1270.3	53.6	1295.2	29.8	1296.9	22.0	1278.0	25.4	1163.6	17.9
Net lifetime income	2308.6	52.8	2589.8	30.3	2752.7	30.9	2739.1	50.3	2344.6	22.5

Employers' contributions amounted to 8.4% of the (employees') gross wage for the cohort 1930, 8.1% for 1940, 8.0% for 1950 and 7.5% for 1960. Persons living during 1970 received an average of 7.5% of their gross wage as employers' contribution. The differences are, of course, related to governmental policy with respect to the financing of the social security system and to the year in which the various social security schemes were introduced.

To complete the picture we repeat that the AOW was introduced in 1957, the AWW in 1959, the AAW in 1976, the AKW in 1963, the ABW in 1965, the AWBZ in 1968, the WW in 1952, the WWV in 1965 and the WAO in 1967. Schemes such as the ABP, other family allowances, ZW and ZFW (ZFB) were already in existence when the first cohort entered the labour market. The employers' contributions to the ABP are almost constant: about Dfl. 68 000 for the four cohorts. The contributions to the AKW are about Dfl. 16 000 on average, whereas those to the KW/KWL/KBWL/KTO are decreasing. This decrease is caused by the abolition of these schemes in 1979. Employers' contributions to the AAW amounted to Dfl. 23 000 for the oldest three cohorts and Dfl. 20 000 for the cohort 1960. The cohort 1960 also contains the first group of persons who could apply for the AAW from the beginning of the scheme. The employees' contributions to the WAO increased gradually at first but then declined. The ZW contributions gradually increased from Dfl. 48 800 for the cohort 1930 to Dfl. 64 800 for the cohort 1960. The (N)WW contributions almost doubled and the ZFW contributions increased by about 50%, although the amounts were limited, Dfl. 14 000 and Dfl. 32 000, respectively, for the cohort 1960. For those living during 1970, it holds that the concerned contributions are comparable with the results of the first two cohorts.

These employers' contributions resulted in a lifetime employers' gross wage of Dfl. 3 148 500 for the cohort 1930, Dfl. 3 466 700 (cohort 1940), Dfl. 3 721 700 (cohort 1950), Dfl. 3 719 300 (cohort 1960) and Dfl. 3 146 500 for persons living during 1970. This implies growth figures which hardly differ from the growth figures for employees' gross wages: 10.1% for the cohort 1940 in comparison with the cohort 1930, 7.4% (cohort 1950 versus 1940) and – 0.1% (cohort 1960 versus 1950).

Employees' social security contributions are shown in the second panel of table 8.2. These are larger than the employers' contributions. The younger the cohort, the larger the difference. This, of course, is connected with the developments in employees' and employers' premium percentages. Employees' contributions amounted to Dfl. 337 100 for cohort 1930, being 10.7% of employees' gross wage, Dfl. 446 500 for 1940 (12.9% of employees' gross wages), Dfl. 573 600 for 1950 (15.4%), Dfl. 705 700 (19.0%) for 1960 and Dfl. 440 600 on average for those living during 1970, being 14.0% of the employees' gross wages. The AOW accounts for almost half of these contributions. The employees' contributions are Dfl. 166 500 for the cohort 1930 and the contribution increases to Dfl. 326 100 for cohort 1960. The next largest contributions are for the AWBZ and WAO, but they are considerably less, about a quarter to one-third of those for the AOW. The contributions to the WAO rise almost equally to those for the AOW, but the size is rather limited. It grows from Dfl. 35 700 for cohort 1930 to Dfl. 86 500 for the youngest cohort. The contributions to the AAW and the AWBZ increase even faster. The employees' contributions to the ABP are almost constant: about Dfl. 35 000 for the four cohorts. The same holds for the AKW with Dfl. 3000. The younger the cohort, the larger are the employees' contributions to the other social security schemes (ZW, (N)WW and ZFW). Again, it also holds that the employees' contributions to persons alive during 1970 are generally comparable with the results for the two oldest cohorts.

Next, we look at the lifetime social security benefits as given in the third panel of table 8.2. These successively amount to Dfl. 1 012 300 for the cohort 1930, being 32.0% of employers' gross wages, Dfl. 1 125 500 for 1940 (32.2%), Dfl. 1 177 800 for 1950 (31.3%) and Dfl. 1 262 400 for the youngest cohort (33.5%). Again, AOW benefits are the largest and are fairly constant, being about Dfl. 340 000 for the latest two cohorts. Cohort 1930 and 1940 have a somewhat larger benefit (Dfl. 360 000). This means that the proportion of the AOW in the total benefits declines from 38.9% for cohort 1930 to 30.7% for 1960. This is explained by the introduction of new schemes.

The AWW benefit equals about Dfl. 30 000 for the two oldest cohorts, whereas the benefit is somewhat larger for the youngest cohorts, due to growing differences in life expectations between men and women and to the extension of the coverage of the AWW to widowers. The AKW benefits grow between the oldest (on average Dfl. 70 000) and the youngest cohort (Dfl. 101 000). Here, the extension of the AKW to the first and second child from 1980 plays an important role, in combination with declining fertility. This role returns, but reversed, in the KW/KWL/KWBL/KKZ/KTO, schemes which were abolished on 1 January 1980. For these schemes, we first see an increase, followed by a fast decrease, leading to a situation in which the lowest level is reached by the youngest cohort (Dfl. 40 000).

For the disability schemes, it holds that the AAW continually grows, whereas the WAO differs only slightly between cohorts. For the latter we derive that deductions in benefits almost cancel out the fact that younger cohorts can claim WAO benefits for a longer period. By comparison, the AAW benefits rise from Dfl. 95 000 for cohort 1930 to Dfl. 134 000 for 1960. The AAW is the second largest social security benefit scheme on a lifetime basis. The ZW/DSO benefits are fast growing schemes, with an increase of almost 50%, reaching the level of Dfl. 92 000 for cohort 1960. The average ZW/DSO benefit is almost equal to the WAO benefit for the youngest cohort.

The benefits for the (N)WW also rise quickly: from Dfl. 31 000 for cohort 1930 to Dfl. 60 000 for 1950, but this seems to have stabilized. The WWV – abolished in 1987 – has little impact. It amounts to Dfl. 10 000 on average. The WRO benefits are even smaller. The ABP benefits are more important. Together, they are the second largest scheme, the largest being the AOW. The ABP–OP scheme is the largest of the three ABP types of pensions. The ABP–IP is a little less than the ABP–OP. Together they contribute Dfl. 192 000 to the income of cohort 1960, being 5.1% of their employees' gross wage. For the civil servants in this cohort the average benefit is, of course, considerably higher. The level of the ABW benefits is also fairly high. Lifetime ABW benefits amount to Dfl. 65 800 for the oldest cohort and grow very fast for the two successive cohorts. For the youngest cohort it equals more than Dfl. 140 000. However, we must keep in mind that the ABW benefits are somewhat overestimated. This is caused by the fact that income other than wages and other social security benefits – such as capital income – and wealth have not been included in the model. This absence of capital income and wealth causes an underestimation of total household income, and consequently an overestimation of the ABW benefit. Further, it must be remarked that the aforementioned amounts are gross benefits. The overestimation due to the omission of other income components is about 10%.

These employees' gross wages, employers' contributions and employees' contributions and benefits result in a 'before tax' lifetime income[2] of Dfl. 3 578 800 for cohort 1930, Dfl. 3 885 100 for 1940, Dfl. 4 049 700 for 1950, Dfl. 4 017 000 for 1960 and Dfl. 3 508 400 for those alive during 1970.

Lifetime taxes on labour and social security income amount to Dfl. 1 270 300 for the 1930 cohort. Cohort 1940 and 1950 pay a larger tax: Dfl. 1 295 200 and Dfl. 1 296 900, but the youngest cohort pays only Dfl. 1 278 000. The tax rate (defined as the quotient of taxes and before tax lifetime income) is 0.354 for cohort 1930, 0.333 for 1940, 0.320 for 1950 and 0.318 for 1960. For those living during 1970 this rate amounts to 0.332. The decrease in the tax rate can be explained by the developments in the Dutch tax system. The younger the cohort, the more the cohort gains from the tax reforms in 1990 (the Oort-proposals). The picture is distorted because we are not able to take into account various tax deductions (such as those mentioned in chapter 6, footnote 18), that were also affected by the tax reform and have had to compensate for the cutback in the tax rates.

The resulting net lifetime income amounts to Dfl. 2 308 600 for the cohort 1930 and increases to Dfl. 2 752 700 for 1950, whereafter it declines

[2] We call this **before tax** lifetime income, because taxes are not treated. The private pension premiums for employees are also not included. So, it can be defined as the employers' gross wage plus the net benefits of the schemes in table 8.3 plus the ABW, WWV and WRO benefits minus the ZFW and AWBZ contributions.

somewhat. Discounted net lifetime income was 12.2% higher for the cohort 1940 compared with the cohort of 1930, 6.2% higher for the cohort 1950 compared with the preceding cohort and 0.5% lower for the youngest cohort compared with the cohort of 1950. This implies that the increases in the net lifetime income is comparable with the growth in gross lifetime wages for these cohorts. What is remarkable is that net lifetime income is about 74% of employers' gross wages for all cohorts. So, the tax burden (with social security contributions included) hardly changed between the cohorts.

Table 8.3 *Net social security benefits (in Dfl. 1000 and 1990 prices)*

	Cohort 1930		Cohort 1940		Cohort 1950		Cohort 1960		Year 1970	
	mean	s.d	mean	s.d.	mean	s.d.	mean	s.d.	mean	s.d.
Employers' gross wages	3148.5	93.3	3466.7	56.0	3721.7	49.9	3719.3	76.8	3146.5	39.2
Net Benefits of which	430.3	17.0	418.4	8.1	328.0	12.0	297.7	21.7	361.9	12.9
AOW	200.3	8.2	155.9	6.2	80.6	6.3	18.0	7.2	161.2	3.9
AWW	6.2	3.8	2.0	3.2	0.9	1.3	−7.4	2.9	0.4	1.6
AKW	50.0	2.8	39.9	1.4	38.3	1.3	84.3	2.6	41.6	1.3
AAW	61.6	4.0	63.2	7.7	65.8	4.9	69.4	9.8	52.0	2.0
KW/KWL/KBWL/KKZ/KTO	35.5	0.9	57.0	1.1	45.0	0.8	35.9	0.5	31.1	0.3
WAO	19.2	4.9	3.1	4.6	−13.7	3.4	−17.6	5.0	−0.1	2.1
ZW	−7.0	1.2	−7.5	1.6	−8.3	0.8	−9.6	1.0	−6.6	0.4
(N)WW	11.5	2.4	23.4	4.6	27.2	4.3	23.5	2.2	18.8	2.7
ABP	54.1	14.5	59.5	8.2	84.8	9.3	102.6	10.4	62.0	2.9

The redistributional impact of the social security schemes is shown in table 8.3. The net benefit is the result of receiving benefits and paying premiums. The lifetime calculations have been executed using a real discount rate of 2%. Since this rate looks reasonable for the Netherlands in view of the long-term interest rate, the net benefit can be considered as a real gain from the system. In the terminology of Burkhauser and Warlick (1981) and Wolff (1991) the net benefit can be considered as the transfer component of the scheme under consideration. The total net benefit from the social security system amounts to Dfl. 430 300 for the cohort 1930 (being 13.7% of employers' gross wages), Dfl. 418 400 for 1940 (12.1%), Dfl. 328 000 for 1950 (8.8%) and Dfl. 297 700 for 1960 (8.0%).[3] The gain from the social security system is thus declining rapidly, especially in terms of the percentage of employers' gross wages. The decrease can be related almost completely to the AOW. The oldest generation gains Dfl. 200 000 from the AOW, but the gain for the youngest cohort is only Dfl. 18 000. These

[3] For the sake of completeness we remark that the net gain equals the difference between standardized social security benefits on the one hand and standardized social security premium payments on the other hand. We do not take account of the state contributions (financed via taxes).

findings coincide with the findings in Nelissen (1987), where the net AOW benefit was calculated in a different way.

Family allowances lead to a large net gain for all cohorts, but the gain is the largest for the youngest cohort. For that cohort it amounts to Dfl. 120 000, whereas the oldest cohort gains Dfl. 85 500. Here, we see the effect of the public funding of family allowances premiums in 1988.

The net gain from the disability schemes are, initially, also considerable. The net benefit from the AAW and WAO together are Dfl. 82 000 for the cohort 1930, but decline to Dfl. 52 000 for the cohort 1960. The gain from the AAW is positive for all cohorts, but the cohorts 1950 and 1960 lose on the WAO; their premium contributions are greater than the received benefits.

The net gain from the (N)WW is a positive one for all cohorts and fairly constant (about Dfl. 25 000) with the exception of the oldest cohort. The sickness benefits (ZW) give a negative result for all cohorts. Each cohort pays more premiums than are received in the form of benefits. This is caused by the large administration costs and the abolition in 1981 of contributions from public funds. The net effect from the AWW is very limited. It moves between a net loss of Dfl. 7400 for the youngest cohort and a net gain of Dfl. 6200 for the oldest cohort, but the trend is comparable with that for the AOW: the net gain declines the younger the cohort.

The pension scheme for civil servants, however, shows the reverse: the net gain is larger the younger the cohort is. The net gain for cohort 1930 amounts to Dfl. 54 000, whereas it amounts to Dfl. 103 000 for cohort 1960. The reason for this increase is the reduction in the ABP premiums, for political reasons, in the 1980s.

The average gain from the social security system for persons alive during 1970 amounts to Dfl. 361 900 which is in between the gain for the cohorts 1940 and 1950. The latter also holds for the greater part of the schemes and, if otherwise, the net benefit is of comparable size. The largest deviation occurs in the AAW and KW/KWL/KWBL/KKZ/KTO for which the net benefit for those alive in 1970 is less than for all cohorts. This is because part of this group paid contributions, but did not have a right to claim benefits for themselves or their children. For example, those born before 1890 received no benefit from the KW and related schemes for themselves or their children, if the mother was aged 40 or younger. This did not occur with the AKW, where the low or zero receipts by the elderly were compensated by the large net gain by young persons (who were not required to pay contributions).

8.2.2 The redistributive impact of the social security system

So far we have only looked at the redistributive impact of the social security system in terms of net gains or losses for the complete cohort and compared these gains and losses between cohorts. The next step is the analysis of the impact of social security schemes on income distribution. This is measured by means of the Theil coefficient. The results can be found in tables 8.4 and 8.5. The employers' gross wage is at all times the starting point for our comparisons. In table 8.4 we find the effect on the Theil coefficient for the employers' gross wage, plus a particular benefit or minus a particular contribution, whereas table 8.5 gives us the effect for the employers' gross wages plus the net gain from various social security schemes.

Table 8.4 *Redistributive impact of social security benefits and contributions (Theil coefficients, differences with respect to the Theil coefficient for employers' gross wages and adjusted redistributive impact)*

	Cohort 1930	Cohort 1940	Cohort 1950	Cohort 1960	Year 1970
THEIL COEFFICIENT					
Employees' gross wages	0.171	0.142	0.132	0.122	0.198
Employers' gross wages	0.161	0.133	0.125	0.116	0.192
CHANGES IN THEIL COEFFICIENT					
Benefits					
AOW	-16.4	-15.0	-12.4	-12.7	-17.2
AWW	-2.1	-2.0	-2.0	-2.2	-1.5
AKW	-4.2	-3.4	-2.6	-5.0	-1.9
AAW	-7.1	-7.6	-7.6	-9.1	-4.1
KW/KWL/KBWL/KKZ/KTO	-3.2	-4.1	-2.8	-1.9	-2.0
WAO	-4.0	-3.9	-3.4	-4.3	-2.5
ZW/DSO	-2.3	-2.4	-2.3	-2.6	-1.6
(N)WW	-1.1	-0.4*	-0.9	-1.2	0.0*
WWV	-0.4	-0.5	-0.5	-0.5	-0.3
ABP–OP	3.0	3.0	3.0	3.5	2.1
ABP–WP	0.6	0.4*	0.2*	0.0*	0.1*
ABP–IP	0.5	0.3*	-0.8	-1.3	0.2*
ABW	-7.5	-9.6	-9.8	-11.5	-6.1
General insurances	-25.8	-24.3	-21.3	-24.7	-22.0
Employee insurances	-9.8	-9.9	-8.7	-9.2	-5.5
All insurances	-35.3	-35.5	-32.5	-36.6	-27.8
Employers' contributions					
AKW	0.5	0.5	0.4	0.5	0.3
KW/KWL/KWBL	0.7	0.6	0.4	0.1	0.8
AAW	0.6	0.6	0.5	0.6	0.2
WAO	0.5	0.6	0.6	0.5	0.3
ZW	1.3	1.3	1.3	1.4	0.8
(N)WW	0.2	0.2	0.2	0.3	0.1
ZFW	1.5	1.6	1.7	1.8	1.1
AWBZ	1.0	1.0	0.9	0.8	-0.4
ABP	-1.0	-0.8	-0.7	-0.9	-0.7
Employees' contributions					
AOW	5.2	6.0	7.0	9.3	2.0
AWW	0.8	0.9	1.0	1.2	0.1*

Table 8.4 (*Contd.*)

	Cohort 1930	Cohort 1940	Cohort 1950	Cohort 1960	Year 1970
AKW	0.1	0.1	0.1	0.1	0.1
AAW	0.2	0.3	0.5	0.8	0.0
WAO	0.1	0.1*	0.3	0.5	– 0.3
ZW	0.3	0.3	0.3	0.3	0.2
(N)WW	0.3	0.3	0.4	0.4	0.1
ZFW	1.4	1.5	1.4	1.3	1.0
AWBZ	0.6	1.1	1.6	2.4	0.1*
ABP	– 1.0	– 0.8	– 0.8	– 1.0	– 0.6
All contributions					
AOW	5.2	6.0	7.0	9.3	2.0
AWW	0.8	0.9	1.0	1.2	0.1*
AKW	0.6	0.6	0.5	0.6	0.4
AAW	0.8	0.8	1.0	1.4	0.2
KW/KWL/KWBL	0.7	0.6	0.4	0.1	0.8
WAO	0.6	0.7	0.9	1.1	0.0*
ZW	1.7	1.7	1.6	1.8	1.0
(N)WW	0.5	0.5	0.6	0.7	0.2
ZFW	3.0	3.1	3.1	3.1	2.1
AWBZ	1.7	2.0	2.6	3.1	– 0.2*
ABP	– 1.8	– 1.4	– 1.5	– 1.7	– 1.1
General insurances	7.7	9.1	10.4	14.7	3.7
Employee insurances	3.8	3.8	3.9	4.0	2.2
All insurances	12.3	14.2	16.1	21.8	6.9
ADJUSTED REDISTRIBUTIVE IMPACT					
Benefits					
AOW	– 1.42	– 1.43	– 1.36	– 1.39	– 1.47
AWW	– 2.19	– 1.99	– 1.89	– 2.08	– 1.61
AKW	– 1.91	– 1.98	– 1.71	– 1.86	– 1.04
AAW	– 2.36	– 2.42	– 2.39	– 2.56	– 1.42
KW/KWL/KBWL/KKZ/KTO	– 1.93	– 1.99	– 1.87	– 1.85	– 1.45
WAO	– 1.66	– 1.71	– 1.62	– 1.87	– 1.14
ZW/DSO	– 1.17	– 1.12	– 1.02	– 1.08	– 0.75
(N)WW	– 1.09	– 0.30*	– 0.61	– 0.78	– 0.33
WWV	– 1.45	– 1.67	– 1.79	– 1.87	– 1.08
ABP–OP	+ 1.28	+ 1.40	+ 1.26	+ 1.30	+ 0.84
ABP–WP	+ 0.91	+ 0.88*	+ 0.39*	– 0.12*	+ 0.32*
ABP–IP	+ 0.21	+ 0.15*	– 0.37	– 0.54	+ 0.11*
ABW	– 3.67	– 3.17	– 2.72	– 2.96	– 2.06
General insurances	– 1.45	– 1.49	– 1.44	– 1.51	– 1.28
Employee insurances	– 1.39	– 1.25	– 1.17	– 1.25	– 0.85
All insurances	– 1.32	– 1.32	– 1.20	– 1.34	– 1.06
Contributions					
AOW	0.98	1.00	1.01	1.08	0.31
AWW	1.08	1.00	0.98	1.03	0.10
AKW	0.93	1.01	1.04	1.25	0.78
KW/KWL/KWBL	1.32	1.47	1.37	1.35	1.99

Table 8.4 (*Contd.*)

	Cohort 1930	Cohort 1940	Cohort 1950	Cohort 1960	Year 1970
AAW	0.69	0.63	0.70	0.79	0.19
WAO	0.34	0.32	0.36	0.38	0.01*
ZW	0.75	0.69	0.63	0.62	0.40
(N)WW	0.78	0.66	0.70	0.78	0.32
ZFW	2.54	2.46	2.20	2.16	1.66
AWBZ	0.99	0.94	0.94	0.97	- 0.07*
ABP	- 0.58	- 0.52	- 0.47	- 0.55	- 0.37
General insurances	0.98	1.01	1.11	1.23	0.36
Employee insurances	0.72	0.65	0.62	0.61	0.38
All insurances	0.95	0.98	1.00	1.15	0.46

* = not significant at the 0.05 level

The Theil coefficient for the employers' gross wages is 0.161 for cohort 1930, 0.133 for 1940, 0.125 for 1950 and 0.116 for 1960, whereas the Theil coefficient for all those alive during 1970 amounts to 0.192. Hence, income inequality within a cohort is considerably lower than for the whole population. Income inequality within cohorts decreases very fast. The Theil coefficient for the cohort 1940 is 17% less than that for 1930, whereas the Theil coefficient for the cohort 1960 is 7% less than that for 1950. The difference in income inequality for the cohorts 1940 and 1950 is about the same, the latter being 6% lower. This implies a decrease in income inequality in employers' gross wages of 28% between the oldest and youngest cohort.

The first part of table 8.4 gives us the impact of the social security benefits on the income inequality (as measured by the Theil coefficient). With the exception of the pension scheme for civil servants (ABP), all benefits have an equalizing effect. The AOW benefit has the largest effect, diminishing income inequality by 16.4% for the oldest cohort and 12.7% for the youngest cohort. The AAW also has a comparatively large effect. This benefit has an equalizing effect of 7 to 9%. In view of its contribution to the lifetime income, its effect is even larger than that for the AOW. In order to compensate the differences in the size of the schemes under consideration, we introduce the **adjusted redistributive impact**, which we define as the quotient of the proportional change in the Theil coefficient (with respect to the Theil coefficient for the employers' gross wage) and of the proportion of the scheme involved in the employers' gross wage. So, the adjusted redistributive impact of a scheme shows how much the scheme affects the lifetime income distribution, assuming that the scheme amounts to 1 per cent of employers' gross lifetime wages. In this way, the measure offers the possibility to compare the redistributive impact of the various schemes in a more sophisticated way, because it compares the redistributive impact under the assumption that the various schemes do not differ with respect to their size.

The adjusted redistributive impact of the AOW benefit amounts to about – 1.4%[4][5] for all cohorts, whereas the adjusted redistributive impact of the AAW benefit varies between – 2.3 and – 2.6% for the four cohorts. The WAO benefit has a somewhat less equalizing effect. It lowers the Theil coefficient, varying from 3.4% for cohort 1950 to 4.3% for the youngest cohort. The adjusted redistributive impact is somewhat larger than that for the AOW benefit.

The family allowances have a large adjusted redistributive impact. The AKW benefits result in an adjusted redistributive impact of – 1.9% for the cohort 1930, – 2.0% for 1940, – 1.7% for 1950 and – 1.9% for the youngest cohort. For the KW and related schemes we successively have – 1.9, – 2.0, – 1.9 and – 1.9%. The lower redistributive impact after cohort 1950 can be explained by the limitation of the AKW benefit to third and subsequent children up to 1980 and by the strong decrease in fertility for the generations born after about 1950. In terms of the Theil coefficient, the role of the KW and related schemes diminishes as a consequence of its abolition. After a decline in the impact of the AKW, we see an increase for the youngest cohort, probably due to the increases in the benefit per child in the 1980s.

The effect of the AWW benefit is limited, which is, of course, related to the fact that the average benefit is very small (*e.g.* Dfl. 29 900 for cohort 1930, being less than 1% of the before tax lifetime income). If we look at the adjusted redistributive impact, the effect is even larger than the AOW benefit. The AWW benefit is received by widowed women and their income is often less than the income of the aged, especially when young children are still living at home.

The effect of the (N)WW benefit on the Theil coefficient is very limited. Generally, the equalizing effect amounts to less than 1% and is sometimes not significant. The effect of the ZW/DSO benefit is somewhat larger, but remains less than 3%. The adjusted redistributive impact of the ZW/DSO and (N)WW benefits is also small. In both cases, the impact is lower than that for the AOW. The (N)WW has the smallest impact of both schemes.

By comparison, the adjusted redistributive impact of the WWV is proportionally large, varying from – 1.5% for cohort 1930 to – 1.9% for 1960. Here, we leave the WRO outside of consideration because of the very small amounts involved.

As we saw, the ABP benefits lead to an increase of income inequality. This is not surprising, given that the ABP–OP and ABP–WP benefits have a lower

[4] *E.g.* for cohort 1930 we have a benefit of Dfl. 369 000 and the employers' gross wages amounts to Dfl. 3 148 500 (see table 8.2), whereas the change in the Theil coefficient is – 16.4 per cent. So, the adjusted redistributive impact equals – 0.164/(369 000/3 148 500) = – 0.164/0.117 = – 1.42

[5] The negative sign indicates that the scheme has an equalizing effect. If the sign is positive, this implies that the scheme enlarges income inequality.

bound (generally 10/7 times the AOW or AWW benefit) but no upper bound. Moreover, the benefits are related to the wages earned during the last two years of being a civil servant and index-linked. The average adjusted redistributive impact for the ABP–OP benefit is about + 1.3%. The value of the ABP–WP benefit moves between – 0.1 and + 0.9%. The adjusted redistributive impact of the disability pension (ABP–IP) varies between + 0.2% for cohort 1930 and – 0.5% for 1960. So, for older cohorts the ABP–IP benefit enlarges income inequality, whereas it equalizes incomes for the younger cohorts.

The ABW – as may be expected – has a large redistributive impact. The Theil coefficient is reduced by 7.5% for cohort 1930 and by almost 12% for the youngest cohort. The adjusted redistributive impact is also very large.

For all benefits under the general insurances we find that the Theil coefficient decreases by about 25%, whereas the benefits under the employee insurances lead to a decline of about 10%. In terms of the adjusted redistributive impact we find that general insurance benefits have an effect of – 1.5%. For the employee insurance benefits we find equalizing effects of – 1.4% for the cohort 1930, – 1.3% for 1940 and 1960 and – 1.2% for 1950. The difference between both is, of course, caused by the fact that general insurance benefits are flat-rated, whereas the employee insurance benefits are wage-related schemes, but have a maximum benefit.

With the exception of the ABP premiums, all contributions lead to an increase of income inequality. One reason for this is the existence of a maximum premium income. By comparison, the ABP has a franchise as a consequence of the fact that the ABP benefits are reduced by the AOW and AWW benefits (chapter 7). Moreover, no upper limit exists. This explains its equalizing nature.

Excluding the AOW, all contributions affect the Theil coefficient only slightly: the premium payments raise the Theil coefficient by less than 3%. We find an increase in the Theil coefficient caused by the AOW of 5.2% for cohort 1930, 6.0% for 1940, 7.0% for 1950 and 9.3% for 1960. However, if we look at the adjusted redistributive impact,[6] we find figures that are more in line with those for the benefits. The ZFW has the largest impact. The ZFW contributions lead to a serious increase of income inequality. This can be explained by its maximum premium limit, which is lower than the limit for the other insurances, by the fact that (former) employees with an income above a certain level are not eligible to be insured (and thus do not pay premiums any more) and by the fixed amounts which have to be paid from 1989 onwards.

The former family allowances (KW/KWL/KWBL) also lead to a considerable increase of income inequality. Their impact is about two-thirds that of the ZFW, but larger than all other social security premium payments. This

[6] Now defined as the quotient of the procentual change in the Theil coefficient (with respect to the Theil coefficient for the employers' gross wages) and the contributions as a percentage of the employers' gross wages.

enlargement of income inequality is caused by the fact that the larger part of the premium contributors are employees who are, on average, in a lower income decile than civil servants and self-employed persons.[7]

The AOW contributions lead to an adjusted redistributive impact of about + 1.0%. The values for the AWW and AWBZ are of the same magnitude. This finding is what one could expect, in view of the method of finance, which is the same for all three schemes. Differences can be explained by the changes in the mutual ratio of the premium percentages in the course of time and by the different years in which the schemes came into force. Another reason for the difference between the AWBZ and the other two schemes is the Oort-operation which also implied a levying of AWBZ (and also AAW) premiums on the income of the aged.

Although the way in which contributions are levied does not differ for the AOW, AWW and AWBZ, the AAW and AKW show a different picture. The AKW leads to a much greater increase of income inequality than the other schemes. Here, also, changes in the premium percentage are considerable. An additional explanation is the public funding of the premiums. As of 1 July 1988 benefits are financed by public funds. Before that time, premium percentages were already declining, as a consequence also of the decreasing average number of children per female. This development implied that the contributions were comparatively high when income was low and the proportional contribution lowered as a cohort aged and, on average, earned a higher income. This effect increases, the younger the cohort is. For the AAW the reverse is true and the premium percentage has increased, which explains the somewhat smaller adjusted redistributive impact.

The effect of the WAO is a minor one. It is limited as a consequence of the franchise: low income earners do not pay WAO premiums. Neither can they claim a benefit. The other general and employee insurances have about the same impact. The adjusted redistributive impact is about 0.75. All general insurances together show a redistributive effect which increases from 1.0 to 1.2, whereas that for the employee insurances decreases and for the youngest cohort it amounts to about half the value for the general insurances. Finally, we see that the contributions to the ABP scheme form an exception and diminish income inequality.

For those living during 1970 we observe a somewhat different picture. We leave it to the reader to draw his or her own conclusions.

The net redistributive effects for the various social security schemes is given in table 8.5. This net impact is the result of the impact of both the benefits received and the contributions paid. The upper part, again, gives us the effect on the Theil coefficient. Most noteworthy is that the AAW reduces the Theil coefficient for cohort 1960 more than the AOW does. The AKW and WAO also lead to a considerable decline of the Theil coefficient.

[7] Recipients of an unemployment or a disability benefit generally did not pay premiums.

The effect of the former family allowances (KW and so on) is somewhat less, whereas the effects of the (N)WW and ZW are very limited. As we could expect, the ABP leads to an increase of income inequality.

Table 8.5 *Redistributive impact of social security schemes (Theil coefficient, differences with respect to the Theil coefficient for employers' gross wages and the adjusted redistributive impact)*

	Cohort 1930	Cohort 1940	Cohort 1950	Cohort 1960	Year 1970
THEIL COEFFICIENT					
Wages incl. employers' contr.	0.161	0.133	0.125	0.116	0.192
CHANGES IN THEIL COEFFICIENT					
AOW	− 13.0	− 10.8	− 7.4	− 6.1	− 15.7
AWW	− 1.3	− 1.0	− 1.0	− 0.9	− 1.4
AKW	− 3.7	− 2.9	− 2.1	− 4.5	− 1.5
AAW	− 6.4	− 7.0	− 6.8	− 8.1	− 4.1
KW/KWL/KBWL/KKZ/KTO	− 2.5	− 3.5	− 2.4	− 1.8	− 1.2
WAO	− 3.2	− 3.4	− 2.7	− 3.4	− 2.6
ZW	− 0.8	− 0.9	− 0.9	− 1.0	− 0.8
(N)WW	− 0.6	+ 0.1*	− 0.4*	− 0.5*	− 0.2
ABP	+ 1.5	+ 1.8	+ 0.7*	+ 0.4*	+ 0.9
Family allow.	− 6.0	− 6.2	− 4.5	− 6.2	− 2.7
AAW/WAO	− 8.8	− 9.3	− 8.6	− 10.5	− 6.0
General ins.	− 21.9	− 19.8	− 15.5	− 18.2	− 21.1
Employee ins.	− 7.1	− 7.3	− 6.0	− 6.4	− 4.7
Before tax lifetime income	− 26.2	− 26.7	− 22.1	− 24.8	− 25.5
THEIL COEFFICIENT					
Before tax	0.119	0.097	0.097	0.087	0.143
ADJUSTED REDISTRIBUTIVE IMPACT					
AOW	− 1.11	− 1.04	− 0.81	− 0.67	− 1.36
AWW	− 1.36	− 1.09	− 0.98	− 0.90	− 1.54
AKW	− 1.66	− 1.67	− 1.39	− 1.67	− 0.85
AAW	− 2.11	− 2.20	− 2.13	− 2.26	− 1.39
KW/KWL/KBWL/KKZ/KTO	− 1.53	− 1.71	− 1.60	− 1.72	− 0.92
WAO	− 1.44	− 1.47	− 1.27	− 1.50	− 1.17
ZW	− 0.39	− 0.42	− 0.38	− 0.41	− 0.36
(N)WW	− 0.62	+ 0.04*	− 0.26	− 0.34	− 0.17
ABP	+ 0.30	+ 0.40	+ 0.19	+ 0.08*	+ 0.21
Family allow.	− 1.56	− 1.65	− 1.48	− 1.66	− 0.85
AAW/WAO	− 1.62	− 1.69	− 1.62	− 1.79	− 1.20
General ins.	− 1.23	− 1.22	− 1.08	− 1.11	− 1.23
Employee ins.	− 1.00	− 0.92	− 0.80	− 0.88	− 1.23
All schemes	− 0.84	− 0.82	− 0.78	− 0.74	− 0.57

*not significant at the 0.05 level

The adjusted redistributive impact gives us more information and is shown in the lower panel of table 8.5. The adjusted redistributive impact has now been calculated as the quotient of the relative change in the Theil coefficient (with respect to the Theil coefficient for the employers' gross wages) and the proportion of the benefits as compared with employers' gross wages. This is because the benefits form the goal of the schemes and it is, therefore, rational to compare the change in the Theil coefficient with the size of the benefit. The contributions are levied into service of the benefits.

Most striking is the reduction in the effect of the AOW on income inequality. Its effect is less than two-thirds for the cohort 1960 compared with cohort 1930. In view of the large decline in the average net benefit (table 8.3), this decline is less than one would expect. The adjusted redistributive impact of the AWW is of a somewhat larger magnitude than that for the AOW. The other general insurances, the AKW and AAW, have a strong effect. The adjusted redistributive impact of the AKW amounts to about – 1.7%. The impact of the AAW is even larger and amounts to about – 2.2%. This implies that the adjusted impact for the AAW and AKW is considerably larger than for the AOW. However, the effect on the Theil coefficient is minor as a consequence of the limited amounts involved in the AKW and AAW (*e.g.* benefits are Dfl. 100 900 and 133 500, respectively and premium payments are Dfl. 16 900 and Dfl. 63 800, respectively for cohort 1960) compared with the AOW (benefits amount to Dfl. 344 100 and contributions are Dfl. 326 100).

The family allowances belonging to the employee insurances reduce the Theil coefficient by 1.8 to 3.5%. Its impact lowers from cohort 1940 onwards, which is, of course, related to its abolition. In terms of the adjusted redistributive impact, the effect is also very large, being about – 1.5 to – 1.7% and, thus, larger than the effect for the AOW. The adjusted redistributive impact for the WAO is about two-thirds of that of the impact for the AAW, whereas the reduction of the Theil coefficient by the WAO is less than half the reduction for the AAW, especially for the two youngest cohorts. The extent to which lifetime income inequality is affected by the WAO is comparable with the influence of the AKW (in terms of the adjusted redistributive impact) and, thus, also greater than those for the AOW. This is rather surprising, but in agreement with our findings in table 8.4. The ZW has hardly any redistributive impact; the Theil coefficient is lowered by less than 1% and the adjusted redistributive impact is also very small. The effect of the (N)WW is still smaller and also considerably less than the effect of *e.g.* the AOW or the WAO.

If we look at all the family allowances schemes together, we find a reduction of the Theil coefficient of about 6% for all cohorts. The adjusted redistributive impact is on average – 1.6% and the largest for the oldest cohort. The disability schemes AAW and WAO together lead to a reduction of 10% in income inequality as measured by the Theil coefficient. When speaking of the adjusted redistributive impact, the income equalizing effect is somewhat larger than for the family allowances. So, the disability schemes and family allowances are the most redistributive schemes.

The ABP is the only scheme in which the net benefit enlarges income inequality. The increase is limited and not always significant. The Theil coefficient is raised by 0.4 to 1.8%, while the adjusted redistributive impact amounts to a maximum of + 0.4%. We have to bear in mind, however, that the ABP is a private pension scheme and does not aim at a redistribution between (groups of) persons. However, the finance method includes some pay-as-you-go elements and these introduce the possibility of an income redistribution between generations.

All general insurances taken together lead to a reduction in the Theil coefficient of 15 to 22%, whereas employee insurances reduce income inequality by 6 to 7%. The adjusted redistributive impact of the general insurances diminishes from – 1.23% for the oldest cohort to – 1.11% for the youngest cohort. For the employee insurances this impact amounts to about – 1.0% for the oldest two cohorts and about – 0.85% for the youngest two cohorts. So, the impact for *e.g.* the totality of general insurances is less than the average value, which is, of course, because the individual schemes cater for different groups. These figures thus show that the redistributional impact of the general insurances is partly mutually compensated. This holds even stronger for the employees' schemes, of which the total effect is considerably lower than the average for the various schemes.

The before-tax lifetime income results from the employers' gross wages and the schemes discussed hitherto. The social security schemes lead to a reduction in income inequality of 26% for cohort 1930, 27% for 1940, 22% for 1950 and 25% for 1960. In terms of the adjusted redistributive impact, the redistribution is limited. Its value is between – 0.74 and – 0.84%. The decline in the income inequality of the before-tax lifetime income in the course of time is comparable with the developments in the Theil coefficient for employers' gross wages, albeit somewhat less. The difference between the cohorts 1930 and 1940 amounts to 18%, whereas income equality for the cohort 1960 is 10% less than that for 1950. Both cohort 1940 and 1950, again, have about the same income inequality.

To summarize, the social security system reduces income inequality in terms of the Theil coefficient by about 26% for the two oldest cohorts and somewhat less for the other two cohorts. This reduction is due, in particular, to the AOW, ABW and the AAW. The ZW and (N)WW have hardly any effect, whereas the ABP enlarges income inequality somewhat. If we look at the adjusted redistributive impact, in which the redistribution is corrected for the amounts involved, and as a consequence can be considered to show the **potential** redistributive impact, it appears that the ABW has the largest impact (varying between – 2.7 and – 3.7%). Next, the family allowances (both the AKW and the employees schemes) and the AAW have the largest income equalizing effect, being on average about – 1.6 and – 2.1%, respectively. The third group is formed by the WAO, AOW and AWW. The ZW/DSO has a somewhat smaller impact (– 0.4%). The (N)WW scheme follows with an impact of – 0.3% on average. Then we have the ABP scheme which has a small income inequality increasing effect. Finally, we have the ZFW and AWBZ contributions, of which the former has a large income inequality increasing impact. However, we do not know the distribution of the benefits of these schemes. So, it is not possible to give a definite answer on the net effect of these schemes.[8] [9]

8.2.3 Social security benefits and contributions by decile

We now discuss the third element with respect to the redistributional impact of the social security system, the contribution of the various social security benefits and premium payments towards income per decile. This is shown in figure 8.1. The deciles are determined on the basis of the employers' gross wages. In interpreting this figure we must realize that the premiums paid and the benefits received within a year are adjusted for household composition (section 4.4). For example, for pension schemes this implies that the standardized premiums are generally lower than the non-standardized premiums, whereas the standardized benefits are sometimes higher than the non-standardized benefits. This means that the pension premiums have been paid during a period in which the cohort's average household size is relatively large, whereas benefits have been received when the average cohort's household size is relatively small. This partly explains the fact that (standardized) lifetime benefits for the ABP pensions are larger than the (standardized) lifetime premium payments. We look at the effect of the standardization in section 8.4.

The relatively large role of the pension schemes becomes immediately clear in figure 8.1. Both contributions and benefits from the AOW – and to a lesser extent the ABP – rise high above the other schemes. The AOW benefits are almost equally distributed over the deciles. Only the first decile – which contains a relatively large number of people who die at a young age – gets a somewhat smaller average benefit. By comparison, we find that the higher the decile the more the contributions increase. The result is that for the higher deciles, there is a smaller benefit for the AOW net. The monotonic increase of the premium contributions by decile is also found for the other general insurances (AWW, AKW, AAW and AWBZ). The lower the decile, the higher the average AWW benefit, with the exception of the first decile in the cohorts 1940, 1950 and 1960. Widows are to be found more

[8] This will be possible after the NEDYMAS model has been further extended. See Nelissen (1991a).

[9] Because of the small amounts involved, we do not discuss here the effect of the WRO, WWV, TW and IOAW.

in the lower deciles than in the higher ones. There is a positive net benefit up to decile 6, whereafter, on average, the benefit is lower than the premium contribution. However, the differences are rather small. The lowest and highest decile have the smallest AKW benefit, whereas this benefit does not differ between the other deciles in the youngest two cohorts. For the older two cohorts, we find a somewhat higher benefit for the deciles 2 up to 6. An analogous development is found for the AAW. This scheme is very beneficial for the lower deciles. The net benefit for them is the highest, but one (the AOW). The net yield for decile 10 is negative: this decile pays more than is received via benefits.

The employee insurances show a somewhat similar picture, with respect to the KW and related schemes, to that for the AKW. However, for the other schemes some clear differences exist. This is partly caused by the structure of the benefits. The linkage of the benefit to the (previous) income is clearly illustrated; roughly, we find the higher the decile, the higher is the average benefit. This holds for the WAO and (N)WW benefits up to decile 6 or 7 and for the ZW almost generally. The average WAO benefit for the deciles 2 up to and including 8 is substantially larger than that for the deciles 9 and 10, whereas the differences between the deciles 2 up to and including

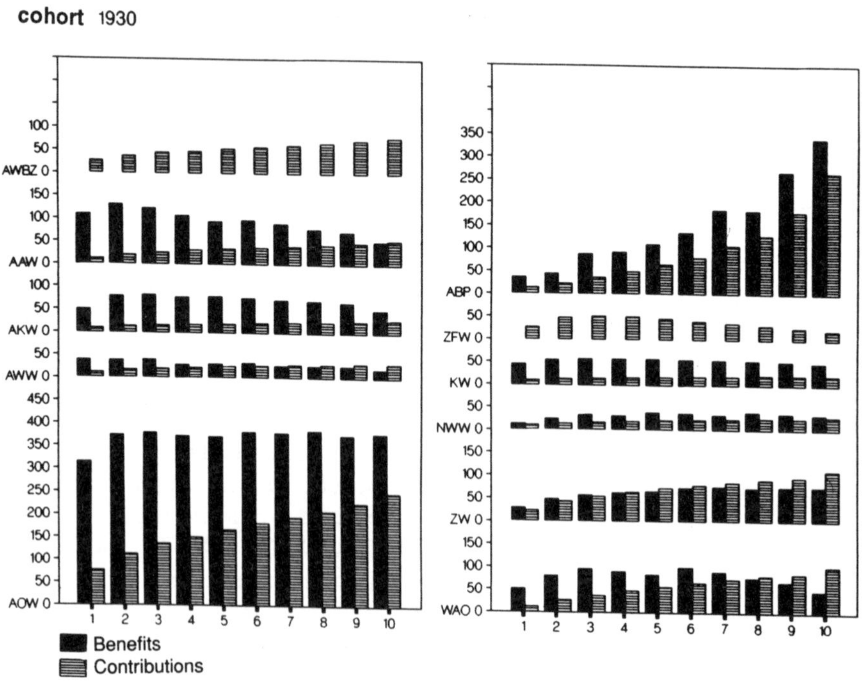

Figure 8.1a Social security benefits and contributions by decile: cohort 1930.

8 are rather limited. The younger the cohort, the faster the net benefit is negative. In the case of cohort 1930, decile 8 is the first one that pays more than it receives from the scheme, whereas this holds for decile 5 in cohort 1960. The (N)WW benefit is in the higher deciles somewhat decreasing, but the average benefit in decile 10 is about equal to the average benefit in decile 4. The (N)WW results in a positive net benefit for all deciles in all four cohorts. The ZW already results in a negative yield from decile 4 on. However, the loss is rather limited. The ZFW clearly shows the existence of an upper income limit. Premium payments increase up to decile 5 and decrease thereafter.

The picture for the ABP shows that the higher the income, the higher are both benefits and contributions. This is what might be expected, in view of the fact that the contribution is a percentage of the income, as is the benefit, whereas for both, an upper limit does not exist. The net benefit is postive for all deciles, but very small for the two lowest deciles.

The results for 1970 (figure 8.1e) are again comparable to those for the youngest cohorts. The exception here is the lowest deciles, which, of course, again contain persons who die at relatively young ages.

Finally, the results for the ABW are shown in figure 8.2. This scheme yields the highest benefits after the pension schemes (AOW and ABP). The ABW benefit is, of course, most beneficial for the lower income groups. But

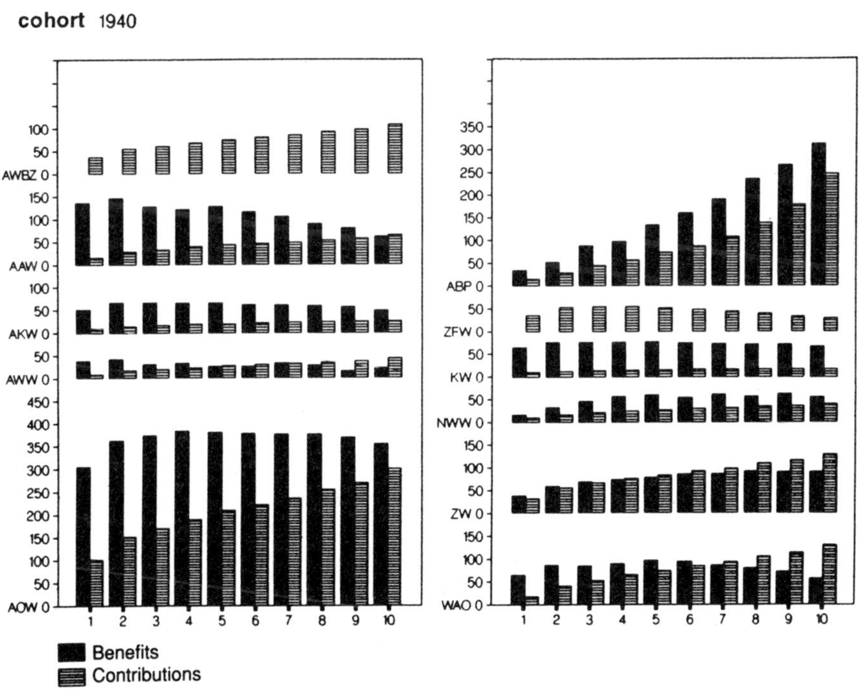

Figure 8.1b Social security benefits and contributions by decile: cohort 1940.

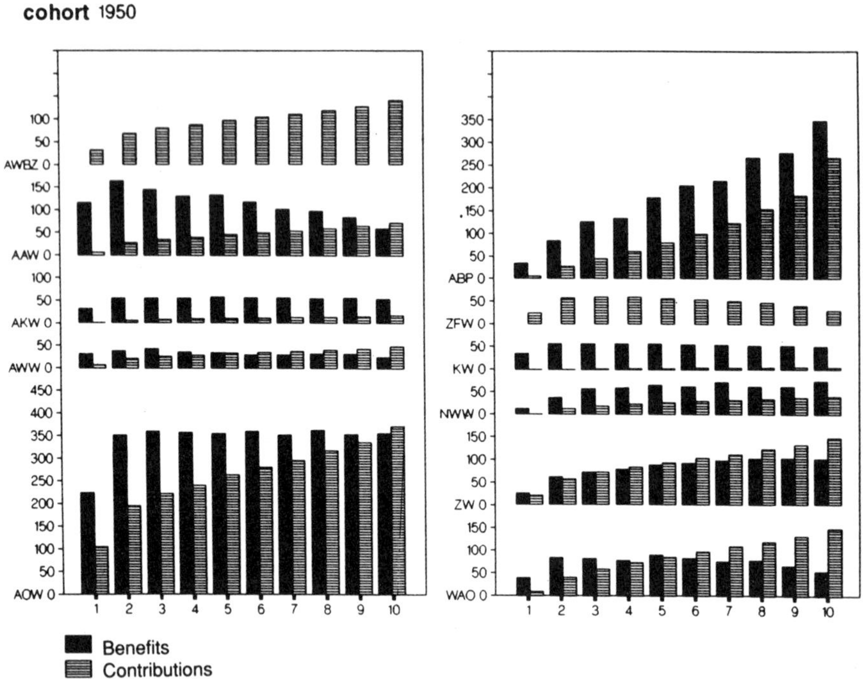

Figure 8.1c Social security benefits and contributions by decile: cohort 1950.

the higher deciles also get a substantial benefit from the scheme. This result is somewhat clouded by the fact that we overestimated the ABW benefit as a consequence of the absence of wealth and other income, such as capital income, in the simulation model.

The net benefits and employers' gross wages by decile are given in table 8.6. This clearly shows that the net effect of the social security system for almost all deciles diminishes in the course of time. The only exception is decile 1 in the youngest cohort. This group is better off than the same group in the foregoing generation. The social security system raises the income of decile 1 in cohort 1930 by about 74% of the employers' gross wages. The increase for decile 5 amounts to only 15%, for decile 9 almost 6% and for the highest decile the gain from the social security system amounts to 1%. In the case of the youngest cohort, decile 1 again receives a relative large gain from the system, 60% (in terms of the employers' gross wages), but for the other deciles the effect of the social security system is rather limited. The income after social security for decile 5 is only 10% higher than before social security. The deciles 9 and 10 experience a net loss, which amounts to almost 4% of the gross wages for decile 10.

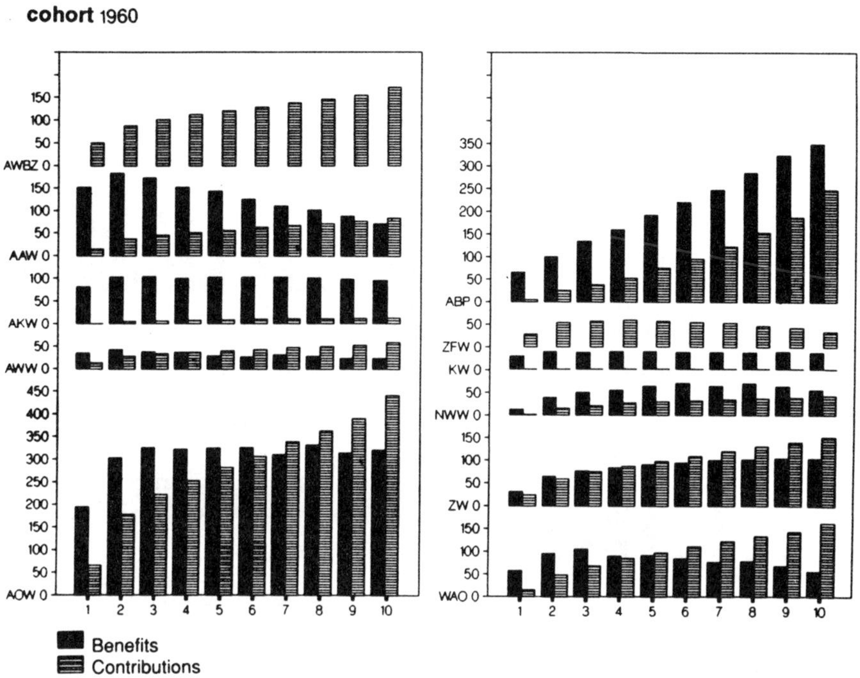

Figure 8.1d Social security benefits and contributions by decile: cohort 1960.

Table 8.6 *Net benefits and employers' gross wages by decile and cohort*

	Decile	1930	1940	1950	1960
Net Benefits	1	622	659	484	602
	2	605	599	583	576
	3	569	543	525	493
	4	516	498	394	371
	5	402	457	383	328
	6	420	385	291	231
	7	370	352	208	130
	8	286	282	184	95
	9	281	189	70	– 18
	10	74	– 12	– 82	– 209
Wages	1	835	1019	870	1000
	2	1441	1739	1901	1956
	3	1835	2164	2401	2462
	4	2213	2549	2848	2894
	5	2607	2936	3274	3302
	6	3016	3334	3719	3741
	7	3512	3817	4203	4237
	8	4117	4439	4810	4819
	9	5034	5308	5682	5631
	10	7331	7392	7737	7476

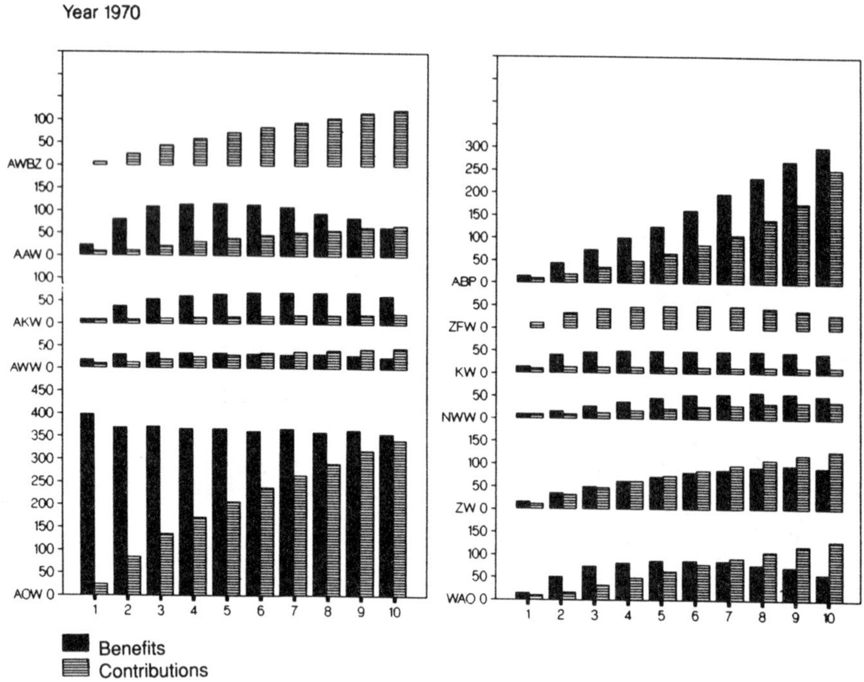

Figure 8.1e Social security benefits and contributions by decile: year 1970.

The employers' gross wage of decile 2 up to and including decile 8 is larger, the younger the cohort is. However, the deciles 9 and 10 of cohort 1960 have a lower wage than the comparable deciles of cohort 1950. The lowest

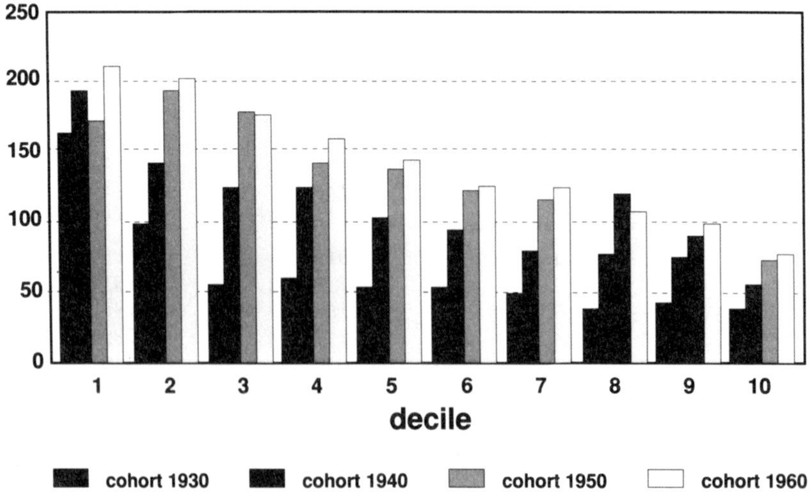

Figure 8.2 ABW benefits by decile: cohort 1930, 1940, 1950 and 1960.

decile exhibits a somewhat different picture. If we look at the ratio of the wages in decile 10 and decile 2, we see that this ratio is lower, the younger the cohort is. It amounts to 5.1 for cohort 1930, 4.3 for 1940, 4.1 for 1950 and 3.8 for 1960. After social security, these ratios are as follows: 2.7 for cohort 1930, 2.5 for both 1940 and 1950 and 2.4 for the youngest cohort. Here, we also see that the redistributive impact of the social security system reduces over time.

8.2.4 The benefit–tax ratio

From the figures underlying figure 8.1 we can derive benefit–tax ratios (defined as the quotient of the social security benefits on the one hand and the social security contributions on the other hand). These are given for each income decile and for the total population, both for the four cohorts and 1970, in table 8.7. We concentrate on the development within and between cohorts, because the benefit–tax ratio for the persons alive in 1970 is comparable to that of persons born around 1940.

For the total of all social security schemes involved here (AOW, AWW, AKW, AAW, WAO, ZW, (N)WW and KW and related schemes), the benefit–tax ratio decreases. For cohort 1930, the benefit–tax ratio amounts to 1.91, for 1940 1.67, for 1950 1.38 and for 1960 1.27. This means that the cohort 1930 gets Dfl. 1.91 for each Dutch guilder invested in the social security system, so that the net gain amounts 91%, whereas this is only 27% for the cohort 1960. The largest reduction takes place between the cohorts 1940 and 1950 with a decrease of 17%. The cohorts 1940 and 1960 are confronted with a decrease of 13 and 8%, respectively, compared with their preceding cohort. The lower benefit–tax ratio for cohort 1940 compared with cohort 1930 is entirely due to the general insurances. This benefit–tax ratio declines by 19%, whereas that for the employee insurances is almost constant. For the cohort with the largest decrease in the total benefit–tax ratio (cohort 1950), the decrease via the general insurances is about twice that of the employee insurances: 20 and 11%, respectively. The drop in the ratio for the youngest cohort is the result of a decline of 9% for the general insurances and a decline of 8% for the employee insurances.

Comparing the results for cohort 1960 with those of cohort 1930 shows that the benefit–tax ratio for all insurances decreased by 34%. For the general insurances the decline amounts to 41% and for employee insurances 18%. As a result of this, the benefit–tax ratios of both types of insurances do not show any more serious differences. For the youngest cohort the benefit–tax ratio for the general insurances is 1.36 and for the employee insurances 1.11, being 18% less. For the cohort 1930 the benefit–tax ratios amount to 2.29 and 1.35 respectively, so that the latter is 41% less.

This decline is reflected in the development in the benefit–tax ratio for the various schemes. The benefit–tax ratio for the AOW declines steeply,

Table 8.7 *Benefit–tax ratios*

Cohort 1930	Decile 1	2	3	4	5	6	7	8	9	10	All
AOW	4.12	3.35	2.81	2.49	2.24	2.11	1.96	1.85	1.67	1.53	2.19
AWW	3.45	2.31	1.95	1.27	1.25	1.19	0.93	0.90	0.81	0.59	1.26
AKW	6.44	5.66	5.01	4.22	4.03	3.47	3.03	2.86	2.56	1.77	3.49
AAW	10.26	6.95	4.97	3.58	2.83	2.69	2.30	1.85	1.51	0.97	2.86
KW/*etc.*	4.44	4.18	3.86	3.42	3.19	2.95	2.80	2.55	2.46	2.28	3.07
WAO	4.73	3.10	2.62	1.92	1.49	1.51	1.22	0.94	0.79	0.46	1.33
ZW	1.27	1.12	1.04	0.98	0.90	0.92	0.89	0.80	0.78	0.67	0.88
(N)WW	2.10	2.02	2.10	1.70	1.87	1.65	1.39	1.55	1.38	1.15	1.59
ABP	2.69	2.06	2.51	1.91	1.70	1.70	1.75	1.43	1.49	1.28	1.57
Fam. all.	5.28	4.95	4.46	3.85	3.61	3.22	2.93	2.71	2.52	1.98	3.29
AAW/WAO	7.32	4.93	3.76	2.75	1.96	1.93	1.53	1.20	1.04	0.65	1.90
General ins.[1]	4.83	3.91	3.19	2.67	2.29	2.25	2.03	1.79	1.63	1.40	2.29
Empl. ins.[2]	2.68	2.21	1.99	1.66	1.48	1.41	1.25	1.11	1.01	0.77	1.35
Total[3]	4.20	3.32	2.75	2.28	1.94	1.87	1.71	1.50	1.38	1.14	1.91

Cohort 1940	Decile 1	2	3	4	5	6	7	8	9	10	All
AOW	3.01	2.39	2.19	2.04	1.82	1.71	1.60	1.48	1.38	1.19	1.75
AWW	2.57	1.84	1.34	1.30	0.96	0.93	1.03	0.86	0.56	0.62	1.07
AKW	5.33	4.30	3.89	3.47	3.18	2.84	2.70	2.43	2.29	1.78	2.98
AAW	8.83	5.23	3.96	3.11	3.00	2.52	2.18	1.67	1.40	0.96	2.62
KW/*etc.*	6.40	6.20	5.62	5.20	4.98	4.73	4.47	4.20	4.15	3.82	4.85
WAO	3.69	2.18	1.62	1.38	1.29	1.12	0.93	0.75	0.63	0.43	1.04
ZW	1.26	1.07	1.03	0.97	0.93	0.93	0.87	0.83	0.78	0.70	0.89
(N)WW	1.81	1.98	2.17	2.32	2.25	1.83	1.95	1.62	1.74	1.38	1.88
ABP	2.34	1.80	1.99	1.75	1.83	1.86	1.78	1.70	1.49	1.27	1.61
Fam. all.	5.88	5.13	4.67	4.23	3.95	3.64	3.43	3.16	2.92	2.56	3.76
AAW/WAO	6.39	3.51	2.52	1.94	1.96	1.61	1.38	1.08	0.88	0.61	1.61

Table 8.7 (*Contd.*)

General ins.	3.83	2.74	2.39	2.23	1.97	1.80	1.67	1.55	1.35	1.14	1.87
Empl. ins.	2.77	2.13	1.81	1.64	1.55	1.39	1.28	1.12	1.05	0.85	1.36
Total	3.52	2.54	2.16	2.00	1.82	1.63	1.50	1.38	1.23	1.00	1.67

Cohort 1950	Decile 1	2	3	4	5	6	7	8	9	10	All
AOW	2.15	1.81	1.62	1.49	1.35	1.29	1.19	1.14	1.05	0.96	1.31
AWW	2.43	1.51	1.46	1.20	1.05	0.87	0.85	0.83	0.78	0.60	1.02
AKW	5.06	3.96	3.59	3.33	3.21	3.00	2.84	2.64	2.55	2.30	3.06
AAW	7.34	4.59	3.43	2.78	2.51	2.09	1.75	1.55	1.26	0.85	2.23
KW/*etc.*	6.99	6.31	5.67	5.18	4.98	4.71	4.42	4.33	4.14	4.09	4.90
WAO	2.57	1.82	1.33	1.05	1.03	0.88	0.72	0.68	0.54	0.41	0.86
ZW	1.17	1.07	1.01	0.96	0.96	0.90	0.89	0.84	0.80	0.70	0.89
(N)WW	2.35	2.07	2.35	2.09	2.07	1.81	1.91	1.58	1.49	1.54	1.85
ABP	3.20	2.62	2.53	2.06	2.12	1.97	1.70	1.69	1.49	1.29	1.68
Fam. all.	5.91	4.89	4.41	4.07	3.89	3.67	3.44	3.29	3.13	2.92	3.76
AAW/WAO	4.73	3.07	2.24	1.70	1.53	1.35	1.10	0.95	0.80	0.58	1.37
General ins.	2.78	2.21	1.93	1.72	1.58	1.45	1.31	1.25	1.14	1.00	1.50
Empl. ins.	2.32	1.83	1.61	1.40	1.35	1.21	1.12	1.03	0.92	0.82	1.21
Total	2.65	2.11	1.82	1.59	1.47	1.35	1.29	1.18	1.04	0.92	1.38

Cohort 1960	Decile 1	2	3	4	5	6	7	8	9	10	All
AOW	1.68	1.41	1.29	1.18	1.11	1.04	0.94	0.93	0.85	0.78	1.06
AWW	1.90	1.38	1.10	1.01	0.80	0.71	0.74	0.66	0.54	0.50	0.84
AKW	9.25	7.47	6.86	6.21	6.11	5.83	5.62	5.38	5.15	4.64	6.03
AAW	6.46	4.05	3.25	2.60	2.26	1.86	1.56	1.37	1.13	0.87	2.08
KW/*etc.*	14.94	12.55	11.21	10.84	10.45	9.80	9.39	8.95	8.78	8.70	10.15
WAO	2.63	1.79	1.47	1.04	0.94	0.78	0.66	0.62	0.51	0.38	0.83
ZW	1.19	1.08	1.01	0.96	0.93	0.88	0.85	0.80	0.77	0.71	0.88

Table 8.7 (*Contd.*)

(N)WW	1.88	1.88	1.88	1.74	1.82	1.87	1.62	1.68	1.49	1.24	1.67
ABP	5.12	3.05	2.94	2.66	2.37	2.20	1.95	1.81	1.69	1.39	1.89
Fam. all.	10.41	8.44	7.66	7.10	6.92	6.58	6.35	6.08	5.86	5.36	6.81
AAW/WAO	4.59	2.87	2.23	1.60	1.45	1.17	0.96	0.88	0.70	0.55	1.30
General ins.	2.51	1.97	1.73	1.51	1.41	1.29	1.19	1.13	1.03	0.92	1.36
Empl. ins.	2.20	1.72	1.54	1.28	1.21	1.12	1.00	0.96	0.86	0.74	1.11
Total	2.43	1.90	1.66	1.41	1.33	1.22	1.11	1.06	0.97	0.84	1.27

Year 1970	Decile 1	2	3	4	5	6	7	8	9	10	All
AOW	16.75	4.37	2.76	2.13	1.78	1.53	1.39	1.24	1.14	1.04	1.78
AWW	5.08	2.45	1.68	1.34	1.12	0.96	0.81	0.77	0.65	0.54	1.00
AKW	3.45	4.33	4.38	4.16	3.99	3.88	3.74	3.55	3.32	2.74	3.70
AAW	11.35	7.46	5.14	3.81	3.01	2.52	2.09	1.67	1.34	0.95	2.33
KW/*etc.*	1.92	2.96	3.45	3.70	3.82	3.95	3.95	3.82	3.94	3.55	3.57
WAO	5.07	3.16	2.31	1.71	1.37	1.10	0.93	0.73	0.61	0.44	1.00
ZW	1.54	1.12	1.06	1.01	0.97	0.95	0.89	0.85	0.81	0.71	0.89
(N)WW	2.55	2.08	2.09	2.06	1.96	1.96	1.78	1.72	1.53	1.36	1.77
ABP	2.08	2.40	2.22	2.05	1.94	1.93	1.87	1.66	1.52	1.20	1.69
Fam. all.	2.42	3.54	3.89	3.95	3.93	3.92	3.81	3.64	3.57	3.03	3.64
AAW/WAO	8.11	4.92	3.44	2.58	1.97	1.60	1.34	1.05	0.86	0.62	1.48
Gen. ins.	14.33	4.44	3.01	2.35	1.99	1.71	1.54	1.36	1.24	1.08	1.88
Empl. ins.	2.21	2.08	1.88	1.65	1.46	1.32	1.18	1.05	0.95	0.80	1.23
Total	9.32	3.59	2.61	2.10	1.78	1.56	1.39	1.27	1.12	0.98	1.63

1 AOW, AWW, AKW and AAW
2 WAO, ZW, (N)WW and KW and related schemes
3 AOW, AWW, AKW, AAW, WAO, ZW, (N)WW and KW and related schemes

the younger the cohort is – by 20% or even more between successive cohorts. In the case of cohort 1960 the benefit–tax ratio for the AOW is 52% lower than for the cohort 1930. The latter receives 2.19 times the premiums paid, whereas the former receives only 6% more than the contributions.

The decline in the AWW is particularly evident at the change-over from cohort 1930 to cohort 1940 and the change-over from cohort 1950 to 1960. The youngest cohort pays more for the AWW than will be received; the benefit–tax ratio amounts to 0.84.

By contrast, the youngest cohort has a higher benefit–tax ratio for the AKW than the oldest cohort. The ratio is 6.03 and 3.49, respectively, thus 73% higher. This is because the AKW is financed from 1988 by public funds. The benefit–tax ratio for the AKW for the cohort 1940 is about one quarter smaller than that for the cohort 1930. On the other hand the benefit–tax ratio increases, the younger the cohort is. It is almost twice that for the cohort 1950.

The total decrease in the benefit–tax ratio for the AAW is considerably below that of the AOW (the benefit–tax ratio for the youngest cohort is 28% below that for the oldest one), but the difference in the benefit–tax ratio is larger between the cohorts 1930 and 1940 than between the cohorts 1940 and 1950 and between 1950 and 1960; 15 and 8%, respectively.

For the individual employee insurances we find that only the benefit–tax ratio for the WAO declines. This ratio is 38% lower for cohort 1960 (0.83) compared with cohort 1930 (1.33). The WAO shows a declining benefit–tax ratio up to and including cohort 1950. This is partly the result of the reform of the social security system in 1987, when the wage-related benefits (ZW, WW and WAO) were decreased by 10 percentage points. Another reason is that these cohorts paid high contributions during the 1980s when the number of disabled persons was extremely high. The youngest cohort was less affected by this element. The cohort 1930 has the largest benefit–tax ratio. During the economic crisis in the early 1980s a relatively large number of persons in this cohort – and to a lesser extent in cohort 1940, which partly explains the differences between the cohorts 1940 and 1950 – entered the disability schemes [Aarts and De Jong (1990)]. The net benefit is negative both for cohort 1950 and cohort 1960. Their benefit–tax ratio amounts to 0.86 and 0.83, respectively.

For the KW/KWL/KWBL it appears that for the youngest cohort the benefit–tax ratio is twice that of the cohort 1950. Here, the abolition of this scheme plays an important role. The youngest cohort averages 19 years of age at the time of this abolition. This implies that the benefits earmarked for them as a child have been received (but, of course, not the benefits earmarked for their children), whereas premium payments can only be imputed during those 19 years on average. The benefit–tax ratio for the intermediate cohorts 1940 and 1950 is about the same size, both being roughly 40% larger than the ratio for the oldest cohort.

The benefit–tax ratio for the (N)WW is the largest, at 1.88, for the cohort 1940. This cohort made a relatively large claim on these schemes during the economic crisis in the early 1980s. The younger cohorts were also affected by the cuts in the benefit level and the changes in the duration of the benefit as a consequence of the adoption of the NWW. The younger the cohort the larger are these negative implications.

The ZW shows a stable pattern. These schemes do not imply intergenerational redistributions. Each generation has about the same net result, about minus 12% of the contributions. All cohorts pay more contributions to the ZW than they receive as a benefit. This is caused by high administration and transaction costs.

The ABP shows an equal benefit–tax ratio for the cohort 1930 and the cohort 1940, whereas the ratio rises for the other two cohorts. This is caused by the decrease in the premium percentage in the 1980s in order to limit public expenditures and to finance temporarily the rise in civil servants' wages (without additional costs for the government).

For persons alive in 1970 the benefit–tax ratio amounts to 1.63 and is thus of about the same size as for the cohort 1940. Generally, the ratio for those living during 1970 is of comparable size as for the cohort 1940.

In general, the benefit–tax ratio is larger as the decile is lower. Significant deviations occur for:

(1) The **(N)WW** with respect to the increase in the benefit–tax ratio from decile 1 to 4 of cohort 1940 and the difference in the ratio between decile 2 and 3 in cohort 1950. The latter is caused by the fact that the benefits fall behind and not because of high contributions. An explanation for this is the relatively large number of (unmarried) women in these lower deciles, who have, on average, a lower benefit–tax ratio for the (N)WW (section 8.3.1 and 8.3.2).
(2) The **ABP** results in a relatively low benefit–tax ratio for decile 2 of the cohorts 1930 and 1940. Here also, the over-representation of unmarried women is a partial explanation.

Most striking when comparing the benefit–tax ratio by deciles is the low ratio for the disability schemes (AAW and WAO) and, to a lesser extent, the AWW for decile 10. For example, in cohort 1960 this decile receives only 87% of the contributions paid to the AAW, whereas the cohort as a whole receives more than double the amount paid in contributions. For the WAO this decile receives 38%, while the cohort's average amounts to 83%. By comparison, the lowest decile receives a relatively large gain from these schemes. This can be illustrated by comparing the benefit–tax ratio for the first decile with the ratio for the tenth decile. This proportion is the highest for the disability schemes. Decile 1 in cohort 1930 has a benefit–tax ratio more than ten times that of decile 10. This proportion decreases over time, but is still about 7 for both schemes. This proportion for the AWW amounts to almost 6 for cohort 1930 and declines to almost 4. The proportion for the AKW also decreases; from almost 4 for cohort 1930 to 2 for the youngest one. The proportion for the AOW declines slightly and remains above 2.15. The ABP shows the reverse picture. Its proportion increases from 2.1 to 3.7. The other schemes (KW and related schemes, ZW and (N)WW) are rather constant; their proportion varies between 1.31 and 1.90. Taking all the schemes together, the benefit–tax ratio for the first decile is 3.68 times the ratio for the tenth decile in cohort 1930. This proportion decreases to 3.52 for cohort 1940 and to 2.89 for the two youngest cohorts.

8.3 HORIZONTAL REDISTRIBUTION

This section treats the redistribution by social security schemes between various groups within the four distinguished cohorts. The following groups are considered:

(a) Sex;
(b) Marital status;
(c) Employment status at the age of 45; and
(d) Number of children.

8.3.1 Horizontal redistribution by sex

The equivalent household income components for men and women are given in table 8.8. With respect to the employers' gross wages we find that women's wages are lower. This is, of course, related to the lower labour force participation of female-headed one-parent families and one-person households compared with male-headed ones. With the exception of the youngest cohort, the differences between wages of men and women become smaller as the cohort becomes younger. The proportional difference for cohort 1960 is about equal that for cohort 1940. Standardized household (employers' gross) wages for women are 16% lower than for men for the cohort 1930, 14% for 1940, 9% for 1950 and 13% for 1960. By comparison, the net benefits from social security schemes (defined as the difference between the benefits and the contributions as given in table 8.3) are higher for women than for men. The women in the two oldest cohorts receive about Dfl. 310 000 more from social security schemes than men. The difference for the cohort 1950 amounts to Dfl. 273 000 and for the youngest cohort to Dfl. 259 000. As a result, differences in the income between men and women became considerably less after social security transfers. This now varies between 2 (cohort 1950) and 7% (cohort 1930). So, social security results in a redistribution from men to women. The younger the cohort, the smaller this redistribution becomes. The 'profit' – measured as the quotient of the difference between the net benefits for women and that for the whole group, on the one hand, and employers' gross wages of women, on the other hand – amounts to 5.4% for the cohort 1930, 4.9% for the cohort 1940, 3.9% for the cohort 1950 and 3.7% for the cohort 1960.[10]

Table 8.8 *Composition of equivalent household income by sex and cohort*

Cohort		Employers' gross wages	Net benefits	Income after social security	Taxes	Net lifetime income
1930	Men	3429	279	3708	1436	2272
	Women	2864	585	3449	1101	2348
	All	3149	430	3579	1270	2309
1940	Men	3719	266	3985	1398	2587
	Women	3204	575	3780	1188	2592
	All	3467	418	3885	1295	2590
1950	Men	3899	194	4093	1345	2748
	Women	3574	467	4005	1247	2758
	All	3722	328	4050	1297	2753
1960	Men	3962	178	4140	1363	2777
	Women	3458	427	3883	1188	2695
	All	3719	298	4017	1278	2739

The differences in net gain from the social security system are broken down in table 8.9. The gain is mainly due to the AOW, which is, of course, related to the longer life expectation for women. A second important scheme in explaining the difference is the ABW. Women in the youngest two cohorts receive over Dfl. 100 000 more than men. For the oldest generation the relative gain is about half that amount. The next important scheme with respect to the difference between men and women is the AWW. Women receive more benefits than men from this scheme. The later even have a loss, varying between Dfl. 13 000 and Dfl. 17 000 for the various cohorts. Here also, differences in death rates play an important role. Also important is the fact that until recently men could not claim a widower's benefit. This also explains why the difference in net gain from the social security system between men and women is smaller for the younger cohorts than for the older ones. The older cohorts show a modest gain from the AKW and KW and related schemes for women, whereas for the younger generations there are no significant differences. Here, the explanation is found in the presence of relatively more one-parent families with a woman rather than a man as head of the family. For the older cohorts widowhood plays a more import-

[10] Because we emphasize redistribution by means of social security, we will also mention the level of the taxes and net lifetime income in the relevant tables, but will not go into it further.

ant role than for the younger cohorts, whereas divorce is relatively more relevant for the latter. We find also that because men spend, on average, a longer period in the educational process, the benefit received as a child will be larger for men than for women.

Women gain less from the AAW than men. The difference amounts to about Dfl. 12 000 in men's favour. This is the consequence of the lower eligibility rate for women. The WAO shows no significant differences in net benefits between men and women. Here, the lower average benefit for females as a consequence of their lower disability rate has been compensated by a lower premium contribution. The latter is caused by the average lower income of women in combination with the existence of a franchise. The ZW has hardly any impact. The (N)WW is more favourable for men than for women. This is especially relevant in the case of the intermediate cohorts. The conditions under which an (N)WW benefit is received do not favour women. On the other hand, the ABP widows and old age pensions favour women, while the ABP disability pensions favour men. Overall, this results in a higher net gain for women.

Table 8.9 *The difference in net gain from various social security schemes between men and women by cohort*

Cohort	AOW	AWW	AKW	AAW	KW/	WAO	ZW	NWW	ABP	ABW	Net gain
1930	174	50	11	−12	5	−1	2	−9	39	48	306
1940	152	44	16	−13	6	6	3	−29	46	74	309
1950	138	27	4	−12	−4	−1	4	−13	16	103	273
1960	125	17	−3	−11	0	−1	6	−3	18	102	259

Table 8.10 *Income inequality by sex and cohort*

Cohort	Within men	Women	Between	Total
employers' gross wages				
1930	0.144	0.174	0.002	0.161
1940	0.130	0.130	0.003	0.133
1950	0.131	0.115	0.002	0.125
1960	0.109	0.108	0.007	0.116
after social security				
1930	0.116	0.120	0.001	0.119
1940	0.106	0.090	0.001	0.097
1950	0.110	0.085	0.001	0.097
1960	0.090	0.078	0.004	0.087

The income inequality of employers' gross wages – as measured by the Theil coefficient – is shown in table 8.10. Total income inequality has been decreased by 28% between the oldest and youngest cohort. It appears that the decline for men was smaller than for women, 24 and 38% respectively, whereby the inequality of the groups in between has risen somewhat (from a little less than 1% of the total inequality to about 6%). Inequality within groups in the youngest cohort does not differ between men and women. The drop in women's income inequality is especially noticeable in the cohort 1940, whereas the decline in the males' income inequality occurs at two stages (at the transition from cohort 1930 to cohort 1940 and from cohort 1950 to cohort 1960, respectively).

If we look at the redistributive impact of the various schemes,[11] it appears that the impact of the AOW is about eight percentage points higher for women than for men, as is the case for all four cohorts. Taking men and women together, we find that the AWW scheme reduces income inequality. Distinguishing between men and women shows that the AWW decreases lifetime income inequality among women, but that the effect on men is absent or even slightly regressive (cohort 1940). The AKW shows hardly any differences in its effect on income inequality between men and women. The AAW leads to a larger decline in income inequality for men than for women and the (absolute) difference between both is greater as the cohort becomes younger. The relative difference remains about constant and amounts to 25 to 30% of the equalizing effect for the cohort as a whole. The result is that the general insurances combined have a larger income equalizing effect on the lifetime income of women. The difference is 38% (with respect to the equalizing effect for men and women together) for cohort 1930 and diminishes to 30% for the two youngest cohorts.

The KW and related schemes also do not show any significant differences between men and women. The differences in the equalizing effect of the WAO are limited. The decrease in income inequality from the WAO for females is about 15% lower than for men (on average 3.8 as opposed to 3.3%). The ZW shows almost no difference between both groups. The (N)WW scheme works more progressively for women than for men for the oldest three cohorts, but the differences are small (generally less than half a percentage point). However, for the youngest cohort we find that the (N)WW decreases income inequality for men, but increases income inequality for women. The ABP schemes lead to a larger income inequality and the increase is greater for women than for men. The difference in the income equalizing effect between males and females reduces over time, but is still present. The employee insurances combined (with inclusion of the ABP) result in a decrease of income inequality which does not differ between men and women in the cohorts 1930, 1940 and 1950. In the youngest cohort, however, the income equalizing effect is somewhat larger for men than for women.

The ABW shows a redistributive impact that is about eight percentage points higher for women than for men in all cohorts. The ABW diminishes

[11] The relevant figures are not presented here. Tables are available from the author on request.

female income inequality as measured by the Theil coefficient by 11.7% (cohort 1930) to 15.3% (cohort 1960).

All of the aforementioned schemes together result in a larger income equalizing effect for women than for men, but the difference between both groups is reducing. Social security decreased the Theil coefficient by 19.4% for men and 31.0% for women in cohort 1930, so that the Theil coefficient amounted to 0.116 and 0.120, respectively. For 1960, we find a 17.4% and a 27.8% decrease in the Theil coefficient as a consequence of social security benefits and contributions.

The differences in the benefit–tax ratio between men and women reflect the redistributions between both. So, the benefit–tax ratio for the AOW is considerably higher for women than for men. Whereas the benefit–tax ratio for the cohort 1930 amounts to 1.60 for men, it is 2.92 for women (the average value for the cohort is 2.17). For the youngest cohort the figures are 1.29 for women, 0.85 for men and 1.06 for both groups together. This implies that the difference is getting smaller over time. This can be largely explained by the increasing labour force participation of women, which means that they contribute more than in the past. For the AWW it will be clear that the benefit–tax ratio is higher for women than for men. Large differences in the benefit–tax ratio can also be found for the (N)WW and the ABP. The cohort 1930, in particular, shows a much larger ratio for the (N)WW for men (2.60) compared with that for women (1.67). For the cohorts 1940 and 1950, the difference is somewhat smaller – 1.83 and 1.93 for men, respectively, and 1.43 and 1.59 for women, respectively – but for the youngest cohort, the benefit–tax ratio for men equals that for women (1.64). With respect to the ABP, women in the oldest two cohorts have about a 45% higher return than men, whereas this amounts to about 20% for the cohorts 1950 and 1960. The family allowances show a larger benefit–tax ratio for women in the older cohorts, but the difference between men and women has almost completely disappeared in the youngest cohorts. The other schemes do not show significant differences between males and females.

Taking all general insurances together, we find that the benefit–tax ratio for women amounts to 2.96 for the cohort 1930, 2.39 for the cohort 1940 and 1.84 and 1.57 for the youngest two cohorts. For men the ratio is 1.78, 1.51, 1.26 and 1.21, respectively. Consequently, women in the subsequent cohorts receive 66, 58, 46 and 30%, respectively, more than men. Thus, women still gain more than men from the general insurances, but the difference is becoming smaller. With respect to all the employee insurances, there are hardly any differences in the benefit–tax ratio between men and women. The social insurances together result in a benefit–tax ratio which is, of course, higher for women than for men. These ratios are given in table 8.11. It appears that the ratio for men declined by 27% and for women by 39%, but the latter group still profits more from the system.

Table 8.11 *Benefit–tax ratio by sex and cohort*

Cohort	Men	Women	Total
1930	1.59	2.31	1.91
1940	1.43	1.95	1.67
1950	1.22	1.57	1.38
1960	1.16	1.40	1.27

To conclude: the redistributive impact of the social security system is greater for women than for men, and the difference remains about 10%. The employee insurances together have about the same effect for women as for men (only the cohort 1960 shows a somewhat larger effect for males), whereas the general insurances have a smaller effect for men than for women. When we look at the individual schemes, we find that the AOW, ABW, AWW and (N)WW have a larger redistributive impact on females in equalizing incomes, whereas the AAW and WAO affect men's income inequality to a larger degree. The ABP enlarges income differences and its effect is greater for women than for men. The social security system results in a redistribution from males to females. The AOW, AWW, ABP and – to a declining extent – the family allowances redistribute income from men to women, whereas the opposite is true for the (N)WW.

8.3.2 Horizontal redistribution by marital status

Here, we distinguish three groups: unmarried persons, who have never cohabitated; persons who have been married or have been living together and have not separated; and persons who have been married or have been living together and who have separated. To simplify matters, we will call these groups singles, married persons and separated persons, respectively. One difficulty is that the number of female singles in the simulation is small (54 at most). Therefore, we only report on this group for the youngest cohort. The equivalent household income components for the three groups are given for both men and women in table 8.12. If we look at the employers' gross wages we see that the wages for single men are larger than those for married men for the two oldest cohorts, but less for the two youngest cohorts. Separated men have the highest wages, with the exception of the oldest cohort. Single men from cohort 1930 have about a 19% higher lifetime wage than married men. For the cohort 1940 this percentage amounts to 4, whereas the youngest two cohorts show a 21% lower lifetime wage for single compared with married men. Women show a somewhat different picture. Single women have the lowest lifetime wages, followed by separated women, whereas the highest wages are earned by married women (with the exception of the oldest cohort, where separated women have a somewhat higher average wage income). The difference between married and separated women rises in the course of time. We attribute this to a multitude of factors and developments, such as labour force participation, partner's earnings (if present), duration of marriage or cohabitation, presence of (minor) children, and so on.

Table 8.12 *Composition of equivalent household income by marital status, sex and cohort*

Cohort			Employers' gross wages	Net benefits	Income after social security	Taxes	Net lifetime income
1930	Men	(1)	3929	175	4104	1998	2106
		(2)	3312	263	3575	1372	2203
		(3)	3881	427	4308	1538	2770
	Women	(2)	2914	590	3504	1120	2384
		(3)	2971	341	3312	1204	2108
	All		3149	430	3579	1270	2309
1940	Men	(1)	3808	185	3994	1549	2445
		(2)	3664	278	3942	1355	2587
		(3)	3945	256	4201	1524	2677
	Women	(2)	3390	568	3957	1265	2692
		(3)	2983	526	3508	1028	2480
	All		3467	418	3885	1295	2590
1950	Men	(1)	3109	115	3224	1088	2136
		(2)	3924	241	4165	1352	2812
		(3)	4206	118	4324	1447	2877
	Women	(2)	3746	483	4229	1399	2830
		(3)	3397	417	3814	1176	2638
	All		3722	328	4050	1297	2753
1960	Men	(1)	3169	95	3262	1108	2154
		(2)	4001	190	4191	1363	2827
		(3)	4249	196	4445	1489	2956
	Women	(1)	1238	315	1553	356	1197
		(2)	3733	440	4173	1313	2860
		(3)	3056	395	3452	977	2475
	All		3719	298	4017	1278	2739

(1) single
(2) married, not separated
(3) separated

Married women receive the highest net benefits from social security schemes. The married women in the oldest cohort receive Dfl. 590 000 more than they pay into the social security schemes. The net benefit for the youngest cohort amounts to Dfl. 440 000. Separated women receive the second largest net benefits and the difference with married women decreases from

Dfl. 249 000 for the oldest cohort to Dfl. 45 000 for the youngest one. The single women in the youngest cohort again receive somewhat less, almost Dfl. 315 000. The group with the smallest gains from the social security system are single men who receive, on average, Dfl. 142 500.

The profit or loss measured as the quotient of the difference between the net benefits for the group in question and the average net benefits (differentiated by sex), on the one hand, and the average employers' gross wages, on the other hand, is limited for men. With one exception (separated men from cohort 1930) the gain or loss is below 2.5%. For females, however, the loss can be much greater. For single females in the youngest cohort it amounts to 8.9%. There is also a relatively large loss for separated females in the oldest cohort. Single males, single females and separated women show a loss on average, whereas married persons gain. So, the social security system results in a redistribution from single men and separated and single women to married persons and, for some cohorts, to separated men.

The net gain with respect to the average for the cohort and how this is broken down are given in table 8.13. The AOW redistributes income from men to women. Separated men pay most, followed by single men. On average, married women receive most and single women the least, although the latter group shows strong differences between cohorts. This is probably due to the limited number of observations in the simulation. The AWW only shows a net gain for married women and for single women in the youngest cohort. All others will pay more than they will receive. This is, of course, inherent in the nature of the AWW. Separated men and women pay most and married men have the smallest loss. The AKW redistributes income from singles to married and separated persons. Married women have the highest relative return from the AKW (Dfl. 7000 above the average). The net gain for separated women amounts to only Dfl. 1000. The amount single persons contribute to the social security schemes is larger than the amount they receive from the system and their loss, as compared with the average gain, is considerable. The AAW is particularly favourable for separated men. They receive, on average, almost Dfl. 18 000 more than the cohort's average. Single men receive, on average, somewhat less, Dfl. 14 000. And this is especially paid by single and separated women (with a loss of Dfl. 38 500 and Dfl. 27 500 with respect to the average). Married men and women have about the same net gain as the cohort's average.

Singles and separated men receive less than the average from the KW and related schemes, whereas the other groups have a (relatively small) profit, which is the largest for separated women. The picture is comparable to that for the AKW. The picture for the WAO is rather capricious. On average, separated men have the largest profit, followed by single men and single women. This has been paid by married men and separated women. The role of the ZW in the horizontal redistributional process is considerably more limited than the aforementioned schemes. The average difference between

Table 8.13 *The difference in net gain (with respect to the average for the cohort) from various social security schemes for the various marital status groups*

Cohort			AOW	AWW	AKW	AAW	KW/	WAO	ZW	NWW	ABP	ABW	Net gain
1930	M	(1)	−102	−40	−74	16	−43	27	10	8	−48	−56	−265
		(2)	−101	−28	1	−2	0	−12	−3	3	−40	−21	−167
		(3)	−189	−56	−25	22	−14	71	9	−16	17	−23	−3
	F	(2)	110	39	10	0	4	2	−1	−2	58	−11	160
		(3)	123	−32	1	−23	11	13	9	−2	−207	121	−89
1940	M	(1)	−111	−28	−55	32	−28	20	−3	−3	−2	−92	−233
		(2)	−84	−16	1	1	1	−2	−3	3	−33	−29	−140
		(3)	−112	−39	−16	14	−1	12	−2	0	4	−31	−162
	F	(2)	89	33	13	−2	4	−5	1	−2	58	−17	150
		(3)	109	−28	−4	−34	7	−15	5	0	−104	173	108
1950	M	(1)	−86	−22	−31	1	−21	−14	−6	−5	−2	−118	−213
		(2)	−67	−10	0	2	2	−9	−3	14	−18	−36	−87
		(3)	−80	−24	−3	14	−2	19	−3	−3	28	−43	−210
	F	(2)	92	31	4	5	3	6	2	−9	47	−1	155
		(3)	73	−31	8	−28	4	−11	5	0	−70	171	89
1960	M	(1)	−75	−8	−15	8	−6	7	−4	−8	−26	−111	−203
		(2)	−37	0	4	3	1	−3	−1	12	−39	−37	−108
		(3)	−98	−24	2	21	0	−9	−8	11	43	−36	−102
	F	(1)	3	8	−51	−25	−14	32	11	−24	−129	144	17
		(2)	87	21	0	−1	1	0	1	−9	65	3	142
		(3)	71	−20	−1	−25	1	−1	6	−10	−87	160	97

(1) single
(2) married, not separated
(3) separated

the group with the largest net gain (single women) and the largest loss (married men) is less than Dfl. 17 000. For the AOW this difference amounts to Dfl. 199 000, for the AAW, AKW and AWW between Dfl. 50 500 and Dfl. 67 000, for the KW and related schemes. Dfl. 30 000 and for the WAO about Dfl. 34 000. Single and separated women have a net gain from the ZW, whereas married men pay relatively more. The NWW shows a redistribution from women to men. Single women pay most, whereas married men receive the largest amount on average.

The ABP results in a redistribution from separated women (– Dfl. 117 000 on average over the four cohorts), single women (– Dfl. 97 000), married men (– Dfl. 32 500) and single men (– Dfl. 22 000) to separated men and married women, who receive about Dfl. 20 500 and Dfl. 57 000, respectively, more than the average over all persons in the four cohorts.

The ABW benefits single and separated women. There is a slight loss for married women. Single men get relatively the smallest amount. Married and separated men get somewhat below the average.

Income inequality – as measured by the Theil coefficient – is shown in table 8.14. Income inequality is largest for single women, although we have to remember that the number of observations is very small. The same is true for single men. Here, the decrease in inequality is less than for single females (– 33 and – 49%, respectively). All groups show a decline in income inequality. The largest decrease occurs for single females, followed by married women (– 37%) and separated women (– 35%). Income inequality among married men declines by 31%. The smallest decrease is for separated men, 28%. Income inequality within the group for married and separated men and women is of the same magnitude as that for the youngest generation in the complete cohort (between 0.088 and 0.105), whereas that for singles is substantially higher. Inequality between the groups remains limited.

If we look at the redistributive impact of the various schemes, it appears that the redistributive impact of the AOW is especially large for separated women and to a lesser extent for married women. Single and separated men show a very small redistributive effect. For these men in the youngest cohort the effect of the AOW on income distribution is even positive, which means that the AOW raises income inequality within this group. The AWW diminishes income inequality only for married women in all four cohorts. The scheme is most regressive for married men and separated persons, especially separated women. For single persons, the AWW is progressive for the three oldest cohorts and degressive for the youngest cohort, although the absolute effect is very limited. The AKW hardly shows any differences in its effect on income inequality between the various groups in the youngest cohort, with the exception of single women, who show a lower redistributive effect. However, for the other cohorts the equalizing effect for married and separated persons is greater than for single persons. The redistributive effect is somewhat larger for women than for men. The AAW diminishes income

Table 8.14 *Income inequality by marital status, sex and cohort*

Cohort	Men within (1)	(2)	(3)	Between	Total	Women within (1)	(2)	(3)	Between	Total	Total between 6 groups m.s.	Total
employers' gross wages												
1930	0.325	0.127	0.146	0.002	0.144	–	0.155	0.156	0.003	0.174	0.005	0.161
1940	0.293	0.109	0.125	0.002	0.130	–	0.114	0.103	0.011	0.130	0.009	0.133
1950	0.329	0.104	0.100	0.003	0.131	–	0.103	0.091	0.005	0.115	0.006	0.125
1960	0.218	0.088	0.105	0.002	0.109	0.241	0.097	0.102	0.004	0.108	0.010	0.116
after social security												
1930	0.276	0.105	0.112	0.001	0.116	–	0.111	0.115	0.005	0.120	0.003	0.119
1940	0.268	0.085	0.102	0.002	0.106	–	0.086	0.062	0.011	0.090	0.007	0.097
1950	0.299	0.089	0.087	0.001	0.110	–	0.076	0.056	0.007	0.085	0.004	0.097
1960	0.190	0.065	0.090	0.001	0.090	0.212	0.072	0.063	0.006	0.078	0.006	0.087

(1) single
(2) married, not separated
(3) separated

inequality within all groups. The largest effect is found for separated men, followed by married men and women, then single men and separated women. The effect for single women is the smallest. Consequently, the general insurances together have the largest income equalizing effect for married and separated women, on average 25 and 20%, respectively. The reduction in income inequality of married and separated men amounts to 13% and about 7% for single men.

The KW and related schemes also only show small differences between the various groups in the youngest cohort. For the other cohorts, we find that the equalizing effect is somewhat larger for married and separated persons than for single ones. The effect is always somewhat larger for women than for men in comparable groups. At present, the largest effect is for separated women, on average 3.4%. The differences in the equalizing effect of the WAO are also limited. The largest effect is found for separated men (on average a 4.8% decline in the Theil coefficient) and separated women (3.8%). The smallest effect is shown by single women (at an average of 0.4%). Income inequality for married persons declines by 3% by means of the WAO. For single men, the effect is somewhat less (2.3%). The ZW shows a smaller difference between the groups and has the largest impact on separated men (on average an equalizing effect of 0.95%). Single women show the smallest effect (0.3%). The change for the other groups amounts to around 3%. The (N)WW has a slight equalizing effect on men and married women. For separated women the (N)WW enlarges income inequality. The effect for married men and single women is ambiguous. The ABP schemes lead to a larger inequality among married women and separated men. For separated women and single men the ABP reduces income inequality. In totality, this results for the employee insurances (with inclusion of the ABP) in a decrease of income inequality which ranges from 6.3 to 8.6% for non-singles. For singles, the reduction amounts to about 4% for men and 2% for women.

The younger the cohort, the larger is the redistributive impact of the ABW. Its effect is very small for single men and rather high for separated women. The income inequality among the latter group decreases in terms of the Theil coefficient by 25.0% in the youngest cohort. For the oldest one, the impact amounts to – 15.7%. The redistributive impact for married women is about half this value (for example 11.0% for the youngest cohort). The figures for married and separated men remain below this percentage. Here, income inequality is diminished by 3.3 and 3.2%, respectively, for cohort 1930 and 8.9 and 8.0, respectively, for 1960.

The aforementioned schemes together result in a larger income equalizing effect for women than for men. Within these groups the reduction is the largest for married and separated women (about 26.3 and 35.7% on average, respectively). The reduction for separated males declines as the cohort becames younger. Married and separated men also show a large reduction (about 20 and 17% on average, respectively). The reduction is the smallest for single men, being 12%. The resulting Theil coefficient for the income after social security is shown in the lower panel of table 8.14.

Table 8.15 *Benefit–tax ratio by marital status, sex and cohort*

Cohort	Men (1)	(2)	(3)	Women (1)	(2)	(3)	Total
1930	1.42	1.53	1.45	2.32	2.46	2.25	1.91
1940	1.32	1.45	1.35	2.93	1.98	1.86	1.67
1950	1.13	1.24	1.21	1.60	1.66	1.44	1.38
1960	1.14	1.22	1.10	1.45	1.41	1.34	1.27

(1) single
(2) married, not separated
(3) separated

The benefit–tax ratio for the AOW is considerably higher for women than for men. And within these groups married men and single women have the highest return. Separated persons have a lower profit, but the differences are small. With respect to the AWW we find that only married women have a positive return on the premiums. All other groups pay on balance. The AKW and KW and related schemes, of course, result in higher net returns for married and separated persons. Single men and married women gain most from the AAW, whereas separated persons profit the least. However, the differences are small. The benefit–tax ratio for the WAO, ZW and (N)WW does not strongly differ between the various groups within the subgroups men and women. Larger differences can be found in the ABP. Here, married women gain relatively more than other groups.

For all general insurances together we find that the benefit–tax ratio for married men is somewhat higher than for single and separated men. Married women receive relatively more than single and separated women. With respect to the employee insurances we find that the differences are very small. This means that the general and employee insurances under consideration result in analogous conclusions as under the general insurances. These ratios are given in table 8.15.

To conclude: the social security system has the largest redistributive effect on married and separated women, whereas single men are least affected. The combined employee insurances have about the same effect for women as for men: they are more equalizing for separated and married than for single persons. The general insurances show the largest effect for married and separated women and the lowest effect for single men. With respect to the individual schemes, we find that the AOW, AWW and (N)WW have a larger redistributive impact on married women in equalizing incomes, the AOW, ABW, WAO and ABP on separated women, whereas the AAW, WAO and (N)WW affect separated men's income inequality to a larger degree (in reducing inequality). The (N)WW and ABP also reduce income inequality of single men by more than the average. The same is true for the (N)WW with respect to married men. A relatively low equalizing effect is present for the AOW and ABW with respect to single men, the AWW with respect to married men and separated persons, the AAW and WAO with respect to single women, the (N)WW with respect to separated women and the ABP with respect to separated men and married women.

The social security system is beneficial to married and separated persons. The most important redistributions occur in the AOW (separated persons to married men and single women), AKW and KW and related schemes (to married and separated women by all others), AAW (separated persons to single men and married women), ABP (married women for which all other groups contribute) and the ABW (which is beneficial in particular to single and separated women).

8.3.3 Horizontal redistribution by employment status at age 45

Here we look at the redistribution by employment status. Employment status has been defined as the labour market position at the age of 45. We distinguish four groups:

(1) employees in private firms and persons who became unemployed or disabled from the state 'employee'; (2) civil servants and persons who became unemployed or disabled from the state 'civil servant'; (3) persons who were self-employed at the age of 45; and (4) all other persons (*e.g.* housewives, housemen, early-disabled persons, unemployed school-leavers, but also unemployed persons who were once self-employed).

For the sake of convenience, we will call these groups employees, civil servants, self-employed persons and nonworkers, respectively. The equivalent household income components for the four groups are given for both men and women in table 8.16. Because of the small number of observations for women in category (2) in cohort 1930 and 1940, no figures are given for this group. With respect to the lifetime employers' gross wages we find that the wages for self-employed persons are, on average, the highest from cohort 1940 onwards. This holds both for men and women. It goes without saying that nonworkers have the lowest wages. Generally, civil servants have a higher wage income than the employees, which is in accordance with their higher level of education. Civil servants' wages are about 32% above those of male employees in the two oldest cohorts and about 19% higher than males in the two youngest cohorts. The difference between the wages of nonworkers and employees increases over time for males (from about 15% to 40%). The differences are smaller for females. The youngest two cohorts show a 14% lower lifetime wages for female nonworkers compared with employees.

Table 8.16 *Composition of equivalent household income by employment status, sex and cohort*

Cohort			Employers' gross wages	Net benefits	of which ABP	Income after social security	Taxes	Net lifetime income
1930	M	(1)	3218	280	19	3498	1375	2123
		(2)	4267	272	107	4539	1976	2564
		(3)	3943	235	48	4178	1123	3055
		(4)	2731	356	79	3088	1145	1943
	W	(1)	3701	459	16	4160	1474	2734
		(3)	3445	413	66	3858	1029	2828
		(4)	2648	631	−1	3279	1045	2234
	All		3149	430	54	3579	1270	2309
1940	M	(1)	3535	275	21	3810	1337	2473
		(2)	4680	302	171	4982	1989	2993
		(3)	4824	57	−3	4881	1481	3400
		(4)	2866	327	20	3193	1034	2159
	W	(1)	3358	527	69	3885	1209	2676
		(3)	3840	327	30	4167	1243	2924
		(4)	3072	628	92	3700	1175	2525
	All		3467	418	60	3885	1295	2590
1950	M	(1)	4001	160	36	4161	1318	2843
		(2)	4801	247	245	5048	1810	3237
		(3)	4880	130	35	5009	1679	3330
		(4)	2583	247	57	2830	911	1919
	W	(1)	3869	428	108	4297	1353	2944
		(2)	3610	320	131	3930	1069	2861
		(3)	3694	484	52	4178	1278	2900
		(4)	3312	497	88	3809	1191	2618

Table 8.16 (*Contd.*)

Cohort			Employers' gross wages	Net benefits	of which ABP	Income after social security	Taxes	Net lifetime income
	All		3722	328	85	4050	1297	2753
1960	M	(1)	4035	93	24	4128	1277	2851
		(2)	4781	340	377	5120	1853	3267
		(3)	5177	74	35	5251	1890	3361
		(4)	2468	314	52	2782	890	1892
	W	(1)	3698	430	164	4128	1253	2875
		(2)	3813	426	212	4239	1226	3013
		(3)	3840	260	54	4100	1277	2823
		(4)	3184	447	79	3631	1123	2508
	All		3719	298	103	4017	1278	2739

(1) (former) employee
(2) (former) civil servant
(3) self-employed
(4) nonworker

The net benefits from the social security schemes are highest for nonworkers in the oldest cohort, but in the youngest cohort, male civil servants profit most from the system. However, only ABP pensions are considered, whereas all other private pension schemes are not included. This means that civil servants' net gain is not completely comparable with the other groups.[12] If we adjust the net benefits for this, nonworkers have the highest return from the social security system. With the exception of the youngest cohort, the (adjusted) net gain for employees is only slightly below those of the nonworkers. Self-employed men get the lowest return from the system. Self-employed women also have a low profit on average. Employees are always better off than civil servants if we adjust for the ABP scheme. Further, we find that women have a higher net benefit in all four groups in each cohort.

The profit or loss measured as the quotient of the difference between the net benefits for the group in question and the average net benefits (differentiated by sex, see table 8.8), on the one hand, and the average employers' gross wages on the other hand, is generally limited. This measure – which can be considered as a measure for the relative gain or loss for a group – is, in absolute terms, at maximum 4.6% (the loss for self-employed women in the cohort 1940). Again, nonworkers have the highest profit, whereas civil servants and self-employed persons generally lose, with the latter showing the largest loss. Male employees generally have a slight gain, whereas female employees show a small loss.

The net gain with respect to the average for the cohort, and how this is broken down, is given in table 8.17. Because of their low income, nonworkers benefit most from the AOW in the sense that they contribute less than the other three groups. Employees in the two oldest cohorts also gain in relative terms from the AOW, just as do self-employed men in the cohorts 1950 and 1960.

Generally, civil servants are worse off; their net AOW benefit is smaller than for other groups. The AWW is beneficial to male employees, but the younger the cohort, the lower the gain. Nonworkers are best off in the youngest two cohorts. Self-employed persons have the largest loss. Among women, the AWW is most profitable to civil servants, but the employees' and nonworkers' return is slightly lower. The redistribution by the AKW over the socio-economic groups is very small. The same goes for the KW and related groups. The AAW particularly benefits male nonworkers and, to a lesser extent male employees. Again, self-employed persons both men and women pay the most. However, it must be borne in mind that a self-employed person who became disabled before the age of 45 is classified as a nonworker, whereas comparable employees and civil servants keep

[12] Other groups can also receive ABP benefits via other household members.

Table 8.17 *The difference in net gain (with respect to the average for the cohort) from various social security schemes for the various socio-economic groups*

Cohort		AOW	AWW	AKW	AAW	KW/	WAO	ZW	NWW	ABP	ABW	Net gain
1930	(1)	-81	-24	-6	9	0	8	-2	13	-37	-25	-150
	(2)	-117	-28	-4	-2	-11	-24	-6	5	49	-27	-158
	(3)	-104	-29	-7	-34	-8	0	8	-4	11	-19	-195
	(4)	-23	-34	6	85	6	-23	4	-17	-63	-8	-74
	(1)	94	32	-5	-19	2	-17	-1	-5	-17	-11	29
	(3)	64	14	6	-23	-11	-25	-7	-9	-23	0	-17
	(4)	91	26	8	2	5	6	3	-4	32	35	201
1940	(1)	-66	-17	-8	11	-3	11	-1	21	-42	-41	-143
	(2)	-98	-32	-5	-6	-5	-27	-9	-9	119	-50	-116
	(3)	-118	-35	-14	-58	-3	-33	-3	6	-67	-35	-361
	(4)	-52	-20	-5	39	-3	-23	-3	8	-43	+5	-91
	(1)	92	22	3	10	3	0	2	-14	9	-5	109
	(3)	23	-1	7	-43	-4	-17	-1	-12	-29	-12	-91
	(4)	80	24	11	-10	3	6	2	-15	33	63	210
1950	(1)	-68	-12	-3	7	-1	7	-3	16	-43	-55	-168
	(2)	-105	-11	-3	-9	-3	-7	-7	-5	138	-70	-81
	(3)	-51	-31	2	-51	1	-8	2	13	-46	-43	-198
	(4)	-39	-9	-2	33	-4	-6	3	-11	-33	-30	-81
	(1)	62	4	0	6	2	-1	0	9	20	11	100
	(2)	-2	30	13	-34	-4	-25	-5	-8	49	-8	-8
	(3)	120	24	5	-20	0	3	-3	-4	-29	63	156
	(4)	76	17	2	-11	1	1	3	-15	2	80	169

Table 8.17 (*Contd.*)

Cohort		AOW	AWW	AKW	AAW	KW/	WAO	ZW	NWW	ABP	ABW	Net gain
1960	(1)	−74	−15	5	−2	1	−2	−5	13	−58	−53	−205
	(2)	−87	−5	−1	−1	0	4	−7	−10	200	−61	42
	(3)	−64	−6	4	−65	2	2	0	−4	−50	−56	−224
	(4)	−2	5	−6	66	−3	−1	6	−14	−37	−21	16
	(1)	65	11	6	−4	0	−13	2	9	44	25	132
	(2)	38	19	−2	8	−1	−14	11	−10	79	7	128
	(3)	60	−23	−16	−48	0	12	−4	−14	−43	16	−28
	(4)	69	9	−5	−4	−1	9	4	−6	−17	83	149

(1) (former) employee
(2) (former) civil servant
(3) self-employed
(4) nonworker

their status. For the rest, we cannot discriminate between the various other female groups.

The picture for the WAO, is again, rather capricious. On average, male employees profit from the WAO. The same holds, but with a lower gain, for female nonworkers. Averaged over the four cohorts, the other groups lose. However, in the youngest cohort, there are no significant differences between the male groups, whereas self-employed women in the two youngest cohorts also benefit from the WAO. The differences for the ZW, again, are minor. Nonworkers profit to some extent from these schemes, whereas self-employed women and male employees and civil servants are worse off. The (N)WW leads to a relative gain for employees, whereas the largest loss is for nonworkers, male civil servants and self-employed women.

The ABP, of course, is beneficial to civil servants. Also female employee and nonworkers gain – via their partner – from the ABP. Nonworkers generally lose. Furthermore, the younger the cohort, the greater increase there is in the net gain. The ABW is beneficial to females, nonworkers in particular. Male nonworkers have a lower loss (and a profit for cohort 1940) than the other male groups, with respect to the cohort's average.

The income inequality – as measured by the Theil coefficient – is shown in table 8.18. Income inequality is the largest among nonworkers. This holds for all cohorts. It is clear that the diversity within this group plays a role here. Further, it is striking that income inequality among self-employed men in the youngest cohort is larger than for the oldest cohort. The between-group component of the Theil coefficient also increases among men. The largest declines in income inequality take place among male employees and civil servants (in both cases the Theil coefficient almost halves).

If we look at the redistributive impact of the various schemes, it appears that the redistributive impact of the AOW is especially large for nonworkers and self-employed persons, and that it is the lowest for civil servants. The redistributive effect of the AOW is positive for male employees and male civil servants, which means that the AOW increases income inequality within these groups. The AWW particularly diminishes income inequality for female nonworkers in the older cohorts. The AWW further shows an income equalizing effect for female employees (cohort 1950 excluded) and female civil servants. By comparison, it increases income inequality among male civil servants and, to a lesser extent, among male nonworkers. The AKW is more progressive among female civil servants, self-employed women and male nonworkers. The redistributive impact is relatively small for male civil servants, female employees and female nonworkers. The AAW affects female employees in particular, whereas the income equalizing effect for self-employed men and female civil servants is

Table 8.18 *The income inequality decomposed by employment status, sex and cohort*

Cohort	Men within (1)	(2)	(3)	(4)	Between	total	Women within (1)	(2)	(3)	(4)	Between	Total	Total between 8 groups	Total
employers' gross wages														
1930	0.148	0.120	0.070	0.211	0.005	0.144	0.129	–	0.134	0.180	0.004	0.174	0.007	0.161
1940	0.116	0.108	0.095	0.164	0.010	0.130	0.111	–	0.105	0.140	0.001	0.130	0.008	0.133
1950	0.106	0.090	0.101	0.187	0.010	0.131	0.105	0.075	0.105	0.122	0.002	0.115	0.008	0.125
1960	0.082	0.062	0.089	0.169	0.012	0.109	0.097	0.080	0.083	0.120	0.002	0.108	0.014	0.116
after social security														
1930	0.119	0.100	0.069	0.157	0.005	0.116	0.098	–	0.097	0.122	0.003	0.120	0.004	0.119
1940	0.092	0.093	0.089	0.133	0.009	0.106	0.083	–	0.075	0.096	0.001	0.090	0.006	0.097
1950	0.088	0.076	0.086	0.166	0.009	0.110	0.080	0.075	0.071	0.089	0.001	0.085	0.005	0.097
1960	0.066	0.049	0.077	0.129	0.012	0.090	0.069	0.050	0.062	0.089	0.002	0.078	0.011	0.087

(1) (former) employee
(2) (former) civil servant
(3) self-employed
(4) nonworker

small. Consequently, general insurances for men have the largest income equalizing effect for the nonworkers (on average 17% reduction in income inequality) and for employees (15%). The equalizing effect for civil servants amounts to 12% on average and the lowest effect occurs for self-employed men (8%). Among women, most affected are nonworkers and employees (both show a reduction of 21%). However, the effect on the two other groups is also considerable, an average of 19% for self-employed women and 15% for civil servants.

The KW and related schemes show only small differences between the various female groups. Among men the effect is somewhat larger, but the differences are small. The equalizing effect is somewhat larger for male nonworkers and, to a lesser extent, for employees, whereas the impact on self-employed men and civil servants is less than the average. The WAO has a relatively large impact on employees, whereas the redistributive impact for self-employed men is limited and is positive in the case of the oldest cohort. This implies an increase in income inequality due to the WAO. The ZW schemes result in a decrease in income inequality, which is the largest among employees and civil servants, whereas the effect is slight among nonworkers and self-employed persons. The (N)WW enlarges income inequality among self-employed men (by on average 0.9%) and male employees (0.5%), whereas income inequality diminishes for male civil servants (0.9%), female civil servants (0.6%) and self-employed women (0.5%). So, although some redistributional differences are present, they are very small.

The ABP schemes lead to a larger inequality among employees and female nonworkers. This also holds for self-employed men in the two oldest cohorts. For male civil servants and self-employed women the ABP reduces income inequality. In totality, for the employee insurances (when we include the ABP) this results in a decrease of income inequality which ranges from 7.5 to 8.2% for women. For men, the differences are larger. The reduction is the largest for employees and amounts to about 10%. The other three male groups show a reduction of about 6.5%. In particular, the ABW leads to a large reduction in income inequality among nonworkers. The decrease in the Theil coefficient of self-employed men is also larger than average.

The aforementioned schemes together result in an income equalizing effect, which is largest for self-employed women and female nonworkers (a reduction by, on average, 29%) and the lowest for self-employed men (9.3%). A relatively low reduction also holds for male civil servants (on average 17%), male employees (18.5%), female civil servants (19%) and male nonworkers (20%) against 25.5% for female employees. This results in a Theil coefficient after social security, which is particularly small for civil servants, whereas that for nonworkers is relatively high.

Table 8.19 *Benefit–tax ratio by employment status, sex and cohort*

Cohort	Men (1)	(2)	(3)	(4)	Women (1)	(2)	(3)	(4)	Total
1930	1.62	1.41	1.43	2.14	1.94	–	1.95	2.46	1.91
1940	1.49	1.24	1.11	1.67	1.91	–	1.56	2.03	1.67
1950	1.23	1.07	1.14	1.44	1.52	1.32	1.70	1.62	1.38
1960	1.12	1.09	1.06	1.51	1.39	1.34	1.25	1.46	1.27

(1) (former) employee
(2) (former) civil servant
(3) self-employed
(4) nonworker

The benefit–tax ratio for the AOW gives nonworkers the highest return and civil servants the lowest profit, but the differences are small. With respect to the AWW female nonworkers and employees have a slightly higher ratio than female nonworkers, whereas self-employed men have a lower return than the other male groups. The AKW results in higher net returns for nonworkers. The other groups show a fairly equal benefit–tax ratio. Nonworkers also gain most from the AAW, whereas self-employed persons have the lowest profit. The KW and related schemes hardly differ between the various occupational states. The WAO is beneficial for male employees (although the difference with other male groups is rather small for the youngest cohort) and female nonworkers. Civil servants are worse off. There are only slight differences between the various groups with respect to the ZW. The (N)WW does not show large differences either. Here, employees have a somewhat higher benefit–ratio than the other groups. Self-employed men have a higher return than the average. Male civil servants have the largest benefit–tax ratio for the ABP. For females we find a somewhat higher ratio for nonworkers and employees compared with civil servants. In this case women receive the benefit via their partner.

For all general insurances combined we find that the largest benefit–tax ratio is for nonworkers, both male and female, followed by employees. With respect to the employee insurances we find very small differences. Self-employed men and female nonworkers have the highest ratio, whereas civil servants are worse off. This means that all social insurances under consideration (table 8.19) are most advantageous to nonworkers. The benefit–tax ratio is, on average, 1.69 for male nonworkers and 1.89 for females. The lowest ratios are found among self-employed men (1.19) and male civil servants (1.20). Female civil servants in the two youngest cohorts have a benefit–tax ratio of 1.33. For the other groups the ratio amounts to an average of 1.37 (male employees), 1.62 (self-employed women) and 1.69 (female employees).

In conclusion, the redistributive impact of the social security system is the largest for self-employed women and female nonworkers (29%), and the smallest for self-employed men (9%). The employee insurances together have about the same effect for the various female groups. The effect is the largest for male employees (10%), whereas the other male groups are affected somewhat less than females. The general insurances show the largest effect for female nonworkers and employees and the lowest effect for self-employed men.

Male employees' lifetime income inequality is especially diminished by the WAO, ZW and KW and related schemes, whereas the redistribution by the AOW, ABP, ABW and (N)WW is below the general average. The AOW even enlarges income inequality among this group. The redistributive impact of social security on the income of male civil servants is mainly the result of the ABP and, to a much lesser extent, the (N)WW and ZW, whereas the AOW, AWW, AKW, ABW and KW and related schemes have a lower impact on this group than for other groups. Here, the AOW and AWW both increase income inequality. Self-employed men are most affected by the AOW, whereas the effect of the employee insurances on the income inequality is below the average impact. The income inequality among male nonworkers is diminished more than average by the AOW, AKW, ABW and KW and related schemes, whereas the AWW, AAW and ZW cause the reverse effect.

The picture for females is somewhat different. Here, employees' income inequality is especially limited by the AAW, AWW, WAO, ZW and KW and related schemes. However, the effect of the ABP and AKW on this inequality is lower than their average impact. The AWW, AKW, (N)WW and ZW reduce by an above average amount the female civil servants' income inequality. This is partly counterbalanced by the AOW and AAW. Self-employed women are most affected by the AOW, AKW, ABP and (N)WW, whereas only the ZW has a below than average impact. The AOW, ABW and AWW reduce income inequality among female nonworkers more than among other groups, whereas for the ABP, AKW and ZW the opposite holds.

The social security system is especially beneficial to female nonworkers, female employees and male nonworkers. Taking men and women together, nonworkers profit most from the system. The next highest return is obtained by employees. Both civil servants and self-employed persons benefit less than average. The most important redistributions are shown by the AOW (nonworkers gain, whereas civil servants and self-employed persons, in particular, pay), the AAW (a redistribution from self-employed persons to male employees and nonworkers), the ABW (from male employees and civil servants to female nonworkers) and the ABP (from all men, with the exclusion of civil servants, and self-employed women to civil servants and female employees and nonworkers).

8.3.4 Horizontal redistribution by number of children

In this section we look at how the redistributive impact of the social security system differs according to the number of children. For a woman, this is the number of children born plus possible children added to her household by her current partner (*e.g.* children born out of a former cohabitation or marriage). For a man, we take the number of children of his latest partner, if he has not been separated and if otherwise the number of children for which he has been granted custody. The equivalent household income components by number of children are given in table 8.20. The differences in the employers' gross wages are smaller than we found for the subdivisions hitherto. This is in accordance with our expectations. This is because household formation is not determined by behavioural models and household composition only affects labour supply. Of course, household composition does affect social security benefits and – via our choice of the income unit – contributions. The relatively lowest lifetime wages are found with persons with four children in the cohort 1960. Their wages are 11% lower than the highest wages in this cohort. The lowest wages in the other cohorts are less than 10% below the highest ones.

Table 8.20 *Composition of equivalent household income by number of children*

Cohort		Employers' gross wages	Net benefits	Income after social security	Taxes	Net lifetime income
1930	(0)	3286	356	3642	1397	2245
	(1)	3388	263	3651	1274	2377
	(2)	3504	385	3889	1405	2484
	(3)	3179	497	3676	1190	2486
	(4)	3172	533	3703	1181	2522
	All	3149	430	3579	1270	2309
1940	(0)	3425	280	3705	1305	2401
	(1)	3606	350	3956	1359	2597
	(2)	3545	394	3939	1331	2608
	(3)	3368	488	3856	1211	2645
	(4)	3404	561	3965	1295	2670
	All	3467	418	3885	1295	2590
1950	(0)	3501	196	3697	1193	2504
	(1)	3821	353	4174	1352	2822
	(2)	3756	367	4123	1326	2797
	(3)	3772	344	4116	1270	2846
	(4)	3881	386	4267	1392	2875
	All	3722	328	4050	1297	2753
1960	(0)	3620	194	3814	1233	2581
	(1)	3736	327	4062	1255	2807
	(2)	3829	316	4145	1320	2825
	(3)	3812	422	4234	1363	2871
	(4)	3420	365	3785	1122	2663
	All	3719	298	4017	1278	2739

Net benefits generally increase as the number of children increases. The social security system and taxes redistribute income such that the net lifetime income hardly differs between persons with at least one child. However, childless people are worse off than those with children. Their net lifetime income (adjusted for household composition via standardization) is significantly below that of those with children. The profit or loss measured as the quotient of the difference between the net benefits for the group in question and the average net benefits, on the one hand, and the average employers' gross wages on the other hand, varies between – 4.0% (persons with no children in the cohort 1940) and + 4.2% (for persons with four children in the cohort 1940). The differences are rather small in the youngest cohort. Here, it varies between —2.8 and + 3.2%.

The differences in net gain from the social security system are decomposed in table 8.21. We saw earlier that the net gain becomes relatively larger according to the number of children. This is also true in the gain and profit (as compared with the cohort's average) for the AOW, the AWW, the ABP and (with exception of the youngest cohort) the AKW. The latter can be explained by the abolishment of the AKW premium payments in 1988. This implies that contributions have been paid by the youngest generation for only a limited number of years. This means that there is no relative gain in premium contributions via standardization for persons with more children. On the other side, the differences in benefits from the AKW are cancelled out via the standardization. The KW and related schemes are particularly disadvantageous for persons without children, whereas the KW does not discriminate between persons with children. The AAW and to a lesser extent the WAO result in a relative loss for persons with four children; the picture for the other groups is not very clear. The ZW and (N)WW hardly differ between the various groups.

The income inequality – as measured by the Theil coefficient – is shown in table 8.22. Income inequality is the largest among childless people. Here, income inequality is about twice that of the group with the lowest income inequality. The differences between persons with at least one child are limited. This especially holds for those with one, two or three children in the two youngest cohorts.

If we look at the redistributive impact of the various schemes, it appears that the redistributive impact of the AOW is particularly small for childless persons and above average for households with four children. The AWW does not result in an unambiguous result for the two oldest cohorts. But the picture is clear for the two youngest ones: the redistribution is larger as the number of children increases. The latter also holds for the AKW, although the differences are very small for the youngest cohort. The AAW leads to a somewhat smaller reduction in income inequality for childless persons when compared with persons with at least one child. For the general insurances together, redistribution is larger for persons with at least two

Table 8.21 *The difference in net gain (with respect to the average for the cohort) from various social security schemes by number of children*

Cohort		AOW	AWW	AKW	AAW	KW/	WAO	ZW	NWW	ABP	ABW	Net gain
1930	(0)	−56	−18	−63	12	−34	22	8	−4	−21	68	−74
	(1)	−22	−13	−62	0	2	5	−2	−5	2	−11	−167
	(2)	−9	−5	−22	6	6	7	0	2	−10	−18	−45
	(3)	17	6	29	3	6	−3	−2	0	28	−17	67
	(4)	34	12	66	−14	5	−15	−1	−1	22	3	103
1940	(0)	−77	−22	−47	6	−25	4	−1	3	−36	51	−138
	(1)	−16	−6	−43	3	2	−2	3	4	−12	17	−68
	(2)	2	3	−9	5	5	2	1	−5	2	−21	−24
	(3)	34	4	35	−7	4	−5	−2	2	20	−12	70
	(4)	30	1	73	−10	6	6	1	5	38	−4	143
1950	(0)	−64	−15	−18	−9	−11	2	4	−2	−15	−7	−132
	(1)	0	−8	−9	14	1	9	−1	0	9	15	25
	(2)	21	6	3	5	3	−2	−1	0	9	−2	39
	(3)	26	3	15	3	3	0	−1	4	−23	−4	16
	(4)	25	11	22	−16	5	−9	−1	−1	26	4	58
1960	(0)	−58	−22	−4	3	−2	−4	−2	−3	−2	−26	−104
	(1)	14	4	−3	7	1	12	3	−1	−29	24	29
	(2)	7	2	2	−4	1	−3	0	2	1	0	18
	(3)	22	16	5	1	1	3	−2	−5	24	12	124
	(4)	44	25	4	−7	0	0	6	−2	1	2	67

children. Differences hardly exist between persons with two, three or four children in the cohorts 1950 and 1960. On the contrary, the redistribution for persons with four children is larger than for those with three children in the two oldest cohorts. The same holds for persons with three children compared with those with two children. Childless persons show the smallest redistribution by the general insurances.

The KW and related schemes show the same picture as the AKW, but the differences are smaller. The WAO leads to the largest redistribution for persons with one child. No clear picture is available for childless individuals or for those with at least two children. The ZW, (N)WW and ABP do not show systematic significant differences by number of children. The foregoing results for all employee insurances together show for the three oldest cohorts the smallest redistributive impact for childless people and the largest one for persons with four children. The youngest cohort shows a different picture. Here, persons with one child undergo the largest effect and persons with four children the smallest one. The ABW leads to a somewhat larger reduction in income inequality for childless persons in the two oldest cohorts and for persons with one child in the two youngest cohorts.

The aforementioned schemes together result in an increasing income equalizing effect, the larger the number of children. The lower panel of table 8.22 gives the Theil coefficient after social security.

Table 8.22 *Income inequality by number of children and cohort*

Cohort	(0)	(1)	(2)	(3)	(4)	Effect (5^+) + between	Total
employers' gross wages							
1930	0.278	0.136	0.152	0.125	0.128	0.016	0.161
1940	0.242	0.121	0.113	0.107	0.116	0.007	0.133
1950	0.206	0.109	0.106	0.101	0.093	0.003	0.125
1960	0.161	0.101	0.093	0.090	0.079	0.004	0.116
after social security							
1930	0.205	0.099	0.118	0.105	0.088	0.009	0.119
1940	0.168	0.083	0.083	0.073	0.080	0.011	0.097
1950	0.181	0.081	0.083	0.074	0.071	0.009	0.097
1960	0.120	0.070	0.071	0.068	0.050	0.008	0.087

According to our findings in table 8.21, the benefit–tax ratio for the AOW, AWW and AKW (with the exception of the youngest cohort in the case of the AKW, where there are no significant differences) increases as the number of children increases. The AAW shows the reverse for the three oldest cohorts: the benefit–tax ratio declines as the number of children increases. For the youngest cohort we find that the AAW is disadvantageous for persons with two children. The results for the combined general insurances are in line with that for the AOW: the larger the number of children, the larger the benefit–tax ratio. However, the differences are becoming smaller. The benefit–tax ratio for persons with four children is 67% higher than that for childless persons in cohort 1930, whereas the percentage amounts to 36 in cohort 1960.

The KW and related schemes have a larger benefit–tax ratio for persons with children compared with childless persons, but the differences between those with children are very small. The WAO, ZW and (N)WW do not differ according to the number of children. The same holds for the ABP. All employee insurances together also do not show significant differences by number of children. This implies that all the social security schemes under consideration produce conclusions analogous to those for the general insurances: the greater the number of children, the bigger the benefit–tax ratio although the differences are getting smaller. The ratios are shown in table 8.23.

Table 8.23 *Benefit–tax ratio by number of children and cohort*

Cohort	(0)	(1)	(2)	(3)	(4)	Total
1930	1.56	1.60	1.81	2.17	2.07	1.91
1940	1.47	1.45	1.62	1.84	2.03	1.67
1950	1.21	1.35	1.45	1.47	1.39	1.38
1960	1.13	1.33	1.29	1.29	1.49	1.24

In conclusion, the larger the number of children the greater is the redistributive impact of the social security system. This is especially true in the case of the AOW, AWW, AKW and, in a more limited way, the KW and related schemes. The opposite is true for the AAW. Analogous conclusions hold with respect to the benefit–tax ratio. Again, this can be attributed to the AOW, AWW, AKW and KW and related schemes, whereas the AAW is more beneficial to persons with fewer children.

8.4 SOME VARIATIONS

In this section we look at the effect of the income unit and the discount rate. In the foregoing, the income unit has been formed by the household (section 4.3) and we assumed that household members fully share the household income. For that reason, all income components have been standardized (section 4.4) and this standardized income has been given to each household member. An alternative would be to consider the individual as the income unit. In that case, standardization does not have to be applied and household members do not profit from the income of any other household member. The income components are only given to the person who receives that income, which implies that individuals can have zero income. The main results for the simulation in which the individual has been considered as the income unit are shown in table 8.24. These results are also compared with those where the household is the income unit.[13]

If the individual is the income unit, the gross wages are considerably less. This is the result of two counteracting forces. On the one hand, income has not been standardized, which implies that, on average, the accounted income is larger if the individual is the income unit. This is because the standardization factor is mostly less than one. On the other hand, income of other household members is not shared. This means that our individual does not receive a part of the parent's income if (s)he still lives with his or her parents and also does not receive a part of his or her partner's and children's income. The latter apparently dominates. Therefore, women's gross wages decrease more than that of males.

The difference between both income concepts (individual versus standardized household income) increases. The way in which these differences develop also holds when social security contributions and benefits are taken into account. The result is a net lifetime income that decreases from cohort 1940 on. Net benefits are considerably larger for women than for men, whereas the reverse holds for taxes. The result is that the differences in net lifetime income between men and women are smaller than for the gross wages. But the differences between men and women are much larger if the individual rather than the household is the income unit.

The next panel of the table shows us the income inequality as measured by the Theil coefficient. Lifetime income is now distributed more unequally. The Theil coefficient of gross wages where the individual is the income unit is about three times that where the household is the income unit. This proportion has not significantly reduced over time. The reduction in the income inequality as a result of the social security system is about 30% larger. This results in a Theil coefficient which amounts to 0.319 for the cohort 1930, declining to 0.224 for the youngest generation. The income inequality is larger for women than for men and the same holds for the reduction in the income inequality as a consequence of the social security system. The Theil coefficient for gross wages amounts to 0.224 for males in cohort 1930 and 0.537 for women, with a between component of 0.122. The reduction as a result of the social security system is 21.4 and 62.0% respectively, which results in a Theil coefficient for the income after social security of 0.176 and 0.204, respectively. The between component now amounts to 0.080. For the youngest cohort (1960) we find the following figures. The Theil coefficient for gross wages is 0.229 for men and 0.252 for

[13] If the household consists of partners who live together, family allowances have been given to the female partner.

women, whereas the between component is 0.094. The reduction caused by the social security system amounts to 16.8% and 41.6%, respectively, resulting in a Theil coefficient of 0.191 for men and 0.147 for women and a between component of 0.078. The most striking differences in the equalizing effect of the various schemes between the two income concepts are the following:

1. Among **men** the equalizing effect of the AOW increases and the younger the cohort, the larger the increase. The decrease in the Theil coefficient for the youngest cohort now amounts to 8% against 1% if the household is the income unit. The AAW also has a large effect, but it is somewhat less than that of the AOW. The AWW, WAO, (N)WW and ABP also have an income equalizing effect which is larger when the individual is the income unit, but the effect is rather small. The family allowances now result in an increase of income differences among men, whereas before, income inequality was reduced. The redistributive impact of the ABW has now almost disappeared. Its effect amounts to less than 2.5%.
2. Among **women** the equalizing effect of the AOW increases. The Theil coefficient is reduced by 27% in the youngest cohort against 9% when the household is the income unit. The percentages in the oldest cohort amount to 16 and 34, respectively. The ABP is transformed from a scheme that enlarges income differences among women to one that decreases income inequality, but the difference is less than that for the AOW. The redistributive impact of the ABP increases strongly; it almost doubles and amounts to 17 and 29% for the cohorts 1930 and 1960, respectively, if the individual is the income unit. The effect of the ZW is now also somewhat larger. For the family allowances there is a considerably larger equalizing effect among the oldest two cohorts, but this is not true of the youngest cohort. There are various reasons for this, *e.g.* the increased labour force participation of married women and consequently, the higher labour income, which implies that the role of the family allowances in the net lifetime income diminishes. Another aspect is, of course, the decrease in the number of children. With respect to the other schemes we cannot find significant differences in the equalizing effect when we compare the household and the individual as the income unit.

The more unequal distribution of lifetime wages is illustrated in the next panel of table 8.24. If the income unit is formed by the household, then the mean wage for cohort 1930 in decile 10 is 8.8 times that of decile 1 and for 1960 we find a mean wage 7.5 times higher in decile 10. If the individual is the income unit, these proportions are 220.4 and 56.3, respectively. Of course, in the lower deciles we mainly find (married) women, who have only been working for a few years. If we only look at men, then we see that the highest decile of cohort 1930 has on average a wage (Dfl. 7 495 000) that is 14.7

Table 8.24 *Confrontation of results with the household (hh) and the individual (ind) as income unit*

	1930		1940		1950		1960	
	hh	ind	hh	ind	hh	ind	hh	ind
Employers' gross wages	3149	1714	3467	1587	3722	1430	3719	1350
of which men	3429	2800	3719	2708	3898	2323	3962	2069
women	2864	582	3205	723	3537	786	3458	816
Employers' contributions	245	154	261	159	276	153	259	108
Employees' contributions	337	191	447	250	574	303	706	343
Benefits	1012	614	1126	638	1178	611	1262	568
Income after social security	3579	1982	3885	1965	4050	1738	4017	1574
Taxes	1270	719	1295	670	1297	547	1278	459
Net lifetime income	2309	1262	2590	1295	2753	1191	2739	1116
of which men	2272	1720	2587	1705	2748	1507	2777	1371
women	2348	789	2592	867	2758	848	2695	843
Theil coeff. gross wages	0.161	0.498	0.133	0.423	0.125	0.352	0.116	0.334
Theil coeff after soc. sec.	0.119	0.319	0.097	0.271	0.097	0.229	0.087	0.224
	(– 26%)	(– 36%)	(– 27%)	(– 36%)	(– 22%)	(– 35%)	(– 25%)	(– 33%)
Wages decile 1	835	28	1019	81	870	77	1000	79
2	1441	51	1739	259	1901	301	1956	319
3	1835	322	2164	460	2401	509	2462	517
4	2213	582	2549	714	2848	733	2894	720
5	2607	920	2936	1030	3274	1001	3302	942
6	3016	1306	3334	1384	3719	1330	3741	1221
7	3512	1782	3817	1862	4203	1734	4237	1571
8	4117	2457	4439	2476	4810	2228	4819	2036
9	5034	3467	5308	3384	5682	3020	5631	2776
10	7331	6170	7392	5801	7737	4953	7476	4449

Table 8.24 (*Contd.*)

		1930 hh	1930 ind	1940 hh	1940 ind	1950 hh	1950 ind	1960 hh	1960 ind
Net benefits decile	1	622	403	659	437	484	307	602	285
	2	605	488	599	477	583	439	576	392
	3	569	485	543	432	525	365	493	301
	4	516	435	498	374	394	349	371	273
	5	402	349	457	315	383	222	328	230
	6	420	341	385	292	291	186	231	113
	7	370	231	352	147	208	108	130	46
	8	286	82	282	40	184	− 12	95	− 39
	9	281	7	189	− 33	70	− 134	− 18	− 166
	10	74	− 141	− 12	− 198	− 82	− 290	− 209	− 275
Benefit–tax ratio	AOW	2.19	2.23	1.75	1.81	1.31	1.47	1.06	1.30
	AWW	1.26	1.64	1.07	1.33	1.02	1.16	0.84	0.94
	AKW	3.49	2.01	2.98	1.84	3.06	2.53	6.03	5.82
	AAW	2.86	3.04	2.62	2.51	2.23	2.13	2.08	1.99
	KW/*etc.*	3.07	3.09	4.85	4.08	4.90	4.11	10.15	8.74
	WAO	1.33	1.56	1.04	0.97	0.86	0.77	0.83	0.76
	ZW	0.88	0.87	0.89	0.86	0.89	0.85	0.88	0.89
	(N)WW	1.59	1.75	1.88	2.07	1.85	2.14	1.67	1.99
	ABP	1.57	1.34	1.61	1.76	1.68	2.03	1.89	2.40
	Gen. ins.	2.29	2.50	1.87	2.00	1.50	1.56	1.36	1.36
	Empl. ins.	1.35	1.42	1.36	1.23	1.21	1.07	1.11	1.02
	All ins.	1.91	2.06	1.67	1.68	1.38	1.36	1.27	1.25

times that of the average wage in the lowest decile (Dfl. 511 000). If a woman received the latter income, she would belong to decile 7 among the women. In the course of time, the differences get smaller. We also find persons with relatively low lifetime earnings among males in the youngest cohort. So, the proportion between the highest (with an average wage of Dfl. 5 175 000) and lowest decile (Dfl. 93 000) increases among men and amounts to 55.6 in that cohort. Among women this proportion is even smaller than among men, while the wage income in the lowest decile hardly differs among men and women. However, the average income in the highest decile is considerably higher for men than for women: Dfl. 5 175 000 against Dfl. 2 239 000, respectively.

Net benefits are decomposed by decile in the penultimate panel of the table. Here, we find that the lowest and highest decile have a larger (absolute) loss than the middle deciles. It is striking that the highest decile does not generally have the largest loss. Another point to note is the relatively small loss for the higher deciles in the youngest cohort. Moreover, the foregoing holds for both men and women.

Finally, the benefit–tax ratios are shown in the lowest panel of table 8.24. Using the individual as the income unit leads to an increase in the benefit–tax ratio of the AOW, AWW and (N)WW in all cohorts. The same holds for the AKW in the older cohorts and the ABP in the younger cohorts. The KW and related schemes and, with exception of cohort 1930, the AAW and WAO result in a lower ratio. Men and women differ with respect to the ABP, AWW, family allowances, AAW, ZW and (N)WW. If we compare the individual and household income concept, the ABP leads to a remarkably higher benefit–tax ratio for women in the oldest cohorts, whereas it is lower for men. The benefit–tax ratios for the AWW, ZW and KW and related schemes become smaller for men and larger for women in all four cohorts. The same holds for the AKW with respect to the older cohorts. The reverse is true for the AAW: the benefit–tax ratio for men is higher under the individual income concept, but is lower for women in the oldest cohorts. The (N)WW shows higher benefit–tax ratios for men in all cohorts, whereas women in older cohorts show a lower one and no difference exists for women in the youngest cohorts.

In our analyses up to now we used a discount rate of 2%. We now look at the effect of the choice of the discount factor via comparing the aforementioned results with those which are obtained from a discount rate of 3%. This comparison can be found in table 8.25. The use of a higher discount rate implies that future receipts and payments are valued lower, whereas the reverse holds for receipts and payments in the past. This is also reflected in the development of the (employers') gross wages. The difference between the lifetime gross wages discounted by 3% and those discounted by 2% is larger as the cohort becomes older. The difference is negative for the youngest generation, for which males are responsible. There is hardly

Table 8.25 *Confrontation of results with different discount rates (2% versus 3%)*

		1930		1940		1950		1960	
		2%	3%	2%	3%	2%	3%	2%	3%
Employers' gross wages		3149	3861	3467	4142	3722	4178	3719	3742
of which men		3429	4181	3719	4472	3998	4343	3962	3960
women		2864	3538	3205	3800	3537	4007	3458	3524
Employers' contributions		245	299	261	321	276	326	259	291
Employees' contributions		337	374	447	475	574	565	706	637
Benefits		1012	991	1126	1047	1178	1050	1262	1064
Income after social security		3579	4180	3885	4419	4050	4337	4017	3879
Taxes		1270	1493	1295	1517	1297	1441	1278	1224
Net lifetime income		2309	2687	2590	2903	2753	2896	2739	2654
of which men		2272	2664	2587	2911	2748	2900	2777	2691
women		2348	2710	2592	2894	2758	2891	2695	2622
Theil coeff. gross wages		0.161	0.159	0.133	0.131	0.125	0.121	0.116	0.109
Theil coeff after soc. sec.		0.119	0.119	0.097	0.101	0.097	0.097	0.087	0.085
		(– 26%)	(– 25%)	(– 27%)	(– 23%)	(– 22%)	(– 20%)	(– 25%)	(– 22%)
Wages decile	1	835	1014	1019	1267	870	989	1000	1040
	2	1441	1800	1739	2099	1901	2141	1956	2026
	3	1835	2261	2164	2585	2401	2710	2462	2505
	4	2213	2646	2549	3030	2848	3155	2894	2927
	5	2607	3162	2936	3487	3274	3631	3302	3319
	6	3016	3676	3334	3985	3719	4136	3741	3738
	7	3512	4366	3817	4560	4203	4679	4237	4199
	8	4117	5025	4439	5267	4810	5354	4819	4749
	9	5034	6111	5308	6325	5682	6350	5631	5542
	10	7331	8799	7392	8809	7737	8573	7476	7393

Table 8.25 (*Contd.*)

		1930		1940		1950		1960	
		2%	3%	2%	3%	2%	3%	2%	3%
Net benefits decile	1	622	679	659	620	484	413	602	475
	2	605	515	599	549	583	483	576	430
	3	569	458	543	473	525	341	493	321
	4	516	387	498	323	394	281	371	267
	5	402	350	457	335	383	169	328	160
	6	420	320	385	238	291	159	231	92
	7	370	301	352	161	208	69	130	9
	8	286	145	282	141	184	10	95	− 7
	9	281	154	189	84	70	− 127	− 18	− 119
	10	74	− 139	− 12	− 146	− 82	− 195	− 209	− 261
Benefit–tax ratio	AOW	2.19	1.69	1.75	1.26	1.31	0.94	1.06	0.74
	AWW	1.26	1.19	1.07	0.96	1.02	1.02	0.84	0.82
	AKW	3.49	3.54	2.98	3.03	3.06	3.22	6.03	6.23
	AAW	2.86	2.56	2.62	2.51	2.23	2.01	2.08	1.90
	KW/*etc.*	3.07	2.95	4.85	4.55	4.90	4.61	10.15	9.58
	WAO	1.33	1.23	1.04	1.04	0.86	0.82	0.83	0.82
	ZW	0.88	0.86	0.89	0.88	0.89	0.86	0.88	0.86
	(N)WW	1.59	1.61	1.88	1.82	1.85	1.99	1.67	1.73
	ABP	1.57	1.10	1.61	1.17	1.68	1.19	1.89	1.41
	Gen. ins.	2.29	1.91	1.87	1.52	1.50	1.23	1.36	1.16
	Empl. ins.	1.35	1.33	1.36	1.39	1.21	1.24	1.11	1.15
	All ins.	1.91	1.67	1.67	1.47	1.38	1.23	1.27	1.16

any difference for women in the youngest cohort. Employers' contributions are paid at a relatively later stage during one's life than employees' contributions.[14] As a consequence, the employers' contributions are higher when discounting by 3%, whereas those of employees are higher when a discount rate of 2% is used. Benefits discounted by 3% are lower than when a discount rate of 2% is used. Here, the younger the cohort, the larger the difference. This is, of course, related to the fact that a large part of the benefits are received at older ages (*e.g.* AOW and ABP–OP). As a result, income after social security is larger for the three oldest cohorts when a discount rate of 3% is used, whereas for the youngest cohort a discount rate of 2% leads to a larger income. Taxes show the same result and, consequently, so do the net lifetime wages. A discount rate of 3% leads to a 16% higher net lifetime income for the oldest generation compared with a discount rate of 2%. The generation 1940 has a 12% higher net lifetime income, whereas the difference amounts to 5% for 1950. By comparison, cohort 1960 shows a lower income. The difference is minus 3%. These percentages hardly differ between men and women.

The next panel of the table shows us the Theil coefficients. The differences are small. Lifetime gross wages have a somewhat lower Theil coefficient, when a discount rate of 3% is used, and the difference is larger, the younger the cohort. The reduction caused by the social security system is somewhat smaller when the discount rate amounts to 3%. However, the differences between the Theil coefficients as a consequence of different discount rates are minor. The most striking differences in the equalizing effect of the various schemes between the two income concepts are the following:

(1) Among **men** the equalizing effect of the AOW decreases by about 2.5 percentage points. For the generation 1960 the net effect of the AOW becomes positive, which means that the income inequality is enlarged. The AAW is also largely affected. The equalizing effect decreases by about 1 percentage point for the oldest cohort, and by as much as 4% for the youngest generation. The higher discount rate leads to a smaller equalizing effect for the WAO and the ZW. The reverse holds for the AWW, ABW and – with exclusion of the youngest cohort – (N)WW and ABP. The family allowances do not show changes. Taken together, this results in the social security system having less of an impact on income inequality. The Theil coefficient for males is reduced by 1.2 (cohort 1930) to 4.7 (cohort 1960) percentage points if the discount rate increases from 2 to 3%.
(2) Among **women** the equalizing effect of the AOW as measured by the Theil coefficient decreases by on average 5 percentage points. We also find a decrease in the equalizing effect for the AAW (an increase of the Theil

[14] This is connected with the different maximum premium limits, being higher for the employee insurances.

coefficient varying from 1 to 2 percentage points), the WAO (1 percentage point), the ZW (about a half percentage point) and finally for the (N)WW (about 1 percentage point for the two youngest cohorts). The ABP is the only scheme in which income differences among women become smaller in all cohorts when the discount rates increases from 2 to 3%. The decrease amounts to about 3 percentage points. The ABW also results in a further reduction in income inequality, but this is limited to the oldest cohorts.

The effect on the distribution of lifetime wages is illustrated in the following panel of table 8.25. The ratio between the tenth and first decile is affected only marginally. The decrease in the net benefits holds for each decile and is shown in the next panel of the table. There are no striking characteristics.

Finally, the benefit–tax ratios are shown in the lowest panel of table 8.25. These ratios decrease, the later the benefits are received, which is in accordance with our expectations. The largest decreases are shown by the old age pensions (AOW and ABP). By contrast, the benefit–tax ratio for the AKW increases somewhat. Here, the benefits are received by younger people. The KW and related schemes do not have this affect. This is due to the fact that the scheme was abolished on 1 January 1980 and because, in practice, the number of children involved is limited. As a result, the benefit–tax ratio for all insurances is lower as the discount rate increases. This holds, in particular, for the general insurances. The employee insurances are hardly affected by the change in the discount rate.

9

Epilogue

9.1 INTRODUCTION

This book describes the microsimulation model NEDYMAS and its application in the field of income redistribution. The microsimulation model consists of a large number of submodules that aim to trace the developments in the socio-economic characteristics of the Dutch population. NEDYMAS simulates a so-called panel from 1947 on, distinguishing 312 characteristics for each member of the panel in its most recent version.[1]

The current version, NEDYMAS–92/A, is practically complete with respect to the demographic data and the social security module. This makes it probably the most extensive microsimulation model in existence. The DEMOGRAPHIC MODULE contains all possible demographic transitions and household positions, with the exception of cohabiting homosexuals, multi-family households and communes. However, immigration, emigration and transitions into and out of institutional households [Nelissen (1991b)] are explicitly modelled. The SOCIAL SECURITY MODULE covers 96% of the social security benefits [including health care expenditures; Nelissen (1991a)] in the Netherlands from 1970 on. Data on early retirement schemes as well as some social provisions are still lacking. The LABOUR MARKET AND INCOME FORMATION MODULE is somewhat less developed. The most important gap here relates to capital income. Another flow[2] – which is also true of the demographic module – is that many the of transitions have not been based on behavioural equations. From that point of view, the model may be considered an accounting framework. This is the most important challenge for future microsimulators.[3]

The application concerns the research into the redistributive effect of social security schemes on lifetime basis. This is the first time that the effect of the whole social security system on LIFETIME INCOME DISTRIBUTION has

[1] The results in chapter 8 are based on an earlier version.

[2] But, this objection holds for all dynamic microsimulation models.

[3] The funding by the *Research Program for Population Studies* of the Dutch Scientific Organization NWO (grant no. 18.051) makes it possible to take up this challenge.

been studied. Related studies were limited to only old age pensions and were often applied to synthetic cohorts (chapter 2). Only Harding (1992) and Falkingham *et al.* (1993) used a microsimulation approach in order to investigate the social security incidence, but they limited themselves to a synthetic cohort. Here, we follow an actual population – the Dutch population – and also consider the lifetime redistributive effect of the disability schemes, of the sickness schemes, of the family allowances, of the unemployment provisions and of the health care provisions.

9.2 CONCLUSIONS

Although the model has been applied to the Netherlands, it is still possible to generalize the results. The social security system in the Netherlands is very suited for that purpose, in view of its ambiguous nature, consisting of a need-based welfare system (the general insurances and social provisions) and a wage-related social security system for employees and civil servants (the employee insurances and schemes for civil servants). We will refer to these systems in the following as the Atlantic and Continental system, respectively. Other countries generally focused on one of both. For example, Great Britain, Denmark, Norway and Sweden opted for the Atlantic approach, whereas Austria, Belgium and Germany chose the Continental system. In this, almost all countries use the pay-as-you-go system as a method of finance.

In the course of time, elements of the Continental system have been added to the Atlantic system and *vice versa*. In the Atlantic systems additional benefit schemes are created for some categories, *e.g.* for the elderly in the United Kingdom and Sweden. On the other hand, basic allowances have been introduced in the Continental system, like the guaranteed income for the elderly in Belgium. Until the late 1980s this convergent trend of both systems has persisted. In countries with Atlantic schemes we find a fast growth of supplementary occupational arrangements, whereas these arrangements hardly increase in countries with Continental oriented schemes. In the late 1980s and 1990s we see another trend. The retrenchments on government expenditures have also affected the social security system. The cuts in social security schemes have led to a situation in which the relevance of wage-related benefits above the social minimum level is discussed. This has led some to suggest the abolition of the wage-related schemes and to limit the social security system to (sometimes even means-tested) flat-rate benefits. If a person wants a higher benefit, (s)he has to insure the concerning risk at the private insurance market. In other words, it is advocated that government limits itself to the Atlantic-type schemes. We see this development in the United Kingdom where wage-related sickness and unemployment benefits were abolished in the 1980s and in the Netherlands (the proposals for the WAO and the discussion on the so-called '*ministelsel*'). Another trend is to introduce (or to strengthen) the labour history as an element that also determines the level of the benefit in the Continental system, see *e.g.* the discussion on the Old Age Insurance (OAI) in the United States and the reforms of the unemployment insurance in the Netherlands.

What can we conclude from our study for the situation in other countries? We must of course take stock of the fact that all countries differ with respect to socio-demographic context, like age composition of the population, the household composition, the labour force participation of men and women and the primary income distribution. Nevertheless, the results are so clear that generalizations are possible.

First, we compared the impact of flat-rate benefits (AOW, AWW, AKW, AAW and KW and related schemes) with that of wage-related benefits with a maximum benefit level (WAO, ZW, (N)WW and WWV). The most suited comparison can be made between the AOW on the one hand and the ZW on the other hand.[4] If we correct for the size of the total benefits and thus look at the adjusted redistributive impact, then the impact of the ZW amounts to 82% of that of the AOW for the cohort 1930 and 78% for the youngest cohort. So, the redistributive impact via the benefits differs only slightly between the Atlantic-type flat-rate benefits and the Continental-type wage-related benefits. This implies that earnings-related benefits do not necessarily have a much smaller redistributive impact than flat-rated ones. This of course depends on the level of the maximum wage-related benefit. The larger the maximum benefit, the larger the difference between both types. If the benefit has no limit, than the income equalizing effect of the Continental-type scheme becomes very small, *e.g.* the effect of the ABP–IP benefits on the income inequality.

Second, the social assistance scheme (ABW) makes clear that means-tested schemes have a relatively large redistributive impact. The size of the ABW benefits is comparable with those of the AAW, but the adjusted redistributive impact of the former is about 50% greater. Moreover, the redistributional impact of the ABW is underestimated, because NEDYMAS contains no capital income and wealth module.

Third, we look at the impact of the role of premium ceilings. Both general and employee insurances have wage-related contributions, whereby the ceiling for the employee insurances is considerably higher than that for the general insurances (from 1967 on). Between 1967 and 1981, the ceilings for the employee insurances were about one-third above those for the general insurances; between 1982 and 1989 it was less than 10%, but from 1990 onwards the difference is over 60%. The existence of a ceiling results in an increase of income inequality and the lower the ceiling, the larger the

[4] For, these two schemes are most uniformly distributed over the income groups. Everyone receives an AOW benefit (unless one dies before the age of 65) and sickness incidence is distributed more equally by income than unemployment and disability incidence.

increase is. Again comparing the AOW and ZW, we see that the adjusted redistributive impact of the ZW is about 77% of that of the AOW for generation 1930 and about 57% for generation 1960. So, the level of premium ceilings has a large effect on the redistributive impact. Because Atlantic-type schemes generally have a lower ceiling than Continental-type schemes, we can conclude that income inequality is enlarged more among the former type via the contributions than for the latter type.

Fourth, we see that the existence of a franchise in the contribution – *e.g.* the National Insurance in the United Kingdom, where the franchise amounted to £46 per week on 1 January 1991 – importantly reduces the increase in income inequality. The WAO has a premium franchise which amounts to about 35% of the ceiling from 1982 onwards and about 25% in the period therefore. The premium ceiling for the (N)WW, for example, equals that of the WAO, but the adjusted redistributive impact of the WAO premiums is only half that of the (N)WW premiums.

Fifth, if no ceiling exists, the levying of contributions in combination with a franchise, results in a decrease of income inequality, but the decrease is small in comparison with the effect of flat-rate benefits. See the ABP scheme.

Sixth, we see that the existence of a franchise in the benefits in combination with no upper bound for the benefit, can result in an enlargement of income inequality, like the ABP–OP benefits show in the Netherlands.

So, the Dutch social security system shows that the redistributive impact of Atlantic-type schemes does not necessarily largely differ from Continental-type schemes. The income equalizing effect of the flat-rate benefit in comparison with a wage-related benefit (in combination with a maximum level of the benefit) can be neutralized by a lower contribution ceiling. That is why we find for the Netherlands only a relatively small difference in the redistributive impact between the general and employee insurances.

The benefits and contributions structure of the Dutch social security system results in an only limited redistribution of income, when emphasis is on lifetime earnings. The schemes under consideration lead to a reduction in the Theil coefficient that varies from 22.1% for cohort 1950 to 26.7% for cohort 1940 (see table 8.5). This reduction is even smaller than the reduction in lifetime wage income inequality between the cohorts 1930 and 1960. The latter amounts to 28%. Of course, the extension of the social security system has diminished income differences, but its effect is smaller than the role that other factors have been playing.[5] This is also illustrated by table 8.6. The ratio between decile 10 and decile 1 for cohort 1930 amounts before social security (so, gross wages) to 8.8 and after social security to 5.1. For the youngest cohort, these figures are 7.5 and 4.5, respectively.

[5] The effect of the social security system is problably somewhat greater if we take account of the ABW. But the effect will not be very large in view of the size of this scheme (less than 10% of all social security benefits).

However, this does not imply that some groups cannot have a large benefit – in relation to their contribution – from the system. But we also find that the differences decrease in the course of time. Decile 1 in cohort 1930 receives about four times more per contributed guilder to the social insurances (and discounted by 2%) than decile 10. For cohort 1960, this ratio is decreased to about two.

It is remarkable that the redistributive impact of the social security system hardly differs between generations. The notion that a comprehensive social security system will result in an extensive change in the income distribution does not necessarily hold for the lifetime income. In spite of this the situation in the Netherlands shows that on an annual basis the redistribution can be large. The scheme that by far results in the largest redistribution on an annual basis – the AOW – has a limited redistributive impact on lifetime basis. In spite of its size, its redistributive impact is smaller than that for the AAW and the combined family allowance schemes in the youngest cohort (see table 8.5). The explanation is simple: all people who are 65 years and older receive AOW, whereas the AAW only benefits people who are disabled, and the higher the income, the lower the probability of becoming disabled is.

Another striking point is that the supplementary pension scheme for civil servants – the ABP pension – results in a significant enlargement of income inequality for the cohorts born around 1930 and 1940. This is an unintended consequence of the low contribution rates in the 1980s and 1990s due to governmental expenditure cuts.

All generations have a benefit–tax ratio that is larger than 1.00, which means that all generations profit from the social security system. But note, we do not take into account the financing via public funds, which amounts to 10 to 15%. Further it holds that a higher discount rate results in a lower benefit–tax ratio. If we use a discount rate of 3% and take account of the public funding, the cohort 1960 breaks even. Younger generations then will probably have a loss from the social security system. Intergenerational redistributions result in a gain for the generations up to cohort 1960, whereas the generations born after about 1965 lose from the system. This type of intergenerational redistribution from younger cohorts to older cohorts is often justified by the increase in the non-transfer income in the course of time. The redistribution would make the lifetime income distributions more equitable, whereas younger cohorts are still better off. But, this reasoning only holds when (non-transfer) income continues increasing. However, table 8.2 shows us that the income growth appears to come to a halt, so that the argument does not hold any more. If the generational losses become steadily larger, this will require a growing solidarity from younger to older generations in the future.

The Dutch system is in particular beneficial to the poor, to older cohorts, to women (via the AOW, AWW, ABP, ABW and family allowances), to married and separated persons (via the same schemes, with the exception of the ABW which is beneficial to separated and single women), to so-called nonworkers and, to a less extent, employees (again via AOW, AWW, ABW and ABP) and to households with a large number of children (via AOW, AWW and family allowances). The (relative) losers are the rich, younger generations, men, single persons, self-employed persons and households with no children.

Looking at the individual schemes, those which are most redistributive with respect to horizontal redistribution are:

1. The AOW redistributes income from single males, separated persons, civil servants, self-employed persons and households with few children to married and single females, married men, nonworkers and households with many children;
2. The AAW redistributes income from separated persons, self-employed persons and households with many children to single men, married females, male nonworkers and male employees and households with few children;
3. The AWW redistributes income from males and households with few children to females and households with many children;
4. The ABP redistributes income from males and self-employed females to females (especially married ones), civil servants and female nonworkers and employees;
5. The family allowances redistribute income from males and households with few children to females (especially married ones) and households with many children;
6. The (N)WW redistributes income from females to males; and finally
7. The ABW results in a relatively high benefit for single and separated women and nonworkers, whereas single men and male employees and civil servants receive considerably less than the average.

We also see that the differences between generations are small or the development in the difference is rather limited for those schemes where we can expect this, *e.g.* the AOW, whereas these differences are large for schemes for which important changes took place, like the KW and related schemes.

Standardized household income after social security and (labour income) taxes for households with at least one child are higher than for households without children. An interesting finding is that the greater the number of children, the larger the standardized net lifetime household income generally is, whereas this does not hold for the lifetime wage income. This implies that on a lifetime basis and after standardization (using a subjective (*sic*) method) the social security and tax system compensates the difference in wage income, and the required higher consumption needs more than would be necessary to generate an income distribution which is independent of the presence of children in a household. This casts doubt on the efforts of some groups in the Netherlands to increase the transfers to households with children, especially via higher family allowances. In view of our results, it can only be defended to additionally support households with four or more children. An objection against the argument can be that the fertility sub-module (see chapter 7) has not been based on a behavioural equation. But advocates of higher family allowances cannot appeal to this because no reliable results are available in this field in the Netherlands. Only further research on the interrelationship in the field of demography, psychology and economics can shed further light on this question.

The confrontation of the results with the household as the income unit on the one hand and with the individual as the income unit on the other hand, shows that income inequality in the latter case is about three times larger in terms of the Theil coefficient, whereas the redistributive impact of the social security system is about one and a half times larger. However, with respect to the benefit–tax ratio we find that the differences are rather small.

The choice of the discount rate (2 or 3%) hardly affects the lifetime wage income inequality. But the redistributive impact of the social security system is diminished somewhat. A higher discount rate also results in a lower benefit–tax ratio of the system. This is mainly caused by the effect of a higher discount rate on the old age pensions. Because we only concern ourselves with cohorts who have not yet reached the age of 65, the benefits are valued lower, the higher the discount rate is. Against the lower benefit–tax ratio of schemes whereof the benefits are received at older ages, we have a higher ratio for those schemes of which the benefits are received relatively early in life.

References

Aaron, H. J. (1977) Demographic effects on the equity of social security benefits, in *The Economics of Public Services*, (eds M.S. Feldstein and R.P. Inman), MacMillan, New York, pp. 151–173.

Aaron, H. J. (1982) *Economic effects of social security*, Brookings Institution, Washington DC.

Aarts, L. J. M. and De Jong, P. R. (1990) *Economic Aspects of Disability Behavior*, Ph.D. Dissertation, Leyden University, Leyden.

Abowd, J. M. and Killingsworth, M. R. (1983) Sex, Discrimination, Atrophy, and the Male–Female Wage Differential. *Industrial Relations*, **22**, 387–402.

Aitchison, J. and Brown, J. A. C. (1957) *The Lognormal Distribution*, Cambridge University Press, Cambridge.

Alessie, R. J. M., Camphuis, H. and Kapteyn, A. (1990) *Een simulatiemodel ter berekening van het sociale risico*, EIT/Tilburg University, Tilburg.

Arrow, K. J. (1980) Microdata Simulation: Current Status, Problems, Prospects, in *Microeconomic Simulation Models for Public Policy Analysis*, vol. 2, (eds R.H. Haveman and K. Hollenbeck), Academic Press, New York, pp. 253–265.

Atkinson, A. B. (1970) National Superannuation: Redistribution and Value for Money. *Bulletin of the Oxford University Institute of Economics and Statistics*, **32**, 171–185.

Atkinson, A. B. (1983) *The Economics of Inequality*, 2nd edn, Clarendon Press, Oxford.

Atkinson, A. B., Bourguignon, F. and Morrisson, C. (1988) Earnings Mobility. *European Economic Review*, **32**, 619–632.

Atkinson, A. B., Bourguignon, F. and Morrisson, C. (1992) *Empirical Studies of Earnings Mobility*, Harwood, Chur.

Barr, N. (1992) Economic Theory and the Welfare State: A Survey and Interpretation. *Journal of Economic Literature*, **30**, 741–803.

Barten, A. P. (1964) Family composition, prices and expenditure patterns, in *Econometric Analysis for National Economic Planning*, (eds P. E. Hart, G. Mills and J. K. Whitaker), Butterworth, London, pp. 277–292.

Bartlema, J. (1987) *Developments in Kinship Networks for the Aged in the Netherlands*, Ph.D. Dissertation, Tilburg University, Tilburg.

Behrens, J. and Smolensky, E. (1973) Alternative Definitions of Income Redistribution. *Public Finance*, **28**, 315–332.

Bekkering, J., Van Schaaijk, M., Verkade, A. and Waaijers, R. (1989) *MIKROPOLIS: Een eenvoudig dynamisch micro-simulatiemodel*, Central Planning Agency, The Hague.

Bennett, R. L. and Bergmann, B. R. (1986) *A Microsimulated Transactions Model of the United States Economy*, John Hopkins University Press, Baltimore/London.

Berends-Ballast, H., Bernelot Moens, W. E., Jansen, R. J. A., Van de Stadt, H. and De Zeeuw, A. E. (1980) Welvaartsverschillen tussen huishoudens van verschillende samenstelling. *CBS Select*, **1**, 291–306.

Berg, G. J. Van den (1988) *Search Behaviour, Transitions to Nonparticipation and the Duration of Unemployment*, FEW 338, Tilburg University, Tilburg.

Bergmann, B. R. (1990) Micro-to-Macro Simulations: A Primer With a Labor Market Example. *Journal of Economic Perspectives*, **4**, 99–116.

Blinder, A. S. (1974) *Toward an Economic Theory of Income Distribution*, MIT University Press, Cambridge.

Blomquist, N. S. (1976) *The Distribution of Lifetime Income; A Case Study of Sweden*, Ph.D. Dissertation, Princeton University, Princeton.

Bolhuis, E. A. (1987) Koopkrachtoverzichten, in *Bouwstenen voor inkomensbeleid en sociale zekerheid*, (eds C. A. de Kam, *et al.*), Vuga, The Hague, pp. 129–40.

Bonsall, P. W. (1979) Microsimulation of Mode Choice: a Model of Organized Car Sharing. *Planning and Transportation Research Conference Proceedings*, Summer Annual Meeting, University of Warwick, pp. 81–102.

Boskin, M. J., Avrin, M. and Cone, K. (1983) Modelling alternative solutions to the long-run social security funding problem, in *Behavioral Simulation Methods in Tax Policy Analysis*, (ed M. Feldstein), The University of Chicago Press, Chicago/London, pp. 211–237.

Boskin, M. J., Kotlikoff, L. J., Puffert, D. J. and Shoven, J. B. (1987) Social Security: a Financial Appraisal Across and Within Generations. *National Tax Journal*, **40**, 19–34.

Bossons, J. (1967) *A General Income Tax Analyzer*, Studies of the Royal Commission on Taxation, No. 25, Queen's Printer, Ottawa.

Bovenkamp, J. F. Van den (1972) Een analyse van de ongelijkheid van de persoonlijke inkomens in 1967. *Statistische en Econometrische Onderzoekingen*, **13**, 47–77.

Brekel, E. J. G. Van den (1986) Ziekteverzuim van de beroepsbevolking 1981–1984. *Maandbericht Gezondheidsstatistiek*, **86/4**, 5–32.

Bridges, B. Jr. (1974) *Redistribution of Transfer Payments Among Age and Economic Status Groups*, Office of Research and Statistics Staff Paper No. 10, US Department of Health, Education and Welfare, Washington DC.

Brittain, J. A. (1972) *The Payroll Tax for Social Security*, Princeton University Press, Princeton.

Browning, M., Deaton, A. and Irish, M. (1985) A Profitable Approach to Labour Supply and Commodity Demand Over the Life Cycle. *Econometrica*, **53(3)**, 503–544.

Burkhauser, R. V. and Warlick, J. L. (1981) Disentangling the Annuity from the Redistributive Aspects of Social Security in the United States. *Review of Income and Wealth*, **27**, 401–421.

Caldwell, S. B. (1987) *How Can Microsimulation Help Develop Better Theories?*, paper International Workshop for Demographic Microsimulation of the IIASA, Budapest.

Caldwell, S. B., Greene, W., Mount, T. and Saltzman, S. (1978) *Forecasting Regional Energy Demand: The Case of New York State*. Technical Report Prepared for the New York State Public Service Commission, Long Range Forecast Hearings, Case No. 27319.

Castellino, O. (1971) Income Redistribution Through Old-Age Pensions: Problems and its Definition and Measurement. *Public Finance*, **26**, 457–471.

Chen, Y.-P. and Chu, K.-W. (1974) Tax-benefit ratios and rates of return under OASI: 1974 retirees and entrants. *Journal of Risk and Insurance*, **41**, 189–206.

Clarke, M. (1986) Demographic processes and household dynamics: a microsimulation approach, in *Population Structures and Models: Developments in Spatial Demography*, (eds R. Woods and P. Rees) Allen & Unwin, London.

Cohen, W. and Friedman, M. (1972) *Social security: universal or selective*, American Enterprise for Public Policy Research.

Corpeleijn, A. (1979) De arbeidsmobiliteit in 1976/'77; enige uitkomsten van de Arbeidskrachtentelling 1977. *Sociale Maandstatistiek*, **27** (**8**), 648–656.

Corpeleijn, A. (1987) Verdiende lonen van werknemers met verschillende opleiding, 1985. *Supplement Sociaal- Economische Maandstatistiek*, **1987** (**8**), 4–21.

Creedy, J. (1974) Income Changes over the Life Cycle. *Oxford Economic Papers*, **26**, 405–423.

Creedy, J. (1975) Aggregation and the Distribution of Income. *Bulletin of the Oxford Institute of Economics and Statistics*, **37**, 91–101.

Creedy, J. and Hart, P. E. (1979) Age and the Distribution of Earnings. *Economic Journal*, **89**, 280–293.

Creedy, J., Hart, P. E., Jonsson, A. and Klevmarken, N. A. (1980) The distribution of cohort incomes in Sweden, 1960–73: a comparative static analysis, in *The Statics and Dynamics of Income*, (eds N. A. Klevmarken and J. A. Lybeck), Tieto Ltd, Clevedon, pp. 55–80.

Danziger, S. (1977) Income Redistribution and Social Security; Further Evidence. *Social Service Review*, **51**, 179–184.

Danziger, S., Haveman, R. and Plotnick, R. (1981) How Income Transfer Programs Affect Work, Savings, and the Income Distribution: A Critical Review. *Journal of Economic Literature*, **19**, 975–1028.

Davies, J. B. (1982) The Relative Impact of Inheritance and Other Factors on Economic Inequality. *Quarterly Journal of Economics*, **97**, 471–498.

Davies, J., St-Hilaire, F. and Whalley, J. (1984) Some Calculations of Lifetime Tax Incidence. *American Economic Review*, **74**, 633–649.

Deaton, A. and Muellbauer, J. (1980) *Economics and Consumer Behavior*, Cambridge University Press, Cambridge.

Deleeck, H. (1974) Sociale Zekerheid en Inkomensverdeling, in *Sociale Zekerheid; enige kwantitatieve, economisch-theoretische en beleidsmatige beschouwingen over de toekomstige ontwikkelingen van de sociale zekerheid*, (ed Vereniging voor de Staathuishoudkunde), Martinus Nijhoff, The Hague, pp. 35–50.

Departementale Werkgroep SZW (1984) *Demografische ontwikkelingen in macro-economisch perspectief*, Ministerie van Sociale Zaken en Werkgelegenheid, The Hague.

Devine, J. and Wertheimer, R. (1981) *Aging Techniques Used by the Major Microsimulation Models*, Working Paper 1453–01, The Urban Institute, Washington DC.

Directoraal-Generaal der Belastingen (1989) *Belastingherziening 1990*, Belastingdienst.

Elseviers (1983) *Almanak voor de Sociale Verzekering 1983*, Annoventura, Amsterdam.

Falkingham, J. Hills, J. and Lessor, C. (1993) *William Beveridge versus Robin Hood: Social Security and Redistribution over the Lifecycle*, Discussion paper WSP/88, London School of Economics, London.

Fase, M. M. G. (1969) *An Econometric Model of Age-Income Profiles*, Ph.D. Dissertation, Universitaire Pers Rotterdam, Rotterdam.

Fase, M. M. G. (1971) On the Estimation of Lifetime Income. *Journal of the American Statistical Association*, **66**, 686–692.

Fase, M. M. G. (1972) The Distribution of Lifetime Earnings: A Problem of Intertemporal Aggregation. *Statistica Neerlandica*, **26**, 103–111.

Feldstein, M. S. and Pellechio, A. (1978) Social security wealth: the impact of alternative inflation adjustments, in *Policy Analysis with Social Security Research Files*, Social Security Administration, Research Report 52, pp. 693–714.

Ferrara, P. J. and Lott, J. R. Jr. (1985) Rates of return promised by social security to today's young workers, in *Social Security, Prospects for Real Reform*, (ed P. J. Ferrara), Cato Institute, pp. 13–32.

Fields, G. S. and Mitchell, O. S. (1984) Determinants of the Optimal Retirement Age: An Empirical Investigation. *Journal of Human Resources*, **19**, 245–262.

Freeman, R. B. (1979) The Effect of Demographic Factors on Age-Earnings Profiles. *Journal of Human Resources*, **14**, 289–318.

Freeman, R. B. (1986) Demand for education, in *Handbook of Labor Economics*, (eds O. Ashenfelter and R. Layard), North-Holland, Amsterdam-New York-Oxford-Tokyo, ch. 6.

Freiden, A., Leimer, D. and Hoffman, R. (1976) *Internal Rates of Return to Retired Worker Only Beneficiaries Under Social Security, 1967–70*, US Social Security Administration, publication no. 77–117776.

Friedman, M. (1957) *A Theory of the Consumption Function*, Princeton University Press, Princeton.

Galler, H. P. (1988) Microsimulation of household formation and dissolution, in *Modelling Household Formation and Dissolution*, (eds N. W. Keilman, A. C. Kuijsten and A. P. Vossen), Oxford University Press, Oxford, pp. 139–159.

Gastwirth, J. L. (1972) The Estimation of the Lorenz Curve and Gini Index. *Review of Economics and Statistics*, **54**, 306–316.

Ghez, G. R. and Becker, G. (1975) *The Allocation of Time and Goods over the Life Cycle*, Colombia University Press, New York.

Göbel, D. (1983) *Lebenseinkommen und Erwerbsbiographie; Eine Längschnittuntersuchung mit Daten der gesetzlichen Rentenversicherung*, Campus Verlag, Frankfurt a.M.

Goedhart, Th., Halberstadt, V., Kapteyn, A. and Van Praag, B. M. S. (1976) Welk inkomen vinden we minimaal? *Economisch Statistische Berichten*, **61**, 620–624.

Goedhart, Th., Halberstadt, V., Kapteyn, A. and Van Praag, B. M. S. (1977) The Poverty Line: Concept and Measurement. *Journal of Human Resources*, **12**, 503–520.

Golladay, F. and Haveman, R. H. (1977) *The Economic Impacts of Tax-Transfer Policy: Regional and Distributional Effects*, Academic Press, New York.

Goodman, L., Keyfitz, N. and Pullum, T. (1974) Family Formation and the Frequency of Various Kinship Relationships. *Theoretical Population Biology*, **5**, 1–27.

Greenberger, M., Crenson, M. and Crissey, B. (1976) *Models in the Policy Process: Public Decision Making in the Computer Era*, Russel Sage Foundation, New York.

Hagenaars, A. J. M., Homan, M. E. and Van Praag, B. M. S. (1984) Draagkrachtverschillen tussen huishoudens met één resp. twee kostwinners. *Economisch Statistische Berichten*, **69**, 552–559.

Hagenaars, A. J. M. and Wunderink-Van Veen, S. R. (1990) *Soo gewonne, soo verteert; economie van de huishoudelijke sector*, Stenfert Kroese, Leyden/Antwerpen.

Hain, W. and Helberger, C. (1986) Longitudinal microsimulation of life income, in *Microanalytic Simulation Models to Support Social and Financial Policy*, (eds G. H. Orcutt, J. Merz and H. Quinke), North-Holland, Amsterdam, pp. 251–270.

Halberstadt, V. (1978) Sociale zekerheid in de openbare financiën, in *Sociale Zekerheid in een periode van economische overgang*, (ed G. M. J. Veldkamp), Kluwer, Deventer, pp. 73–79.

Hancock, K. and Richardson, S. (1985) Discount Rates and the Distribution of Lifetime Earnings. *Journal of Human Resources*, **20**, 346–357.

Hansen, H.-J., Klein, E. and Mannel, D. (1987) *Das makroökonometrische Modell des Sfb3; Version 5.0*, Sonderforschungsbereich 3 Working Paper No. 238, J. W. Goethe-Universität Frankfurt und Universität Mannheim.

Harding, A. (1990) *Dynamic Microsimulation Models: Problems and Prospects*, Discussion Paper WSP/48, London School of Economics, London.

Harding, A. (1992) How Cash Transfers and Income Taxes Affect the Distribution of Lifetime Income. *Social Security Journal*, Autumn 1992, pp. 1–27.

Hart, P. E. (1973) *The Comparative Statics and Dynamics of Income Distribution*, Discussion Paper, Series, A, No. 49, University of Reading, Reading.

Hartog, J. (1980) *Tussen vraag en aanbod*, Stenfert Kroese, Leyden/Antwerpen.

Hausman, J. (1981) Labor supply, in *How Taxes Affect Economic Behavior*, (eds H. Aaron and J. Pechman), The Brookings Institution, Washington DC, pp. 27–83.

Have, Ten, K. and Jehoel, G. (1985) *Werkloze jongeren: een verloren generatie?*, Voorstudie W8, OSA, The Hague.

Haveman, R. H. (1985) *Does the Welfare State Increase Welfare; Reflections on Hidden Negatives and Observed Positives*, Stenfert Kroese, Leyden.

Haveman, R. H. (1987) *Poverty Policy and Poverty Research*, University of Wisconsin Press, Wisconsin.

Haveman, R. H. and Hollenbeck, K. (1980) Preface, in *Microeconomic Simulation Models for Public Policy Analysis*, vol. 2, (eds R. H. Haveman and K. Hollenbeck), Academic Press, New York, pp. xxi–xxvii.

Hayes, B. (1989) *Alternative Methodologies for Life-Cycle Simulations of the Incidence of Taxation and Benefit Systems*, Discussion Paper TIDI/137, London School of Economics, London.

Heida, H. and Gordijn, H. (1985) *PRIMOS Huishoudenmodel; analyse en prognose van de huishoudensontwikkeling in Nederland*, Ministerie van VROM, The Hague.

Hellwig, O. (1988a) *Probleme und Lösungsansätze bei der Datenbeschaffung und Parameterschätzung für Mikrosimulationsmodelle der privaten Haushalte*, Ph.D. Dissertation, Darmstadt University, Darmstadt.

Hellwig, O. (1988b) *Modelling and Software Aspects of Demographic Microsimulation*, Darmstadt University, Darmstadt.

Hellwig, O. (1988c) *Modelling and Software Aspects of Demographic Microsimulation*, Augsburg University, Augsburg.

Hendricks, G., Holden, R. and Johnson, J. (1977) *A File of Simulated Family and Earnings Histories Through the Year 2000*, Working Paper No. 985–3, The Urban Institute, Washington, D.C.

Herwaarden, F. Van, Kapteyn, A. and Van Praag, B. M. S. (1977) Twelve Thousand Individual Welfare Functions. *European Economic Review*, **9**, 283–300.

Hill, T. P. (1959) An Analysis of the Distribution of Wages and Salaries in Great Britain. *Econometrica*, **27**, 355–381.

Hofstra, H. J. (1980) *Inleiding tot het belastingrecht*, Kluwer, Deventer.

Holbrook, R. S. (1967) The Three-Year Horizon: An Analysis of the Evidence. *Journal of Political Economy*, **75**, 750–760.

Holm, E., Mäkilä, K. and Öberg, S. (1987) *ADDRESS – An Applied Relational Micro Simulation Model*, paper International Workshop for Demographic Microsimulation of the IIASA, Budapest.

Hoschka, P. (1986) Requisite research on methods and tools for microanalytic simulation models, in *Microanalytic Simulation Models to Support Social and Financial Policy*, (eds G. H. Orcutt, J. Merz and H. Quinke), North Holland, Amsterdam, pp. 45–54.

Huijser, A. P. and Van Loo, P. D. (1986) *Vergrijzing, pensioenen en contractuele besparingen*, Monetaire Monografieën No. 5, Kluwer, Deventer.

Hurd, M. D. and Shoven, J. B. (1985) The distributional impact of social security, in *Pensions, Labor, and Individual Choice*, (ed D. A. Wise), University of Chicago Press, Chicago/London, pp. 193–215.

Johnson, W. R. (1980) Vintage Effects in the Earnings of White American Men. *Review of Economics and Statistics*, **62**, 399–407.

Kapteyn, A., Kooreman, P., Muffels, R. J. A., Siegers, J. J., Van Soest, A. and Willemse, R. J. M. (1985) *Determinanten van bestaansonzekerheid*, COSZ-rapport no. 10, Ministerie van Sociale Zaken en Werkgelegenheid, The Hague.

Kapteyn, A. and Van Praag, B. M. S. (1976) A New Approach to the Construction of Family Equivalence Scales. *European Economic Review*, **7**, 313–335.

Keilman, N. W. (1987) *Why Microsimulation – Why Not? A Discussion of Simulation Approaches in the Field of Family and Household Demography*, paper International Workshop for Demographic Microsimulation of the IIASA, Budapest.

Kennedy, B. R. (1990) Financial Consistency in Longitudinal Microsimulation: Homemaker Pensions RE-examined. *Review of Income and Wealth*, **36**, 215–221.

Kirman, A. (1989) The Intrinsic Limits of Modern Economic Theory. *Economic Journal*, **99**, 126–139.

Klevmarken, A. (1980) On estimation and other problems of statistical inference in the micro simulation approach, in *Micro Simulation – Models, Methods and Applications*, (eds B. Bergmann, G. Eliasson and G. Orcutt), IUI Conference Reports 1980:1, Industrial Institute for Economic and Social Research, Stockholm, pp. 261–268.

Klevmarken, A. (1983) There is a need for applied microeconometrics; survey research about the household, in *Microeconomics; IUI Yearbook 1982–1983*, (eds G. Eliasson and H. Fries), Industrial Institute for Economic and Social Research, Stockholm, pp. 28–42.

Klevmarken, A. and Quigley, J. M. (1976) Age, Experience, Earnings, and Investments in Human Capital. *Journal of Political Economy*, **84**, 47–72.

Klooster–Van Wingerden, C. M. Van't (1979) *Huishoudensvorming en samenlevingsvormen*, Monografieën Volkstelling 1971, No. 11. Staatsuitgeverij, The Hague.

Kotlikoff, L. J. (1985) The distributional impact of social security: a framework for analysis, in *International Population Conference Florence 1985*, (ed IUSSP), IUSSP, Liège, pp. 485–499.

Layard, R. (1977) On measuring the redistribution of lifetime income, in *The Economics of Public Services*, (eds M. S. Feldstein and R. P. Inman), McMillan Press, London.

Leeuwen, L.Th. Van (1980) *Ontwikkelingsfasen van het gezin*, Monografieën Volkstelling 1971 No. 9, Staatsuitgeverij, The Hague.

Leimer, D. R. (1978) Projected rates of return to future social security retirees under alternative benefit structures, in *Policy Analysis with Social Security Research Files*, Social Security Administration, Research Report 52, pp. 235–267.

Leimer, D. R. and Petri, P. A. (1981) Cohort Specific Effects of Social Security Policy. *National Tax Journal*, **34**, 9–28.

Lillard, L. A. (1977) Inequality: Earnings vs Human Wealth. *American Economic Review*, **67**, 42–53.

Massizzo, A. I. V. (1975) *De personele inkomensverdeling 1952–1967*, CPB Monografie 19, Staatsuitgeverij, The Hague.

McFadden, D. (1982) *An Evaluation of the ORNL Residential Energy Use Model*, EPRI Report EA-2442, Electric Power Research Institute, Palo Alto.

Meerman, J. (1978) Do Empirical Studies of Budget Incidence Make Sense? *Public Finance*, **33**, 295–313.

Meesters, M. J. (1983) In- en uittrede van personeel bij de rijksoverheid, 1978–1982. *Sociale Maandstatistiek*, **31** (9), 77–82.

Merz, J. (1988) *Microsimulation – A Survey of Principles, Developments and Applications with Focus on the Static Case and the Static Sfb3-Microsimulation Model as an Example*, Working Paper No. 268, J. W. Goethe University, Frankfurt.

Meyer, C. W. and Wolff, N. L. (1987a) Intercohort and intracohort redistribution under social security, in *Social Security, a Critique of Radical Reform Proposals*, (ed C. W. Meyer), Lexington Books, Lexington MA/Toronto, pp. 49–68.

Meyer, C. W. and Wolff, N. L. (1987b) Intercohort and Intracohort Redistribution Under Old Age Insurance: The 1962–1972 Retirement Cohorts. *Public Finance Quarterly*, **15**, 259–281.

Mierlo, J. G. A. Van (1978) Meetlatten voor de tertiaire verdeling. *Economisch Statistische Berichten*, **63**, 555–559.

Mincer, J. (1974) *Schooling, Experiences and Earnings*, Columbia University Press, New York/London.

Ministerie van Sociale Zaken en Werkgelegenheid (several years) *Inkomensbeleid 19 . . .*, Tweede Kamer, The Hague.

Ministerie van Sociale Zaken en Werkgelegenheid (1982) *Meerjarenramingen Sociale Zekerheidsregelingen*, Tweede Kamer, vergaderjaar 1981–1982, 17100, nos. 1–2.

Ministerie van Sociale Zaken en Werkgelegenheid (1983) *Notitie Inkomensontwikkeling en -verdeling*, Tweede Kamer, vergaderjaar 1983–1984, 18189, nos. 1–2.

Ministerie van Sociale Zaken en Werkgelegenheid (1984) *Financiële Nota Sociale Zekerheid 1985*, Tweede Kamer, vergaderjaar 1984–1985, 18612, nos. 1–2.

Ministerie van Sociale Zaken en Werkgelegenheid (1986) *Informatiegids Herziening Stelsel Sociale Zekerheid*, The Hague.

Ministerie van Sociale Zaken en Werkgelegenheid (1988) *Financiële Nota Sociale Zekerheid 1989*, Tweede Kamer, vergaderjaar 1988–1989, 20805, nos. 1–2.

Ministerie van Sociale Zaken en Werkgelegenheid (1989) *Inkomensbeleid 1990*, Tweede Kamer, vergaderjaar 1989–1990, 21307, nos. 1–2.

Moffit, R. (1982) Trends in Social Security Wealth, in *Economic Transfers in the United States*, (ed M. Moon), NBER Studies in Income and Wealth, 49, University of Chicago Press, Chicago.

Mookherjee, D. and Shorrocks, A. (1982) A Decomposition Analysis of the Trend in UK Income Inequality. *Economic Journal*, **92**, 886–902.

Moss, M. (1978) Income Distribution Issues Viewed in a Lifetime Income Perspective. *Review of Income and Wealth*, **24**, 119–136.

Muellbauer, J. (1980) The Estimation of the Prais-Houthakker Model of Equivalence Scales. *Econometrica*, **48**, 153–176.

Muffels, R. J. A., Nelissen, J. H. M. and Nuyens, W. J. F. I. (1986) De inkomensherverdelende werking van een aantal sociale zekerheidsregelingen in 1981. *Sociaal Maandblad Arbeid*, **41**, 35–48.

Muffels, R. J. A., Nelissen, J. H. M. and Nuyens, W. J. F. I. (1988) *Social Security and Income Inequality; A Comparative Study*, Reeks Sociale Zekerheidswetenschap, Rapporten no. 4, Tilburg University, Tilburg.

Musgrave, R. A. and Musgrave, P. B. (1976) *Public Finance in Theory and Practice*, McGraw Hill, New York.

NCBS (1), *Overgangen binnen het onderwijs en intrede in de maatschappij; onderwijsmatrix*, Staatsuitgeverij, The Hague (several years).

NCBS (2) *Statistiek van de buitenlandse migratie*, De Haan NV, Utrecht, De Haan NV, Zeist and Staatsuitgeverij, The Hague (several years).

NCBS (3) *Statistiek van het gewoon- en voortgezet lager onderwijs*, Staatsuitgeverij, The Hague (several years).

NCBS (4) *Statistiek van het gewoon lager onderwijs*, Staatsuitgeverij, The Hague (several years).

NCBS (5) *Statistiek van het buitengewoon lager onderwijs*, Staatsuitgeverij, The Hague (several years).

NCBS (6) *Statistiek van het buitengewoon onderwijs*, Staatsuitgeverij, The Hague (several years).

NCBS (7) *Statistiek van het vwo, havo en mavo; in-, door- en uitstroom van de leerlingen*, Staatsuitgeverij, The Hague (several years).

NCBS (8) *Statistiek van het voorbereidend hoger en middelbaar onderwijs*, Staatsuitgeverij, The Hague (several years).

NCBS (9) *Statistiek van het uitgebreid lager onderwijs*, Staatsuitgeverij, The Hague (several years).

NCBS (10) *Statistiek van het beroepsonderwijs; sociaal-pedagogisch onderwijs*, Staatsuitgeverij, The Hague (several years).

NCBS (11) *Statistiek van het beroepsonderwijs; kunstonderwijs*, Staatsuitgeverij, The Hague (several years).

NCBS (12) *Statistiek van het beroepsonderwijs; economisch en administratief onderwijs, middenstandsonderwijs en lager algemeen voortgezet onderwijs*, Staatsuitgeverij, The Hague (several years).

NCBS (13) *Statistiek van het beroepsonderwijs; technisch onderwijs, nautisch onderwijs*, Staatsuitgeverij, The Hague (several years).

NCBS (14) *Statistiek van het beroepsonderwijs; opleidingsscholen voor kleuterleidsters, pedagogische academies*, Staatsuitgeverij, The Hague (several years).

NCBS (15) *Statistiek van het beroepsonderwijs; opleidingsscholen voor onderwijzers*, Staatsuitgeverij, The Hague (several years).

NCBS (16) *Statistiek van het beroepsonderwijs; opleidingsscholen voor kleuterleidsters, opleidingsscholen voor onderwijzers*, Staatsuitgeverij, The Hague (several years).

NCBS (17) *Statistiek van het beroepsonderwijs; agrarisch onderwijs*, Staatsuitgeverij, The Hague (several years).

NCBS (18) *Statistiek van het beroepsonderwijs; landbouwonderwijs*, Staatsuitgeverij, The Hague (several years).

NCBS (19) *Statistiek van het beroepsonderwijs; beroepsbegeleidend onderwijs, leerlingenwezen*, Staatsuitgeverij, The Hague (several years).

NCBS (20) *Statistiek van het beroepsonderwijs; nieuwe lerarenopleidingen*, Staatsuitgeverij, The Hague (several years).

NCBS (21) *Statistiek van het beroepsonderwijs; huishoud- en nijverheidsonderwijs*, Staatsuitgeverij, The Hague (several years).

NCBS (22) *Statistiek van het beroepsonderwijs; land- en tuinbouwonderwijs*, Staatsuitgeverij, The Hague (several years).

NCBS (23) *Statistiek van het nijverheidsonderwijs*, Staatsuitgeverij, The Hague (several years).

NCBS (24) *Statistiek van het wetenschappelijk onderwijs*, Staatsuitgeverij, The Hague (several years).

NCBS (25) *Statistiek van het hoger onderwijs*, Staatsuitgeverij, The Hague (several years).

NCBS (26) *Nationale Rekeningen*, Staatsuitgeverij, The Hague (several years).

NCBS (27) *Sociale Maandstatistiek*, Staatsuitgeverij, The Hague (several years).

NCBS (28) *Belastingdruk in Nederland*, Staatsuitgeverij, The Hague (several years).

NCBS (29) *Statistiek van de uitgaven der overheid voor onderwijs*, Staatsuitgeverij, The Hague (several years).

NCBS (30) *Sociale Verzekering, Pensioenverzekering, Levensverzekering*, Staatsuitgeverij, The Hague (several years).

NCBS (31) *Diagnose statistiek bedrijfsverenigingen: omslagleden*, Staatsuitgeverij, The Hague (several years).

NCBS (1950) *Statistiek van de buitenlandse migratie 1948 en 1949*, Staatsdrukkerij- en uitgeverijbedrijf, The Hague.

NCBS (1951a) *Verzorging van bejaarden in tehuizen naar de toestand op 1 Oktober 1950*, De Haan NV, Utrecht.

NCBS (1951b) *12e Volkstelling, annex woningtelling 31 Mei 1947. Serie A Deel 3 Woning-en gezinstelling*, De Haan NV, Utrecht.

NCBS (1951c) *12e Volkstelling, annex woningtelling 31 Mei 1947. Serie A Deel 4 Statistiek der bestaande huwelijken en van de vruchtbaarheid dezer huwelijken*, De Haan NV, Utrecht.

NCBS (1952) *12e Volkstelling, annex Woningtelling 31 Mei 1947, Serie A Rijks- en provinciale cijfers, Deel 2 Beroepstelling*, De Haan NV, Utrecht.

NCBS (1953a) *Statistiek van de buitenlandse migratie 1950–1952*, De Haan NV, Utrecht.

NCBS (1953b) *Bevolking van Nederland. Leeftijd en geslacht, 1900–1952. Leeftijd, geslacht en burgerlijke staat, 1947–1952*, De Haan NV, Utrecht.

NCBS (1954) *12e Volkstelling, annex woningtelling 31 Mei 1947. Serie A Deel 1 Belangrijkste uitkomsten der eigenlijke Volkstelling*, De Haan NV, Utrecht.

NCBS (1955) *Statistiek van de loop der bevolking 1938–1954*, De Haan NV, Utrecht.

NCBS (1958a) *Statistiek van de buitenlandse migratie 1955–1956*, De Haan NV, Zeist.

NCBS (1958b) *Echtscheidingen in Nederland, 1900–1957*, De Haan NV, Zeist.

NCBS (1962) *Statistiek van de buitenlandse migratie 1959–1960*, De Haan NV, Zeist.

NCBS (1965) *Overheidsfinanciën voor het wetenschappelijk onderwijs 1930–1965*, De Haan NV, Hilversum.

NCBS (1967a) *Inkomensverdeling 1962 en Vermogensverdeling 1963*, Staatsuitgeverij, The Hague.

NCBS (1967b) *Inkomensverdeling van werkende gehuwde vrouwen 1962*, Staatsuitgeverij, The Hague.

NCBS (1967c) *Overgangen binnen het onderwijs en intrede in de maatschappij; 1936, 1956 en 1961–1966 'Matrix'*, Staatsuitgeverij, The Hague.

NCBS (1968a) *Statistiek van de bejaardenoorden 1965*, Staatsuitgeverij, The Hague.

NCBS (1968b) *Statistiek van de buitenlandse migratie 1965–1966*, Staatsuitgeverij, The Hague.

NCBS (1970) *Bevolking van Nederland naar geslacht, leeftijd en burgerlijke staat 1930–1969*, Staatsuitgeverij, The Hague.

NCBS (1972a) *Inkomensverdeling 1967 en Vermogensverdeling 1968*, Staatsuitgeverij, The Hague.

NCBS (1972b) *Inkomensverdeling van werkende gehuwde vrouwen 1967*, Staatsuitgeverij, The Hague.

NCBS (1973) *Statistiek van de bejaardenoorden 1970*, Staatsuitgeverij, The Hague.

NCBS (1974) *Statistiek van de buitenlandse migratie 1970–1971*, Staatsuitgeverij, The Hague.

NCBS (1975) *Buitenechtelijke geboorte 1840–1973*, Staatsuitgeverij, The Hague.

NCBS (1976) *Echtscheidingen in Nederland 1900–1974*, Staatsuitgeverij, The Hague.

NCBS (1977a) *Statistiek van de buitenlandse migratie 1975*, Staatsuitgeverij, The Hague.

NCBS (1977b) *Inkomensverdeling 1970 en Vermogensverdeling 1971*, Staatsuitgeverij, The Hague.

NCBS (1979) *Inkomensverdeling van werkende gehuwde vrouwen 1970 en 1973*, Staatsuitgeverij, The Hague.

NCBS (1980a) *De Personele Inkomensverdeling 1975*, deel I, Staatsuitgeverij, The Hague.

NCBS (1980b) *Statistiek van de bejaardenoorden 1977*, Staatsuitgeverij, The Hague.

NCBS (1980c) *Arbeidskrachtentelling 1977*, Staatsuitgeverij, The Hague.

NCBS (1980d) *14e Algemene Volkstelling annex woningtelling 28 Februari 1971, Deel 5A Het genoten onderwijs en het volgen van onderwijs*, Staatsuitgeverij, The Hague.

NCBS (1981) *14e Algemene Volkstelling 28 Februari 1971. Serie A, deel 2, Bestaande huwelijken en vruchtbaarheid van gehuwde en gehuwd geweest zijnde vrouwen*, Staatsuitgeverij, The Hague.

NCBS (1982a) *Prognose van de bevolking van Nederland na 1980. Deel 1, Uitkomsten en enkele achtergronden*, Staatsuitgeverij, The Hague.

NCBS (1982b) *Statistiek van de buitenlandse migratie 1980*, Staatsuitgeverij, The Hague.

NCBS (1982c) *De Personele Inkomensverdeling; werkende gehuwde vrouwen 1975 en 1976*, Staatsuitgeverij, The Hague.

NCBS (1982d) *Schoolkeuze en schoolloopbaan bij het voortgezet onderwijs, cohort 1964/'65*, Staatsuitgeverij, The Hague.

NCBS (1982e) *Schoolloopbaan en herkomst van leerlingen bij het voortgezet onderwijs, deel 2; cohort 1977, schoolkeuze*, Staatsuitgeverij, The Hague.

NCBS (1983) *De Personele Inkomensverdeling 1977; verdelingen in inkomensklassen en 10%-groepen*, Staatsuitgeverij, The Hague.

NCBS (1984a) *Vijfentachtig jaren statistiek in tijdreeksen*, Staatsuitgeverij, The Hague.

NCBS (1984b) *De Personele Inkomensverdeling 1979*, Staatsuitgeverij, The Hague.

NCBS (1984c) *Onderzoek Gezinsvorming 1982*, Staatsuitgeverij, The Hague.

NCBS (1985a) *Bevolkingsprognose voor Nederland 1984–2035*, Staatsuitgeverij, The Hague.

NCBS (1985b) *De Personele Inkomensverdeling 1981; individuen*, Staatsuitgeverij, The Hague.

NCBS (1985c) Hoe duurzaam is samenwonen. *Maandstatistiek van de Bevolking*, **33** (**1**), 7–8.

NCBS (1986) Buitenechtelijke levendgeborenen naar burgerlijke staat van de moeder, 1975–1984. *Maandstatistiek van de Bevolking*, **34** (**2**), 11–13.

NCBS (1987a) *Statistiek van de bejaardenoorden 1984*, Staatsuitgeverij, The Hague.

NCBS (1987b) *Arbeidskrachtentelling 1985*, Staatsuitgeverij, The Hague.

NCBS (1988) *Schoolloopbaan en herkomst van leerlingen bij het voortgezet onderwijs, SLVO-cohort 1982, deel 1: schoolkeuze*, Staatsuitgeverij, The Hague.

NCBS (1989) *Sociale verzekering, pensioenverzekering en levensverzekering 1984–1988*, Staatsuitgeverij, The Hague.

Nelissen, J. H. M. (1987a) Leeftijd en inkomen. *Bevolking en Gezin*, **1987–3**, 53–71.
Nelissen, J. H. M. (1987b) The Redistributive Impact of the General Old Age Pensions Act on Lifetime Income in the Netherlands. *European Economic Review*, **31**, 1419–1441.
Nelissen, J. H. M. (1989) *Microsimulation of Household and Education Dynamics*, Discussion Paper No. 89/3, Growth Dynamics University Institute, Erasmus University, Rotterdam.
Nelissen, J. H. M. (1991a) *The health care sector in the microsimulation model Nedymas*, Working Paper Series No. 62, Tilburg University, Tilburg.
Nelissen, J. H. M. (1991b) *The modelling of institutional households in the microsimulation model Nedymas*, Working Paper Series No. 63, Tilburg University, Tilburg.
Nelissen, J. H. M. (1991c) Household and Education Projections by Means of a Microsimulation model. *Economic Modelling*, **8**, 480–511.
Nelissen, J. H. M. (1992) *Private pensions schemes in the microsimulation model NEDYMAS*, Working Paper Series No. 69, Tilburg University, Tilburg.
Nelissen, J. H. M. (1993) The Labour Market and Social Security Module in the Microsimulation model NEDYMAS. *Economic Modelling*, **10**, 225–272
Nelissen, J. H. M. and Vossen, A. P. (1985) *Demografische ontwikkelingen en het sociale zekerheidssysteem*, COSZ Rapport No. 9, Ministerie van Sociale Zaken en Werkgelegenheid, The Hague.
Nicholson, J. L. (1949) Variations in the Working Class Family Expenditure. *Journal of the Royal Statistical Society*, **112 (part IV)**, 359–411.
Odink, J. G. (1978) De nieuwste ontwikkelingen in de Nederlandse personele inkomensverdeling. *Economisch Statistische Berichten*, **63**, 320–324.
Odink, J. G. (1979) Inkomensherverdeling door belastingen en sociale zekerheid. *Economisch Statistische Berichten*, **64**, 1230–1234.
Odink, J. G. and Van Imhoff, E. (1984) True versus Measured Inequality. *Statistica Neerlandica*, **38**, 219–232.
Okonkwo, U. (1973) *Individual Equity Under Social Security: some black-white comparisons*, paper Annual Meeting of the AEA, New York, December, 28, 1973.
Okonkwo, U. (1976) *Intragenerational equity under social security*, International Monetary Fund, Washington DC.
Orcutt, G. H. (1957) A New Type of Socio-Economic System. *Review of Economics and Statistics*, **39**, 116–123.
Orcutt, G. H. (1960) Simulation of Economic Systems. *American Economic Review*, **50**, 893–907.
Orcutt, G. H., Caldwell S. and Wertheimer, II R. (1976) *Policy Exploration Through Microanalytic Simulation*, Urban Institute, Washington, DC.
Orcutt, G. and Glazer A. (1980) Microanalytic modelling and simulation, in *Micro Simulation – Models, Methods and Applications*, (eds B. Bergmann, G. Eliasson and G. Orcutt), IUI Conference Reports 1980:1, Industrial Institute for Economic and Social Research, Stockholm, pp. 121–176.
Orcutt, G., Glazer, A., Harris, R. and Wertheimer, II R. (1980) Microanalytic modelling and the analysis of public transfer policies, in *Microeconomic Simulation Models for Public Policy Analysis*, vol. 1, (eds R. H. Haveman, and K. Hollenbeck), Academic Press, New York, pp. 81–106.
Orcutt, G. H., Greenberger, M., Korbel J. and Rivlin A. (1961) *Microanalysis of Socioeconomic System: A Simulation Study*, Harper and Row, New York.
Ozawa, M. N. (1976) Income Redistribution and Social Security. *Social Service Review*, **50**, 209–223.
Parsons, D. O. and Munro, D. R. (1977) Intergenerational Transfer in Social Security, in *The Crisis in Social Security*, (ed M. M. Boskin), Institute for Contemporary Studies, San Fransisco, pp. 65–86.
Pellechio, A. (1983) *Individual Gains and Losses from Social Security and an Agenda for Reform*, Washington D.C.

Pellechio, A. J. and Goodfellow, G. P. (1983) Individual Gaines and Losses from Social Security Before and After the 1983 amendments. *Cato Journal*, Fall.

Pen, J. (1985) Een Amerikaan kijkt naar Nederland. Een kritiek op Robert Havemans rapport over de verzorgingsstaat. *Openbare Uitgaven*, **17**, 96–104.

Pestieau, P. (1989) The Demographics of Inequality. *Journal of Population Economics*, **2**, 3–24.

Pestieau, P. (1990) The economic consequences of demographic change; a comment, in *Emerging Issues in Demographic Research*, (eds C. A. Hazeu and G. A. B. Frinking), Elsevier, Amsterdam, pp. 229–231.

Ploegmakers, M. J. H. and Van Leeuwen L.Th. (1983) *Veranderende huishoudens in Nederland. Statistische analyse over de periode 1960–1977*, Ministerie van VROM, The Hague.

Prest, A. R. (1970) Some Redistributional Aspects of the National Superannuation Fund. *The Three Banks Review*, **86**, 10–14.

Reynolds, M. and Smolensky E. (1977) *Public Expenditures, Taxes, and the Distribution of Income: The United States, 1950, 1961, 1970*, Academic Press, New York.

Ritzen, J. M. M. (1979) De meting van de tertiaire inkomensverdeling, in *Tertiaire Inkomensverdeling*, (ed Van Niekerk N. C. M.), IOO/Kluwer, The Hague, pp. 79–117.

Ritzen, J. M. M., Pommer, E. J., Roelse, W. and Ruitenberg, L. W., (1977) *Profijt van de overheid*, SCP-cahier no. 12, Staatsuitgeverij, The Hague.

Rosen, S. (1976) A Theory of Life Earnings. *Journal of Political Economy*, **84**, S45–S67.

Russell, L. (1982) The Baby Boom Generation and the Economy, Brookings Institution, Washington, DC.

Sadowsky, G. (1977) *MASH – A Computer System for Microanalytic Simulation for Policy Explorations*, The Urban Institute, Washington DC.

Sahota, G. S. (1978) Theories of Personal Income Distribution: A Survey. *Journal of Economic Literature*, **16**, 1–55.

Schulz, J. H. (1982) Problems of American Pensions: Microsimulation Policy Analysis. *Journal of Institutional and Theoretical Economics*, **138**, 527–545.

Shimono, K. and Tachibanaki, T. (1985) Lifetime Income and Public Pension: An Analysis of the Effect on Redistribution Using a Two-Period Analysis. *Journal of Public Economics*, **26**, 75–87.

Smith, J. D. (1986) Microanalytic Simulation and Social Policy, in *Microanalytic Simulation Models to Support Social and Financial Policy*, (eds G. H. Orcutt, J. Merz and H. Quinke), North Holland, Amsterdam, pp. 211–222.

Smith, J. E. (1987) The computer simulation of kin sets and kin counts, in *Family Demography*, (eds J. Bongaarts, T. Burch and K. Wachter), Oxford University Press, New York, pp. 249–266.

Social and Cultural Planning Agency (1981) *Profijt van de overheid*, Staatsuitgeverij, The Hague.

Social and Cultural Planning Agency (1984) *Sociaal Culturele Verkenningen*, Staatsuitgeverij, The Hague.

Social and Cultural Planning Agency (1984b) *Enkele gevolgen van de stelselherziening sociale zekerheid*, Stukwerk 1984/Nr. 21, Social and Cultural Planning Agency, Rijswijk.

Social and Cultural Planning Agency (1985) *Berekend Beleid*, Staatsuitgeverij, The Hague.

Social and Cultural Planning Agency (1986) *Sociaal en Cultureel Rapport 1986*, Staatsuitgeverij, The Hague.

Social and Cultural Planning Agency (1990) *Gecumuleerd Beleid*, Social and Cultural Planning Agency, Rijswijk.

Söderström, L. (1984) *The Redistributive Effects of Social Protection: Sweden*, paper Conference on 'The Future of the Welfare State', December 19–21, 1984, Maastricht.

Soest, A. Van, Woittiez, I. and Kapteyn, A. (1990) Labor Supply, Income Taxes, and Hours Restrictions in The Netherlands. *Journal of Human Resources*, **15** (3), 517–558.

Soltow, L. (1965) *Toward Income Inequality in Norway*, University of Wisconsin Press, Madison.

Spannenburg, P. (1981) De relatie tussen het hoogst behaalde onderwijsniveau en enige aspecten van het arbeidsmarktgedrag. *Sociale Maandstatistiek*, **29** (**2**), 55–60.

Statistics Canada (without date) *SPSD/M – Product Overview, Electronic Data Dissemination Division*, Statistics Canada, Ottawa.

Stadt, H. Van de (1988) *The Dynamics of Income and Welfare*, Ph.D. Dissertation, University of Amsterdam, Amsterdam.

Steger, A. (1980) *Haushalte and Familien bis zum Jahr 2000. Eine mikroanalytische Untersuchung für die Bundesrepublik Deutschland*, Campus Verlag, Frankfurt/New York.

Summers, R. (1956) *An Econometric Investigation of the Size Distribution of Lifetime Average Annual Income*, Ph.D. Dissertation, Stanford University, Stanford.

Taubman, P. (1976) Personal characteristics and the distribution of earnings, in *The Economics of Inequality*, (ed A. B. Atkinson), Allen & Unwin Ltd, London, pp. 193–226.

Thatcher, A. R. (1976) The new earnings survey and the distribution of earnings in *The Economics of Inequality*, (ed A. B. Atkinson), Allen & Unwin Ltd, London, pp. 227–268.

Theeuwes, J., Kerkhofs, M. and Lindeboom, M. (1988) *Toestanden, overgangen en duren op de Nederlandse arbeidsmarkt 1980–1985*, OSA-werkdocument nr. W 49, OSA, The Hague.

Thompson, L. H. (1983) The Social Security Reform Debate. *Journal of Economic Literature*, **21**, 1425–1467.

Veldkamp, G. M. J. (1978) *Inleiding tot de sociale zekerheid en de toepassing ervan in Nederland en België*, Kluwer, Deventer.

Veldkamp, G. M. J. (1984) *Schets van de leer van de sociale zekerheid*, Kluwer, Deventer.

Verbon, H. (1988) *The Evolution of Public Pension Schemes*, Springer Verlag, Berlin.

Wagner, G. (1983) *Ein neues Einkommensmodul auf Basis des Arbeitnehmersurveys 1980 für die Längschnittsversion 82.w des Sfb 3 Mikrosimulationsmodells*, Working Paper No. 128, J. W. Goethe Universität Frankfurt/Universität Mannheim, Frankfurt a.M./Mannheim.

Wagner, G. (1984) *Umverteilung in der gesetzlichen Rentenversicherung – Eine theoretische und empirische Untersuchung zum Versicherungsprinzip in der GRV*, Campus Verlag, Frankfurt a.M.

Weiss, Y. and Lillard, L. A. (1978) Experience, Vintage, and Time Effects in the Growth of Earnings: American Scientists. *Journal of Political Economy*, **86**, 427–447.

Weiszäcker, C. C. Von (1978) Annual income, lifetime income and other income concepts in measuring income distribution, in *Personal Income Distribution*, (eds W. Krelle and A. F. Shorrocks), North-Holland, Amsterdam, pp. 101–111.

Wijngaarden, P. Van (1986) Inkomensverdelingsbeleid in de verzorgingsstaat: Ontwikkeling, doelstellingen en resultaten, in *Visies op Verdeling*, (eds Y. Brenner, J. Reijnders and P. Van Wijngaarden), Vuga, The Hague, pp. 93–121.

Wilms, P. J. M. (1984) *Op waarde geschat. Methoden en technieken ter bepaling van de consumentenwaardering van gesubsidieerde voorzieningen*, Onderzoeksreeks No. 11, IOO, The Hague.

Windmuller, J. P., De Galan, C. and Zweeden, A. F. Van (1983) *Arbeidsverhoudingen in Nederland*, Het Spectrum, Utrecht/Antwerpen.

Wolff, E. N. (1991) *The Distributional Implications of Social Security Annuities and Transfers on Household Wealth and Income*, paper 1991 ESPE Meeting, June 6–8, Pisa.

Wolfson, D. J. (1979a) Zin en onzin van het tertiaire inkomensbegrip, in *Tertiaire Inkomensverdeling*, (ed N. C. M., Van Niekerk), IOO/Kluwer, The Hague, pp. 101–111.

Wolfson, D. J. (1979b) *Public Finance and Development Strategy*, John Hopkins, Baltimore.

Wolfson, M. C. (1988) Homemaker Pensions and Lifetime Redistribution. *Review of Income and Wealth*, **34**, 221–250.

Wolfson, M. C. (1989) Divorce, Homemaker Pensions and Lifecycle Analysis. *Population Research and Policy Review*, **8**, 25–54.

Wulf, De L. (1979) De neerslag van overheidsuitgaven: alternative benaderingen, in *Tertiaire Inkomensverdeling*, (ed. N. C. M. Van Neikerk), IOO/Kluwer, The Hague, pp. 101–111.

Zabalza, A. (1979) A Note on the Estimation of Subjective Rates of Discount from Labour Supply Functions. *Economica*, **46**, 197–201.

Zweeden, A. F. Van (1983) Van nachtwakersstaat naar verzorgingsstaat, in *Onzekere Zekerheid*, (ed F. G. Van den Heuvel), Vuga/Intermediair, The Hague/Amsterdam, pp. 13–29.

Index

Page numbers appearing in **bold** refer to figures and page numbers appearing in *italics* refer to tables.